City Mission

The story of London's Welsh chapels

Huw Edwards

cyflwynedig i
Dan, Sammy, Amos, Rebecca a Hannah
cenhedlaeth newydd o Gymry Llundain

dedicated to
Dan, Sammy, Amos, Rebecca and Hannah
a new generation of London Welsh

CONTENTS

DIOLCHIADAU

Carwn fynegi fy niolch mwyaf diffuant i'r dwsinau o gyfeillion a enwir isod am eu cymorth a'u caredigrwydd wrth baratoi'r gyfrol hon.

Bu Eirian, Lefi a chriw'r Lolfa yn hynod o gefnogol ac amyneddgar gydol y broses: diolch am eu gwaith trylwyr a graenus.

Rhaid cyflwyno diolch arbennig i Simon Davies a chyfeillion Ymddiriedolaeth Radnor Walk am eu cymorth ariannol. Y mae'n amheus a fyddai'r gyfrol wedi gweld golau dydd yn ei ffurf bresennol heb eu cyfraniad hael.

Derbyniais gyngor, gwybodaeth, dogfennau a lluniau gan lu o garedigion. Dibynnais yn llwyr ar eu parodrwydd.

Serch hynny dylwn gyfeirio'n benodol at weinidogion, cyn-weinidogion, swyddogion ac aelodau holl gapeli ac eglwysi Cymraeg Llundain. Dylem gydnabod eu ffydd, eu dycnwch a'u llafur caled mewn dyddiau anodd.

Ar eu cyfer nhw yn bennaf y bwriadwyd y gyfrol hon. Ond gobeithio y bydd hefyd o ddiddordeb i'r miloedd eraill a fu'n gysylltiedig â chapeli Llundain, i gapelwyr ac eglwyswyr o bob traddodiad, ac i'r genhedlaeth newydd sy'n dangos diddordeb yn eu hetifeddiaeth.

THANKS

I am conscious of my debt to so many people during the preparation of this book.

Top of the list is my family, whose tolerance and encouragement made it possible.

Eirian, Lefi and the team at Y Lolfa have been supportive and patient throughout: their professionalism and attention to detail are clear.

Special thanks are due to Simon Davies and his colleagues at the Radnor Walk Trust for their generous sponsorship. Their financial support made it possible to include a range of high quality images in this book.

To all the friends and colleagues who offered their advice, their documents, their recollections, their photographs, not to mention their unfailing encouragement, I offer my warmest thanks. I have relied on their kindness and endless generosity at all times.

It would be quite wrong of me not to mention the ministers, former ministers, officers and members of all the London Welsh chapels and churches. They have demonstrated strong faith, diligence and remarkable courage in difficult times. I am full of admiration for them and the causes they promote.

Professor M. Wynn Thomas of Swansea University generously agreed to read the manuscript and suggest changes. I am hugely grateful to him for sharing his expertise.

Dr Robert Pope, University of Wales Trinity Saint David, was always ready with advice and suggested valuable corrections.

Professor Ralph A. Griffiths of Swansea kindly identified fresh avenues of inquiry which unearthed new information.

The Revd Dr Lord Griffiths of Wesley's Chapel and the Revd Dafydd Owen of Cardiff offered many wise suggestions which improved the text.

The late Siân Busby, who contributed so much to Welsh culture in

London, gave me every encouragement to write this book. She was a clever, accomplished woman who is greatly missed by her family and friends.

John Samuel was unfailingly kind from the earliest days of the project, supplying vital information and guidance.

Angharad Wright provided valuable help with some of the research and dealt patiently with my unreasonable requests for more information.

Any errors that remain are my responsibility. I have done my best to comply with all copyright issues: any transgressions are inadvertent.

My greatest regret is my inability to convey thanks – in person – to a few individuals whose work in this field has been heroic.

The late Revd John Thickens of Willesden Green dedicated many years of his life to the search for the origins of the London Welsh chapels.

The late Morfudd Jenkins of Harrow was no less dedicated: she created a collection of valuable papers on the Independent causes.

The late Revd Dr Gomer Roberts of Llandybïe produced a superb history of Jewin chapel which is rightly regarded as a classic.

And the late Meurig Owen of Lewisham, unflagging researcher and author, deserves our abiding thanks for producing detailed histories of many of the city's chapels.

My admiration for their work is unqualified.

ADVISERS AND CONTRIBUTORS

Revd Richard Brunt, London

The late Revd Geoffrey G. Davies, London

Revd Ieuan Davies, Waunarlwydd

Revd J. E. Wynne Davies, Aberystwyth

Revd D. Gwylfa Evans, London

Revd Dr Aneirin Glyn, London

Revd Dr Lord (Leslie) Griffiths, London

Revd D. Hugh Matthews, Cardiff

Revd Dafydd H. Owen, Cardiff

Revd Dr D. Ben Rees, Liverpool

Revd Ivor Thomas Rees, Swansea

Revd Peter Dewi Richards, London

Revd Lord (Roger) Roberts, Llandudno

Revd Anthony Williams, London

~

David Beasley, Librarian, The Goldsmiths' Company

Dr Lloyd Bowen, Cardiff University

Anna Brueton, London Welsh Family History Society

Prof. Matthew Davies, director, Centre for Metropolitan History

Philip Davies, former director (London Region), English Heritage

Cyril Evans, National Library of Wales

Prof. Emeritus Ralph A. Griffiths, Swansea

Ceris Gruffudd, National Library of Wales

Prof. Medwin Hughes, University of Wales Trinity Saint David

Prof. Emeritus Geraint H. Jenkins, Aberystwyth

Anne Jones, London Welsh Family History Society

Dr John Gwynfor Jones, Cardiff

Paul Joslin, formerly organist and director of music, Holy Trinity Brompton

Robert Lacey, National Library of Wales

Camwy Macdonald, National Library of Wales

Dr Tomos Owen, Bangor University

Eben Phillips, Cardiff

Dr Robert Pope, University of Wales Trinity Saint David

Prof. Andrew Prescott, King's College London

Dyfrig Hughes Roberts, Eisteddfod Genedlaethol Cymru

Prof. Andrew Saint, general editor, *The Survey of London*

Jeremy Smith, London Metropolitan Archive

Prof. M. Wynn Thomas, Swansea University

William Troughton, National Library of Wales

Helen Weller, Cheshunt Foundation, Westminster College, Cambridge

Dr Eryn M. White, Aberystwyth University

Tegid Rhys Williams, Bangor University

~

Eirlys Bebb (Holloway and Eglwys-y-Drindod)

Nest Beynon (Hammersmith)

Iola and Bob Bilson (Willesden)

Gareth Blainey (Chiltern Street)

Mary Bott (Jewin)

Michael Buck (Dewi Sant)

Rita Clark (King's Cross)

Gwynne and Eira Davies (Jewin)

Kathryn Davies (Falmouth Road and Jewin)

Simon Davies (Radnor Walk)

Tom a Myra Davies (Wembley)

Myra Dawson (Jewin)

Beti Gwenfron Evans (Wood Green)

The late Gwen Evans (Wood Green)

Gwyn Evans (Clapham Junction)

Gwyndaf Evans (Lewisham)

Ivor Evans (Jewin)

Mary Evans (Jewin)

Olwen and John Evans (St Benet)

The late Margaret Felix (Clapham Junction)

Catherine Fowler (Shirland Road)

Mary Green (Mile End)

Graham Griffiths (Ealing)

Siôn Griffiths (Dewi Sant)

Eiona Hammond (Radnor Walk)

Marian Howell (King's Cross)

Brian Hughes (Castle Street)

Bill Jenkins (Jewin)

Ann and Trevor Jennett (Clapham Junction)

Cathy Jones (King's Cross)

Eluned Jones (King's Cross)

Eluned Jones (Sibley Grove)

The late Eluned Idris Jones (Clapham Junction)

Marian Jones (Falmouth Road)

Pennant Jones (Wilton Square and Willesden)

The late Wyn Jones (Lewisham)

Richard Killoughery (Kingston)

Ken Kyffin (Charing Cross)

Glyn Lewis (Clapham Junction)

Megan Lewis (Hammersmith and Ealing)

Ane Lloyd (Mile End)

Bryn Lloyd (Sutton)

Delyth Macdonald (Wood Green)

The late Audrey Morgan (Willesden)

Gareth Morgan (Willesden)

Tom and Bethan Morgan (Willesden)

Enid Morris (Charing Cross)

John T. Morris (Hammersmith)

Llinos and John Morris (Jewin)

Meriele Myhre (Radnor Walk)

Glenys Pashley (Walham Green)

Gwynne Pickering (Charing Cross and Jewin)

Anthony Platt (Leytonstone)

Sian Posner (Jewin)

Mrs W. H. Price (Holloway)

Geraint Pritchard (Jewin)

Tim Pryse-Hawkins (St Benet)

Maldwyn Pugh (City Road and Chiltern Street)

Hugh Richards (Falmouth Road)

Glyn and Cathy Roberts (Jewin and Dewi Sant)

Rhian Medi Roberts (Jewin)

Eleri Rowlands (King's Cross)

John Samuel (Woolwich and Castle Street)

Sian Starr (Jewin)

Hywel Thomas (King's Cross)

Hywel and Eleanor Thomas (Clapham Junction)

Lisa Thomas (Jewin)

Maira Thomas (King's Cross)

Margaret Thomas (Falmouth Road)

Catrin Unwin (Falmouth Road)

Bethan Whitall (Walthamstow and Leytonstone)

Bowen Williams (Wood Green)

David Williams (Falmouth Road)

Glynis Williams (Santes Fair)

Lowri Williams (Clapham Junction)

Mary Williams (Clapham Junction)

Mary Williams (Jewin)

Robyn Williams (Charing Cross)

~

Brent Archives

The British Library

Trustees of the Cheshunt Foundation, Westminster College, Cambridge

English Heritage

The Goldsmiths' Company

Haringey Culture, Libraries and Learning

Islington Local History Centre

Lambeth Palace Library

London Borough of Lambeth Archives

London Borough of Newham, Heritage and Archives Team

London Metropolitan Archive

Museum of London

The National Library of Wales

Stone Nest

Surrey History Centre

LOCATIONS OF LONDON WELSH CHAPELS AND CHURCHES

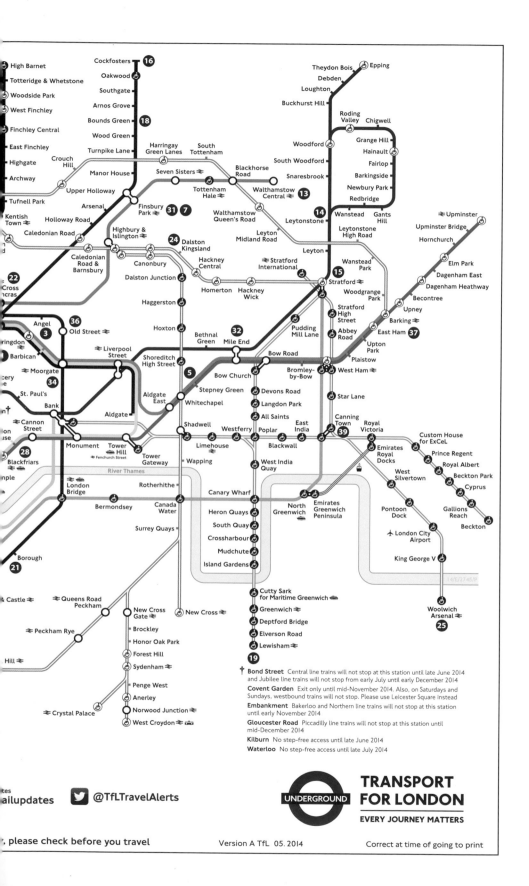

† **Bond Street** Central line trains will not stop at this station until late June 2014 and Jubilee line trains will not stop from early July until early December 2014

Covent Garden Exit only until mid-November 2014. Also, on Saturdays and Sundays, westbound trains will not stop. Please use Leicester Square instead

Embankment Bakerloo and Northern line trains will not stop at this station until early November 2014

Gloucester Road Piccadilly line trains will not stop at this station until mid-December 2014

Kilburn No step-free access until late June 2014

Waterloo No step-free access until late July 2014

, please check before you travel   Version A TfL 05. 2014   Correct at time of going to print

KEY TO MAP

LONDON'S WELSH CHAPELS AND CHURCHES
(BY NEAREST STATION)

1. Jewin (Barbican)
2. Charing Cross Road (Leicester Square)
3. Wilton Square (Angel)
4. Falmouth Road (Elephant & Castle)
5. Mile End Road (Stepney Green)
6. Shirland Road (Warwick Avenue)
7. Holloway (Finsbury Park)
8. Ealing Green (Ealing Broadway)
9. Clapham Junction (Clapham Junction)
10. Hammersmith (Hammersmith)
11. Walham Green (Fulham Broadway)
12. Wembley (Wembley Central)
13. Walthamstow (Walthamstow Central)
14. Leytonstone (Leytonstone)
15. Stratford (Stratford)
16. Cockfosters (Cockfosters)
17. Willesden Green (Willesden Green)
18. Wood Green (Bounds Green)
19. Lewisham (Lewisham)
20. Sutton (Morden★)
21. Borough (Borough)
22. King's Cross (King's Cross)
23. Radnor Walk (Sloane Square)

24. Barrett's Grove (Dalston Kingsland)
25. Woolwich (Woolwich Arsenal)
26. Harrow (South Harrow)
27. Battersea Rise (Clapham Junction)
28. St Benet (Blackfriars)
29. Dewi Sant (Paddington)
30. St Mair (Oval)
31. St Padarn (Finsbury Park)
32. St Rhystyd (Mile End)
33. Castle Street (Oxford Circus)
34. Eldon Street (Moorgate)
35. Chiltern Street (Baker Street)
36. City Road (Old Street)
37. Sibley Grove (East Ham)
38. Brunswick (Marylebone)
39. Cumberland Road (Canning Town)

★ Nearest on Transport for London Map

INTRODUCTION

The story of the Welsh in London spans a thousand years. In many ways, it is still largely untold.

Defining Welshness in a London context is not straightforward. It never has been. Patterns of migration vary; language habits differ; social activities change; loyalties are tested.

But one thing is very clear.

It is impossible to understand the story of the Welsh in London without appreciating the central place of organised religion. The Welsh Nonconformist chapels (and a small number of Welsh-speaking Anglican churches) were far and away the most significant centres of Welsh life in the city throughout the nineteenth century and the first half of the twentieth.

Religious Nonconformity redefined Wales and Welshness. In rejecting the state religion of England, Welsh people built a new identity for themselves. The same process also shaped the London Welsh community in an age when thousands of *Cymry* made for the metropolis. It follows that the chapels are a vital element in the rich story of the Welsh in London.

Without understanding the roots and functions of the chapel network we cannot hope to appreciate the complex dynamics of the London Welsh community over the years.

Writing in 1947, the Revd Llywelyn Williams of King's Cross regretted that only 'a small percentage of the Welsh who come to London remain loyal to the religion of their homeland'. He criticised those who 'shed their Welsh attire and pose as urban Englishmen', while praising the minority whose 'weekly programme includes the Sunday school, the service, the sermon, and the desire to be part of a Christian fellowship'.

The chapels no longer attract crowds of today's London Welsh; their relevance as centres of religious and social life is hugely diminished; their visibility is minimal, to put it kindly. They have been abandoned by the vast majority of those who might be considered potential members. They have rarely featured in serious discussions about the future of the Welsh community in London, though that has now started to change.

So why bother to pay them any attention?

Something has changed appreciably since the start of the new millennium.

A growing interest in the story of Welsh migration around the world, the online availability of genealogical data, and the renewed focus on Welsh identity in a devolved United Kingdom – all of these have created a demand for gaps to be filled, for questions to be answered, for a credible narrative to be constructed.

The first recognised Welsh-speaking religious cause in London was started in the late eighteenth century in Smithfield, generating a network which grew steadily and peaked on the eve of the Second World War. The 'London Welsh Yearbook' for 1938–9 lists no fewer than 31 Welsh-speaking Nonconformist and Anglican causes with an additional six Sunday school vestries. The membership lists of the central London chapels of Jewin, Charing Cross Road, King's Cross and Castle Street each featured more than a thousand names.

The drastic post-war decline experienced in so many parts of Wales took longer to affect the London congregations. There was still growth in the London Welsh chapel scene in the 1950s, thanks in part to the wave of young Welsh men and women taking up teaching posts in London and the surrounding counties.

But the London chapels suffered their own crisis in the 1970s, and by 2014 the number of functioning chapels had fallen to seven. Given the fragility of so many causes in Welsh cities, towns and villages, the survival of as many as seven Welsh chapels in London is surely admirable. But the prospects are patchy, and on current form the forecast for future witness must be unsettling. It is likely that the vibrant, impressive network of the 1950s will be further reduced by the end of the decade.

This narrative is overwhelmingly based on the Nonconformist causes, but I include a chapter on the Welsh-speaking Anglican churches in London. Their important contribution also deserves to be recognised. Some chapters are notably longer than others: it is a fact that Jewin, for example, has a longer and richer history than, say, Stratford. Sadly, time and resources did not allow the inclusion of Welsh causes in Slough, Luton, Croydon, Guildford, Kingston and other centres outside the London area. This is in no way to disregard their importance. They would certainly provide good material for another author.

The main published sources of information are listed in the bibliography. I have relied on a combination of official histories, archive material, press reports, chapel documents and, in many cases, accounts kindly provided by individuals.

This book is aimed at the widest audience: the Welsh chapel community of London, past and present; all those who take an interest in our Welsh heritage; and a younger generation who show signs of appreciating the vision and values of our ancestors.

Quite simply, the story of London's Welsh chapels and churches deserves to be recorded.

How else will future generations understand the forces that shaped the absorbing world of *Cymry Llundain*?

HUW EDWARDS
Llundain, Gorffennaf 2015

CHAPTER 1

FLOW

In the early years of the twentieth century, a tough young farmhand called Daniel Edwards left Dyffryn Aeron in Cardiganshire bound for London.

Daniel Edwards was my great-grandfather.

He and thousands like him were driven from home by extreme hardship. A tenant farmer's life in rural Cardiganshire was brutally unforgiving. Four of his uncles had emigrated to the USA where they suffered yet more poverty and misery before making a success of their lives in Oak Hill, Ohio.

Daniel's story was rather different.

I have spent many hours trying to piece together the sad story of his stay in London. He committed the supreme sin of the Edwardian age: he 'wasted his opportunity' by drinking too much and failing to hold down a regular job as a dairyman's assistant. He was sent home to Wales where he spent the rest of his life as a labourer and roadworker, noted even in old age as a man of extraordinary physical strength.

The person who organised the return to Dyffryn Aeron in 1907 was Jenkin, one of his younger brothers. Here was a strikingly different character who created a thriving dairy business and became a prominent figure in the London Welsh community of the East End.

The story of the two brothers is revealing in so many ways, a tale of fortune and misfortune, of diligence and neglect, of application and carelessness, of success and failure. Indeed, it conveys something of the richly diverse experience of generations of Welsh people in London since Tudor times.

Daniel and Jenkin Edwards are credible representatives of the great mass of Welsh men and women driven from home by hard economic reality. They

Jenkin Edwards on his milk round in London's East End (1908)

tended to settle in some of the poorest areas of the capital where they led a double life as Londoners whose Welshness was irrefutable.

That Welshness found its most complete expression within the home and, crucially, in those all-dominant centres of Welsh life in nineteenth- and twentieth-century London, the Nonconformist chapels. They were divided by denomination (Baptist, Independent, Calvinistic Methodist, Wesleyan Methodist) but there was a considerable degree of cooperation between all the London chapels. The sense of belonging to a London-wide community of exiles tended to weaken the denominational tribalism which dominated chapel life in Wales.

Jenkin Edwards and his extended family became lifelong members of the thriving Welsh chapels of Mile End Road, Walthamstow and Leytonstone in east London. His obituary confirmed his loyalty to the cause in Mile End. He personified a class of business people without whose generosity the huge building costs of the London chapels would never have been met.

The fortunes of the London Welsh fluctuated rather dramatically over the years. When Jenkin died in 1935, chapel membership was peaking and the social life of the London Welsh was vibrant. The 'London Welsh Yearbooks' of the 1930s tell their own story. They carry exhaustive lists of dances, concerts, sports engagements, dinners, talks, excursions, and fundraising bazaars; not to mention details of chapel and church services, 'cymanfaoedd canu' (hymn-singing festivals), the chapels' literary societies, drama and sports clubs, and debating contests.

Is it any wonder that this decade came to be seen by so many as something of a gilded era?

It might even be imagined that this impressive range of activity was sustained by a huge London Welsh population. Not at all. There had been many wild and fanciful estimates of the numbers of Welsh people in London over the centuries, but the coming of the census system in 1841 offered a much more realistic assessment.

In 1851, the census began recording each individual's place or county of birth. This produced the first official measurement of Welsh-born people in London: there were 17,575 (just 0.74%) of the city's population of 2.4 million.

Lloyd's Dairy, Amwell Street, in the 1970s
© London Metropolitan Archive

By the time of Jenkin's death, the numbers of Welsh in London had swollen to around 60,000. More precisely, this was the number of Londoners born in Wales recorded in the census of 1931. It is clearly not a wholly reliable measure of the Welsh presence in the capital: it does not take account of second and third generations whose sense of Welsh identity was still intact. But the census is far and away the best measure available. Sixty thousand might sound impressive but it represents a very modest part (1.36%) of the city's total population of 4.4 million.

By the census of 2011, the proportion of Welsh-born in an ever-growing and changing London had dropped to 0.7%, or 53,828. Fewer than 500 of the London Welsh community in 2011 were members of Welsh chapels or churches, one tenth of the number in the 1930s.

This should be seen against the background of an ever-diversifying London community: the 2011 census found the 'White British' ethnic group to be a minority (44.9%) of the city's population for the very first time. 'Asian' (18.4%), 'Black' (13.3%), 'Other White' (14.9%), 'Mixed' (5.1%), and 'Other' (3.4%) ethnic groups cemented London's status as the most ethnically diverse part of the United Kingdom, and the region with the highest proportion of people identifying themselves as Muslim, Buddhist, Hindu and Jewish. But the same city recorded the lowest level (48%) of Christian belief, while Wales had the highest proportion (32%) of people reporting no religion. Seen in this context, the rapid decline in chapel life, both in Wales and in London, is clear.

Before we get to grips with the origins of London's Welsh chapels and churches, we need a better understanding of the historical context. When did the Welsh become a meaningful presence in the city? Did they live as a discrete ethnic group, or did they rapidly assimilate and conform? How willingly did they assert their Welshness, and how did it manifest itself?

Medieval archives document a Welsh presence in London from the age of the last Welsh princes when Anglo-Welsh relations were, we might say, problematic. Many of the early references feature in legal and court papers. The individuals named range from the prestigious and prominent to the humble and obscure.

Welsh 'guests' at the Tower of London included Gruffydd ap Llewelyn Fawr and his son Owain, imprisoned by Henry III. Gruffydd fell to his death

Mile End Road chapel (1900)
© National Library of Wales

in 1244 as he tried to escape from the White Tower. The bricked-up window of his cell can still be seen today. Another famous member of Welsh royalty to die there was Catrin Glyndŵr, daughter of Owain Glyndŵr. She and her three daughters were captured after the fall of Harlech castle. Catrin died in 1413 and was buried in St Swithin's churchyard in the heart of the City of London. A splendid memorial was placed on the site, off Cannon Street, in 2001.

Legal records contain a wealth of detail about Welsh people in London, as Professor Andrew Prescott of King's College London has explained in his studies. In 1267, two Welshmen convicted of theft were executed on Tower Hill. In 1283, Edward de Dissart was tried 'on suspicion of being a Welshman'. This is hardly surprising: it was a few months after the killing of Llywelyn

('Llywelyn The Last') in December 1282, when Edward I's campaign boosted anti-Welsh sentiment among the English to new heights. In 1384, 'David Welsh of Wales' was accused of facilitating his master's murder in Cranford, a village on the outskirts of London. There are many other examples.

The importance of trade between London and Wales during the fourteenth century is suggested by the appearance of Stephen ap Howell before the Court of Aldermen of the City of London in 1383. He was there to apply for an exemption from cloth duties for the town of Carmarthen. In 1393 we learn of Iorwerth ap Rhys of north Wales travelling to Italy and arranging his currency supply in London en route. Another business case in the early-fifteenth century involves the London glazier, John Forte, providing glass for a grand Welsh home being built by the landowner Sir Richard Harberd.

London, therefore, was hardly a no-go zone for the Welsh in the Plantagenet age. But it is generally accepted by historians that the accession of Henry Tudor in 1485 opened the gates of London to hordes of loyal Welsh servants, soldiers and courtiers. In effect, they suggest this was the year a recognisable London Welsh community was born.

Henry VII, founder of the Tudor dynasty, born at Pembroke castle, a grandson of Owain Tudur (or Owen Tudor), was seen by the Welsh as a national saviour. Had he not chosen to return from exile in France by setting foot on Welsh soil? Had he not gathered Welsh troops on his long march to Bosworth? Had he not proudly proclaimed his Welsh ancestry? His firstborn was called Arthur.

The Welshness of Henry Tudor is not a matter for us, though it has to be said that few historians would describe Henry VII as the saviour or 'son of prophecy' heralded by the Welsh bards. His claim on the throne of England was unconvincing, to say the least. By descent he was a quarter Welsh, a quarter French and half English, but his court included some influential Welsh figures, and London became less hostile to the presence of Welsh people during the Tudor years. In time, they achieved prominence in the military, in Parliament, and the Inns of Court.

The poet John Skelton, one of Henry VIII's favourites, offered an amusing perspective on the heavy Welsh presence in London. He joked that when heaven became overwhelmed with an influx of Welsh people, an angel was posted outside the gates to yell 'Caws Pobi!'. The Welsh addiction to 'Toasted Cheese!' led to a rush for the gates, and heaven's problems were solved. One senses Skelton's desire for a similar solution in the royal court.

Estimating the size of London's Welsh community during the Tudor era is an exercise in sustained guesswork. In a study completed in 1947, Bob Owen of Croesor produced his own estimates based on a detailed search of sixteenth-century archives. He estimated 1,500 Welsh-born Londoners in the city in 1550 (no more than one per cent of the city's population), a figure based on a study of a group of Welsh migrants in the first half of the century.

Intriguingly, Bob Owen found 169 Welsh-born officials and servants at the royal court in 1550, and 393 Welsh-born lawyers, clerks and students at the Inns of Court, a number which grew to 1,012 in the seventeenth century. John Dee, the polymath born in London to parents from Radnorshire, was one of the most learned men of his age and an adviser to Elizabeth I. The queen's chief adviser was William Cecil, whose family came from the Welsh Marches. These figures and others suggest a solid Welsh legacy from the reign of Henry Tudor.

The Lambeth Palace library provides other valuable evidence of Welsh numbers in London. Emrys Jones, who edited and contributed to the pioneering volume *The Welsh in London 1500–2000* (2001), identified as many as 6,000 Welsh surnames in a 1638 church survey of London held in the library's archives. That would correspond to a much stronger 7.3% of the city's population. A similar London survey in 1695 includes 4,353 surnames of recognisably Welsh origin, corresponding to around 7.5% of the population.

The accuracy of numbers based solely on a study of surnames is evidently compromised, but these numbers are probably the best sources available to us. It is a very long wait until 1851 for the first census providing reliable statistical evidence of people's county of birth.

That is not to say, however, that the seventeenth and eighteenth centuries are barren for our purposes. Quite the opposite, in fact. They were centuries which witnessed a remarkable revival of interest in Welsh culture, a revival fostered and driven in London. The city was, in every sense, the capital of Wales. Cardiff would have to wait until 1905 to be granted city status by Edward VII; capital status would be delayed until 1955. Wales lacked the national institutions, including a National Assembly, National Eisteddfod and National Library, so familiar to us today. The list should also feature the University of Wales, for a century the focus of the nation's advanced learning, but a body which has sadly lost its status as our national university.

London was the unavoidable destination for Welsh men and women searching for broader horizons. It provided opportunities on a spectacular scale. It offered employment for all types, a spectrum of social life to suit all pockets, and a vibrant, ever-changing community which rewarded initiative. To say that Wales offered nothing like it is a polite understatement.

Within this seething city community there is vivid evidence of Welsh life. The armies of drovers who brought livestock from Wales to England appear frequently in archives and literature. Bishop John Williams of Bangor called them 'the Spanish fleet of Wales which brings in what little gold and silver we have'. The drovers' numbers were boosted in the eighteenth and early-nineteenth centuries by groups of women from rural Wales (many from Cardiganshire) who made an annual visit to London to work in parks and gardens. They were known as 'merched y gerddi' ('the garden girls') and they built a reputation as hard-working, honest workers.

The drovers and 'merched y gerddi' were visitors to the city. They

travelled by foot along familiar routes from different parts of Wales, spent as much time as was necessary in London, and returned home with their gains. To what extent they were aware of an established London Welsh milieu is anyone's guess. But that milieu was certainly active by the mid-eighteenth century.

Indeed, one of the most decisively vital episodes in the story of Welsh culture was enacted in the heart of eighteenth-century London. On 21 June 1792, Iolo Morganwg

Montgomery drovers (1895)
© National Library of Wales

held a peculiar ceremony on Primrose Hill, a spot on the northern fringe of Regent's Park which affords an impressive panorama of central London. Driven by a high-octane mix of pride, resentment, and creative genius, he had invented 'Gorsedd Beirdd Ynys Prydain' ('The Gorsedd of Bards of the Isle of Britain') which met for the first time on that midsummer day. It is now an indispensable feature of the National Eisteddfod and Welsh life.

Iolo had fabricated a glorious ancient tradition for Wales, fuelled not only by his anger at the endlessly disparaging opinions of the English on Welsh culture, but also by the equally dismissive attitudes of the northern Welsh to their southern brothers and sisters. Iolo's flaming pride in his native county of Glamorgan led him in eccentric directions. He had first come to London in 1773 when he met the wealthy businessman Owen Jones ('Owain Myfyr') and gained an introduction to London's Welsh literary community. Jones had co-founded the Gwyneddigion Society in 1770: he and others were tired of what they considered the snobbish pretensions of the Honourable Society of Cymmrodorion, the society formed by Richard Morris and others in 1751.

Owen Jones, 'Owain Myfyr' (1741–1814)
© National Library of Wales

Jones was also active in the Cymreigyddion Society, formed in *c.*1794, which Iolo joined during one of his stays in London.

The importance of these societies in safeguarding, revitalising and promoting Welsh culture, both in London and in Wales, cannot be overstated. The Gwyneddigion, in particular, financed the publication of some of the most important works of Welsh literature, including *Barddoniaeth Dafydd ab Gwilym* (1789) and *The Myvyrian Archaiology of Wales* (1801–7), a three-volume collection of medieval Welsh works. Most of the works were genuine, but they included some notable forgeries by Iolo Morganwg whose capacity for deception and inventive genius is still hotly debated.

Both Gwyneddigion and Cymreigyddion featured prominently in one of the biggest Welsh public scandals of the early-nineteenth century involving a Methodist preacher called Edward Jones, or 'Ginshop Jones' as he was mercilessly lampooned by the poet and satirist John Jones ('Jac Glan-y-gors'). Edward Jones is a figure of paramount importance in the saga of the Welsh in London.

All of which brings us to the startling starting point of our story.

The founding pastor of the first Welsh chapel in London was, of all things, a former soldier and publican.

The colourful tale of 'Ginshop Jones' unlocks a much bigger adventure.

CHAPTER 2

BEGINNINGS

Edward Jones was an overbearing thug, by most accounts, with a natural gift for upsetting people. He certainly made many enemies. The dreadful reputation he suffered for much of his lifetime has hardly improved in the two centuries since his death. But there is a case for suggesting that his notoriety might be reassessed: his problematic celebrity has tended to obscure his real achievements.

To the best of our knowledge, Edward Jones was born in Llansannan, Denbighshire, in 1741. The young Jones signed up with the Life Guards, and after completing his military service settled in London as an innkeeper and 'rum and brandy merchant'. He joined the congregation of the Tabernacle, Moorfields, one of the churches built by George Whitefield, the prominent evangelist and one of the founders of English Methodism. Jones established himself as a leading member and exhorter, along with a 'ginger-beer manufacturer' called Griffith Jones of Pentre Uchaf, a small village in Llŷn.

Jones and Jones became prime movers in the establishment of the first formally-constituted Welsh Nonconformist cause in London. They took soundings among their fellow London Welsh and decided to look for suitable accommodation in a central location.

It is important to note that the Welsh in London had long enjoyed preaching in their native language. The leading Welsh Methodist revivalist Howell Harris made no fewer than 24 visits to the capital between 1739 and 1767, often preaching to his fellow Welsh in Lambeth, Westminster, Fetter Lane, and in Deptford where many Welsh people worked in the shipyards and royal docks.

Harris's diary on 3 May 1739 notes a visit to a 'farm' in Lambeth to preach to the Welsh. By 1740 the meeting place had moved: Harris records his visit to a 'house in Lambeth over ye bridge with ye Welshmen'. The bridge in question would have to be London Bridge because Westminster Bridge did not open until 1750. An unsigned letter written to Harris in March of that year requests his attendance at the 'Crown house in Lambeth', where the 'poor brethren in the Welch society... continue to meet as usual'.

The Revd John Thickens, in *Howel Harris yn Llundain* (1934), admits great difficulty in locating the 'Crown house'. Other researchers have encountered similar obstacles. The surviving parish records at Lambeth Archives seem to make no mention of a 'Crown house' in this area.

Further digging has nonetheless unearthed some very valuable clues. We can now reveal more information about the likely location. Today's London Borough of Lambeth is based on the ancient parish of Lambeth St Mary, the northern part of which met the River Thames opposite the Palace of Westminster. In the first half of the eighteenth century extensive areas of the parish were marshland criss-crossed by raised roads. Contemporary maps of the area show a few large properties with gardens and some farmhouses dotted around the parish. The 'Crown house' was almost certainly one of the unnamed private residences featured on these maps.

An extensive search of newspaper archives produced a 1736 reference to a robbery 'under Crown-house garden wall between Lambeth and St George's Fields'; another search of land records at Lambeth Archives produced a 1784 reference to 'Crown House, St George's Fields'. In today's London, St George's Fields would roughly correspond to a section of Southwark extending from the

Howell Harris (1714–73) first preached in London in 1739
© National Library of Wales

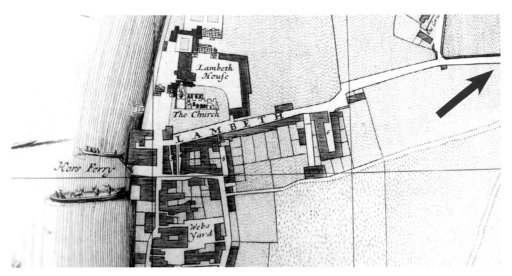

The likely location of 'Crown House, Lambeth' (Morgan, 1682)
© London Metropolitan Archive

Thames end of Blackfriars Road at its northernmost point to West Square (near the Imperial War Museum) at its southernmost.

There are other tantalising clues. Martin Van Butchell, a noted eccentric and dental pioneer, was born in 1735 in central London. But as Kirby notes in *Wonderful and Scientific Museum: Or, Magazine of Remarkable Characters* (Volume 1, 1803), the family soon moved to 'a large house in the parish of Lambeth, between Westminster Bridge and the *Dog and Duck*, to which a very extensive garden was annexed, and was then known by the name of the *Crown House*'. The Dog and Duck was a famous tavern and place of entertainment which stood on land which is now the site of the Imperial War Museum. This likely geographical location of the 'Crown house' becomes more convincing.

That case is further strengthened by a crucial discovery at the Surrey History Centre (Lambeth was at that time in the county of Surrey). In 1767 it records Martin Van Butchell's signature on Dissenters' Certificates relating to three locations: a chapel in his possession in King John's Court, Bermondsey; waste ground near King John's Court; and Kennington Common, Lambeth.

Kennington Common was an important dissenters' venue for open-air meetings. Far more significant at this stage in our story is the revelation that Martin Van Butchell was himself a dissenter whose importance is underlined by the Surrey certificates. Kirby also noted that Van Butchell used to attend the 'Westminster Forum' (a dissenting group) on a Sunday evening 'where he always chose to read a Chapter from the New Testament... and this probably accounts for what some people have said about his occasionally being a *Preacher*'.

This is the same Martin Van Butchell who was living in the 'Crown house' by the late 1730s. It now seems entirely reasonable to conclude that it was to his home that Howell Harris came to preach to the Welsh in 1740.

It might also be reasonable to conclude that this was the very house, with its extensive garden, referred to by the Methodist leader John Wesley in his journal entry for Sunday, 9 September 1739:

> *My mother went with us, about five, to Kennington, where were supposed to be twenty thousand people. I again insisted on that foundation of all our hope, 'Believe in the Lord Jesus, and thou shalt be saved.' From Kennington I went to a society at Lambeth. The house being filled, the rest stood in the garden. The deep attention they showed gave me a good hope that they will not all be forgetful hearers.*

There is other evidence from the following century to help us with the precise location. In 1820 the will of Horatio Goodbehere of China Terrace, Lambeth, mentions 'his estate called the Crown House... on which is situated Lambeth Chapel and three homes of Brixton Place'. If Goodbehere's is indeed Harris's 'Crown house', we can fix its modern location to the south-western corner of the intersection of Lambeth Road and Kennington Road, near the site of today's Lambeth Mission and St Mary's, a shared Anglican and Methodist church.

The China Walk Estate, in the same area, dates from the 1920s and is just a few hundred yards from the southern end of Lambeth Bridge. But that bridge did not exist in Harris's day (it opened in 1862) so his journey would have involved either crossing London Bridge, Westminster Bridge (after 1750), or using the traditional horse ferry to Lambeth Stairs from Millbank.

When Harris visited Lambeth for the first time in May 1739, he had already preached a few times to the Welsh in Fetter Lane, Holborn. This is considerably later than the first recorded instance of a Welsh sermon delivered in London. There were extensive newspaper reports in 1714 (or 1715 by the modern dating) of a sermon delivered by the Revd George Lewis, who preached 'in the British language' at a St David's Day service in St Paul's Church, Covent Garden.

It was an event organised by the newly-created 'Honourable Society of Antient Britons'. The annual service to mark St David's Day in London is still held today, and over the years it has taken place in some grand venues

St Paul's, Covent Garden, where a Welsh sermon was preached in 1715

including St Paul's Cathedral and the church of St Martin-in-the-Fields in Trafalgar Square.

It is surely sensible to assume that Welsh-language sermons had been heard in the capital before 1715, but we have no solid evidence for this. Some of the greatest names in the religious history of Wales had visited or lived in London over the years, including Bishop William Morgan (whose translation of the Bible into Welsh transformed the status of the language), John Penry (Wales's most famous Protestant martyr), Vavasor Powell (the Puritan preacher and evangelist), Stephen Hughes (one of the early apostles of Welsh Nonconformity), Richard Price (the philosopher-preacher, revered in the fledgling United States and widely regarded as the greatest Welsh thinker), and Daniel Williams (the theologian whose vast London library is still a major Nonconformist research facility).

The leading Methodist preachers Daniel Rowland and Howell Davies also visited London in the mid-eighteenth century. It is difficult to believe, for instance, that a preacher of Rowland's evangelical zeal did not avail himself of an opportunity to preach in Welsh during his time in the city. According to one anecdote recorded by James Hughes, pastor of Jewin Crescent chapel from 1823, Daniel Rowland preached in Lambeth and Kennington Common on several occasions.

Without certain proof, we are nonetheless stuck in the realms of the possible and probable. We simply cannot find incontrovertible evidence of a Welsh-language preaching tradition in London before the early-eighteenth century.

What we can say with far more confidence is that the tradition of Welsh preaching in Lambeth and elsewhere led eventually to the decision to rent a room in a narrow, gloomy alleyway near Smithfield in the City of London. Cock Lane curves from Giltspur Street down to Snow Hill, a stone's throw from the famous meat market and the liveried glory of Haberdashers' Hall nearby.

Its modest appearance on the street map of London belies its historical worth: Pye Corner, at the junction of Cock Lane and Giltspur Street, marked the furthest point of the Great Fire of London in 1666; Cock Lane was where John Bunyan died in 1688; and in 1762 the alleyway became famous throughout Britain thanks to the reported appearance of a ghost at number 25.

Modern Cock Lane, with its mix of expensive offices and smart rented apartments, has a soulless, corporate character. The Cock Lane of the mid-eighteenth century was a very different place, crammed with little shops and the grimy homes of the working poor. Earlier still, in medieval times, the graphically-named Cokkes Lane had housed several

Daniel Rowland (1713–90), one of the leaders of the Welsh Calvinistic Methodist revival
© National Library of Wales

Kennington Common, where Daniel Rowland is said to have preached
© Lambeth Archives

brothels. This rather seedy street was where Jones and Jones, after prolonged canvassing among the London Welsh, eventually decided to rent a room to hold religious meetings in the late-eighteenth century.

The challenge of dating the start of the Cock Lane era – one of the biggest milestones in this entire story – has defeated every chronicler. Dr Owen Thomas, James Hughes's successor as pastor of Jewin Crescent, supplied 'around 1774' as his best guess. This was based on anecdotal evidence presented to John Hughes, the author of *Methodistiaeth Cymru* (1851–6), the official history of Welsh Calvinistic Methodism to 1850. All subsequent narrators have accepted 'around 1774' as the most reliable estimate. This is why Jewin Welsh Presbyterian Church – which grew from Cock Lane – celebrated its bicentenary in 1974.

Even allowing for the modest margin implied by 'around', we can now declare that this dating is at least two years adrift. Based on some previously-undiscovered references, it is clear that the Welsh were already gathering for worship in Cock Lane at least as early as 1772. The *Daily Advertiser* on 15 January 1773 carries this simple but significant notice:

*Next Sunday, beginning at Three in the Afternoon, a Sermon is to be preached
in Welch, at the Meeting in Lambeth, by Mr David Jones, of Llangerthro [sic]
in Cardiganshire; also, at Half past Six, the same Evening, he is to preach in the
Great Room over the Earthenware Shop, in Cock-Lane, West-Smithfield.*

Do not be deceived by the apparently sparse nature of the entry: this is the
long-lost key which finally unlocks some stubborn mysteries. It provides
answers to several vital questions.

For the very first time, we have a known date for a meeting in Cock
Lane. For the very first time, we have a precise location within Cock Lane
for these gatherings. And for the very first time, we have evidence that the
Lambeth meetings nurtured by Howell Harris were still in business when
services of worship began to be held in Cock Lane. All of these are significant
discoveries.

It seems safe to assume from the wording of the notice that this meeting
was not the first of its kind in Cock Lane. The new year was barely a fortnight
old when the notice appeared, so the 'Great Room' must have been in use in
1772, if not earlier. We can now demonstrate that Cock Lane was indeed a

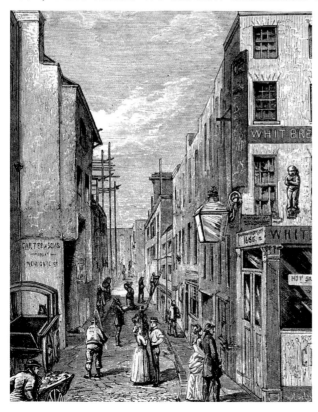

Cock Lane in the 1870s
© National Library of Wales

focal point for dissenting worship in the preceding decade. The *Gazeteer and New Daily Advertiser* on 8 February 1766 carries this report:

> *The New Meeting-house in Cock-lane will be opened to-morrow morning, at half past ten o'clock, by the Rev. Mr. Allen, author of the Christian Pilgrim, just published. As there is no other meeting-house near that place, it will, by desire, be constantly kept open every Lord's Day.*

This sounds like a purpose-built centre, not a meeting room over a shop. It is unlikely to be the space rented by Edward Jones. But the news that Cock Lane saw the opening of a new dissenters' house in 1766 tells us that Jones's choice of location is perhaps not quite as bizarre as it first appears. Sadly, despite thorough searches, there is no documented evidence such as rental agreements or parish land records to help identify a definitive starting date in the 'Great Room over the Earthenware Shop' in Cock Lane.

The preaching was undertaken by Edward Jones, while Griffith Jones took charge of the singing. There were times when the cries of zealous worshippers drew the attention of scornful passers-by in the teeming street below. Some curious souls came to enjoy the singing, but all too often others came to jeer and cause trouble. This intolerance became a familiar problem for Welsh congregations in other parts of London in later years. Despite the challenges presented by this exotic location, the Welsh would continue to meet in Cock Lane for eight years: Robert Jones of Rhos-lan preached there in 1779; Dr William Richards of King's Lynn wrote to a friend in September 1783 describing how he 'preached in Welsh in Cock Lane to a very crowded audience'; Robert Evans of Llanrwst visited Cock Lane in 1782 and lost his life in a road accident on the long and dangerous journey home; other ministers including John Prydderch of Trecastell and Dafydd Cadwaladr of Bala are reported to have visited in those early years.

The crowd, it seems, quickly became too big for the 'Great Room', so the search was on for a bigger space. By 1785 we find the two Joneses and their flock migrating a half-mile northwards to Wilderness Row. This street ceased to exist when the new Clerkenwell Road was laid out in 1879 but some of its features remain. It seems Wilderness Row was originally named after a large, wild garden which belonged to the Charterhouse, the ancient hospital, school and almshouse built on the site of an old Carthusian monastery.

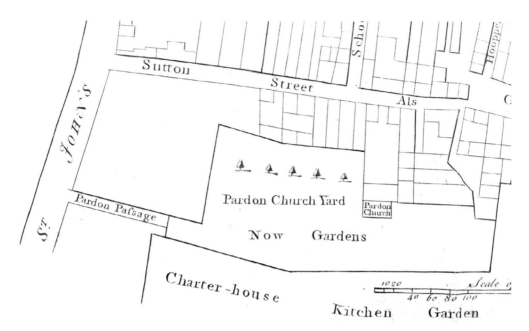

Pardon Churchyard (Charterhouse, 1687)
© London Metropolitan Archive

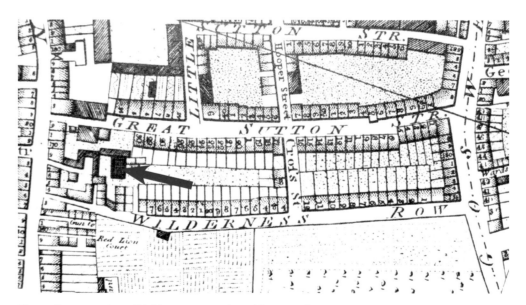

The earliest mapping of Wilderness Row chapel (Horwood, 1799)
© Motco Enterprises Ltd

At the western end of Wilderness Row, clearly visible on early-nineteenth-century maps of Charterhouse lands and properties, was a narrow footpath called Pardon Passage which led to St John Street. This was the surviving section of a medieval alley which gave access to Pardon Churchyard, a fourteenth-century burial site for many thousands of victims of the Black Death. The land had reportedly been bought in 1348 by Ralph de Stratford, Bishop of London, who was keen to bring order and sanctity to the mass burials. He built a small chapel where prayers were offered for the dead. The chronicler Robert Fabyan, writing in the early-sixteenth century, describes 'a Chapell standynge in Pardon Church yarde'. There are countless other historical references which suggest that the chapel was still in use until the mid-sixteenth century before being 'enlarged and made a dwelling house', according to John Stow's *Survey of London* published in 1603.

The great John Wesley mentions in his journal of 1769 that he preached in a place 'built on the very spot of ground whereon... Pardon Church stood'. Maps of late-eighteenth-century Clerkenwell clearly show a spacious yard almost wholly enclosed by buildings at the western end of Wilderness Row. Its location would seem to be very close to that of Pardon Church (but not 'the very spot') within the old medieval confines of Pardon Churchyard. It was in this enclosed yard that the Welsh established their first chapel in London. All accounts say this happened in 1785.

It may, however, have been a few years later than this, if we consider the contents of a letter of application (held at the London Metropolitan Archive) dated 30 May 1788 to the Bishop of London:

> *We whose names are underwritten being Protestant Dissenters living in and about Wilderness Row... Do hereby certify that a certain Building situate in Wilderness Row aforesaid in the Parish of St. James Clerkenwell... in Your Lordships Diocese of London is intended to be appropriated or set apart for a Meeting Place of a certain Congregation of Protestant Dissenters from the Church of England under the Denomination of Independants* [sic]...

This letter, signed by 'Edward Jones, Minister' and eighteen others, has never featured in any previous history and this is the first time its contents have been made public. There is a separate note on the same document:

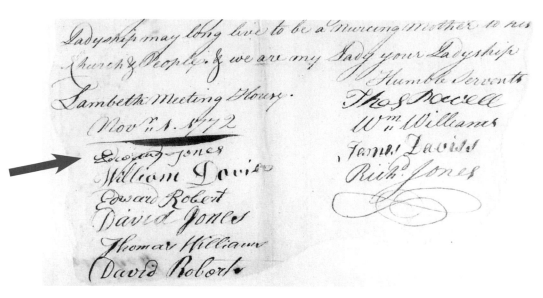

The Lambeth letter signed by Edward Jones and others in 1772
© Trustees of the Cheshunt Foundation

The application signed by Edward Jones and others in 1788
© London Metropolitan Archive

Independants Certificate P(arish) John, Clerkenwell… Registered the 2d June 1788.

This is very significant for several reasons. Accounts of the formation of the Wilderness Row chapel are not rich in detail. The Revd John Thickens, one-time pastor of the Welsh chapel at Willesden Green and an authority on the history of the London Welsh chapels, suggested that the Welsh 'built' their own chapel there. This was always unlikely in the light of Wesley's statement; it is now even more improbable given the letter's strong suggestion ('appropriated or set apart') that a place of worship already existed.

The case is further strengthened by an entry in the report of the Calvinistic Methodist Association held at Llangeitho on 2 August 1785:

Agreed to sign a Petition for a Subscription to purchase a new Chapel for our Welsh friends in London near Blackfriars Bridge.

A 'petition for a subscription' would have taken months to organise and longer still to bring to fruition. This would make a move or opening in 1785 even less credible: 1788 makes far more sense in this regard. Owen Thomas, John Hughes and others may well have based their date for the move to Wilderness Row on the Llangeitho proceedings.

There is now a strong case for asserting that the Welsh 're-opened' a chapel in an obscure yard which can still be roughly located on modern maps. Careful inspection of the space behind today's numbers 64 and 68 Clerkenwell Road will reveal the existence of 'Leo Yard' which is reached by a narrow private alleyway. This would seem to be the location of the yard in which the first London Welsh chapel stood. The basic structure of the chapel building was still there in the early-twentieth century, long after the Welsh had departed for Jewin Crescent. It had been enlarged in 1806, sold to the Wesleyan Methodists in 1823, and occupied by the Baptists after 1849. They owned the place of worship they called 'Zion Chapel' until 1878 when the cause ended and the building was sold for private use.

D. R. Hughes, a London Welshman who took a deep interest in the origins of the city's chapels, described a visit to Wilderness Row in the 1920s when he discovered the decaying structure of the old chapel being used as an engineers' workshop. He took away a section of one of the joists as a treasured souvenir and had it carved into a wooden stool. Embedded in the seat was a

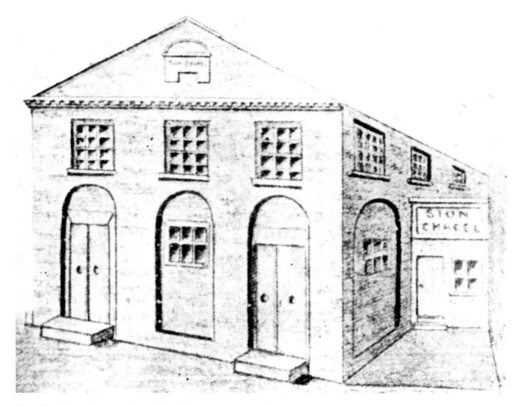

Sketch of Zion Baptist chapel, Wilderness Row, in the 1850s
© National Library of Wales

circular piece of slate engraved with details of the stool's origins in Wilderness Row. The stool was inherited by Hughes's daughter and after her death in 2001 was offered to the National History Museum, St Fagans. Sadly, they rejected this valuable token of Welsh history; despite an extensive subsequent search, its fate remains a mystery.

It is commonly asserted that Wilderness Row was the first Nonconformist cause to be formally constituted by the Welsh in London. This assertion should nonetheless be treated with a degree of caution. John Thickens rightly highlighted the presence of a Welsh religious society in Lambeth for much of the eighteenth century. Howell Harris's visits to Lambeth spanned four decades: he preached there during his last visit in January 1767. By that time, as we have established, Cock Lane already had its own dissenters' meeting house, and the Welsh were holding their own meetings in the 'Great Room over the Earthenware Shop' a few years later.

It is also likely that the Edward Jones who signed a letter in 1772 requesting help to bring Welsh preachers to Lambeth was the same Edward Jones who helped establish Cock Lane. The signatures (see page 44) would seem to match. The letter was sent to the Countess of Huntingdon, another prominent figure in the Methodist movement in England and Wales, founder of a number of chapels and leader of her own Methodist 'Connexion'.

John Thickens always maintained that Cock Lane should not be seen as a 'new' venture: he suggested that the searing spiritual heat of Smithfield had been 'ignited' by an 'ember' from Lambeth. This suggestion, always credible, is now certain: we know from the *Daily Advertiser* that Lambeth was still going in January 1773. In fact, despite unrest and flux, the Lambeth cause would continue in various forms until the 1820s. Thickens was absolutely right when he guessed that the Lambeth society first visited by Howell Harris in 1739 never petered out.

But it remains that the first society to form itself into a discrete 'independent' religious body, petitioning the Bishop of London for a dissenters' licence, was the society which began meeting in Cock Lane and later transferred to Wilderness Row.

In the years that followed the move, some of the best Welsh preachers paid visits to the Welsh in London. Robert Roberts of Clynnog visited Wilderness Row in 1797. David Jones of Llan-gan was often invited to preach at the Countess of Huntingdon's chapel in Spa Fields (near today's Farringdon station) and by all accounts fitted in visits to Wilderness Row. Thomas Charles, a leading Methodist preacher and eminent scholar, visited in 1799 when he laid the foundations for the British and Foreign Bible Society.

The move to Wilderness Row was the start of a turbulent 38-year stretch which featured outbreaks of revivalist zeal peppered with episodes of intense bickering. Edward Jones, whose dictatorial streak offended so many, is generally blamed for a debacle that would paralyse Wilderness Row and virtually destroy the cause that he had worked so hard to develop.

Jones considered himself the undisputed boss whose duty it was to enforce rules and to apply appropriate punishments. When two brothers of his flock decided to marry two sisters who were not members, Jones ordered that the men be excommunicated. It was considered an exceptionally harsh

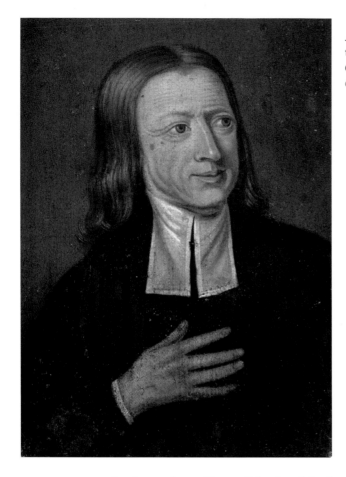

John Wesley (1703–91), one of the founders of the Methodist Church
© National Library of Wales

response even in those days. One of the banished men, Thomas Thomas, was a preacher who helped the cause at Wilderness Row.

The sisters were daughters of another preacher, Daniel Jenkins, whose father-in-law was the great Methodist pioneer Daniel Rowland of Llangeitho. Jenkins was understandably offended by Jones's actions and protested vehemently. Jones brushed aside his opposition, citing rigid Methodist regulations. The venomous dispute between Jones and Jenkins was a prime factor in the separate development of Independent Welsh chapels in London.

Not long after the opening of Wilderness Row, Thomas Thomas and Daniel Jenkins became the driving forces in establishing a branch south of the Thames, in Gravel Lane, Borough. The street survives today as the northern section of Great Suffolk Street. It is a significant location in the religious history of London: a few yards away on Blackfriars Road stood the famous

Surrey Chapel, opened by the famous preacher Rowland Hill in 1783. The familiar circular form of Surrey Chapel survived until the Second World War, though its life as a place of worship had ended by 1880 and it later became a boxing venue.

Gravel Lane would have much in common with old Cock Lane. The author George Godwin offered this description of the neighbourhood in 1854:

An area of dilapidated houses… the drainage is here most defective… [they have] cesspools at the back, many of them without even a covering… the health of the people is very bad… it would be difficult, either by words or illustrations, to give an idea of the squalid and unhealthy condition of this spot. If this disgraceful and unwholesome accumulation be disposed of at the present time, it may be at a loss to the proprietor; but surely this is not to be set against the lives of men, women, and children?

The area colonised by the Welsh chapel-builders in the 1780s was not as densely populated or developed as the one described by Godwin, but by the turn of the nineteenth century it would be heading rapidly in that direction.

It is important to realise that Gravel Lane started life as (essentially) a Methodist meeting house but within a few years had broken away to become a formally-constituted Independent cause. This led eventually to the formation of Borough chapel, the oldest of the Welsh Independent churches in London.

But this is where our story diverges, branching off in different directions, the fallout from which is still with us in modern London.

There were several reasons for this divergence, but one man bore most of the responsibility.

There are no prizes for guessing his name.

Edward Jones.

CHAPTER 3

OUT OF THE WILDERNESS

Jewin, the Welsh chapel which stands today in the shadow of the Barbican Estate, within the ancient boundaries of the City of London, is a supreme symbol of survival. It is an old cause housed in a modern building. This particular set of doors opened in August 1961 after a very long wait.

During the second week of September 1940, in the first days of the Blitz, German bombers destroyed significant areas of the City of London. Sections of Fann Street and Bridgewater Gardens, lying to the east of Aldersgate Street, were reduced to rubble. The official history records that in the early hours of 10 September 1940 the mighty edifice of Jewin Welsh Presbyterian Church was burnt to a shell. It had stood there since 1879, a fortress of Welsh faith in the heart of London.

Bill Jenkins, a Jewin member for over 60 years, has always disputed the precise date. He was twelve years old when Jewin was destroyed and heard the news in Llan-non, Cardiganshire, where he'd been sent to stay with relatives at the start of the war. His parents, Stephen and Annie Jenkins, were at their home in Whidborne Street near King's Cross. Bill describes how his sister, Jane Ann, had been married in Jewin on Saturday, 7 September 1940. Hours later, the Blitz started.

Bill Jenkins contends that Jewin was destroyed in the early hours of Monday, 9 September. He remembers his father describing the events of that night as he saw an immense wall of flames rising above the Aldersgate area. His worst fears were realised when he visited Bridgewater Gardens early on

The remains of Jewin in 1956
© London Metropolitan Archive

Monday morning. He managed to retrieve a piece of lead from the roof and a section of broken glass from one of the lamps.

Lodwick Davies's father managed to find something rather different. Idwal Davies was a native of Tregaron who owned a dairy in Great Sutton Street. He and his wife, Gwyneth, were married in Jewin in 1935. Idwal heard news of the disaster from his fellow reservists in the fire brigade. He visited the site within hours of the attack and found a hymn book lying in a pool of water under some rubble. It is still in Lodwick's possession today, a precious link to the past.

As for the precise date of the bombing, Bill was right. Records at the London Metropolitan Archive include a photograph of Jewin's smoking remains taken at 03:45 on the morning of 9 September 1940.

The Jewin which rose from the ashes of the Second World War was a church full of hope and confidence in the future, despite its traumatic past. Jewin had known many difficult episodes in its long history, including poisonous arguments, theological tangles, organisational disputes, personality clashes, and despotic discipline. The unappealing Welsh chapel tradition of bickering and squabbling has been every bit as robust in London as it has been in Wales.

But Jewin's story is so much more than a list of petty spats. It is the story of religious pioneers in a strange land, a tale of Welsh exiles determined to maintain their traditions in an alien environment. It is a story impressive in scale and heroic in ambition.

Edward Jones, for all his dreadful faults, must be given credit for laying the main foundations. Without his drive and vision it is by no means certain that Wilderness Row would have opened, leading eventually to the founding of Jewin. It is sad that his record as a pioneer has been overshadowed by his unattractive record as a leader.

Jones treated the cause at Wilderness Row as his personal fiefdom. He made the rules. He sat in judgement. He bestowed favours and meted out punishments. Jones liked the limelight and the power of leadership. He was a dictatorial figure who alienated people effortlessly. His dealings with others were coloured by vanity and arrogance. These faults would be the seeds of his eventual downfall.

Jones supervised the move from Cock Lane to the rather primitive building in the yard off Wilderness Row. But what kind of religious cause was it? John Thickens noted that the chapel in those early years was 'Calvinist in outlook', which he defined as 'an absolute conviction that the Bible is the infallible word of God'.

The application letter to the Bishop of London described it as part of a

'Denomination of Independants [*sic*]'. There is no mention here of 'Methodists' or even 'Calvinistic Methodists', the heavily-centralised denomination to which Jewin later belonged before its twentieth-century evolution into the Presbyterian Church of Wales.

There are two vital things to realise here. First, Calvinistic Methodism developed in England as a movement within Anglicanism. In Wales, leaders such as Howell Harris and Daniel Rowland attracted thousands of followers. Both had been converted in 1735 and embarked on a lifetime of itinerant preaching. The Church of England responded with hostility and incomprehension. Harris remained a devoted Anglican throughout his life, but Rowland was thrown out. By the end of the eighteenth century, Calvinistic Methodism was a powerful network. Edward Jones visited Wales regularly and was a well-connected member.

Things came to a head in 1795 when the Calvinistic Methodists realised they had no future in the Church of England. They applied for recognition as a separate grouping under the terms of the Toleration Act 1689. (This was the act which gave freedom of worship to Nonconformists, such as Baptists and Congregationalists, and allowed them to set aside their own chapels.) In Wales, a final, historically momentous, split happened in 1811 when the Calvinistic Methodists ordained their own ministers and effectively formed a 'new' church that became known as Welsh Calvinistic Methodists, or Welsh Presbyterians.

So the move to Wilderness Row happened roughly a decade before the separate status was granted, and this explains why Edward Jones and his colleagues applied to use the chapel as 'Independants'. They saw themselves, in a sense, as 'independent' worshippers within the Anglican family. It was a messy compromise which strained loyalties and tested friendships to breaking point. It can be said that 1811 brought much-needed clarity, marking the start of a period of exponential growth for the Calvinistic Methodist movement.

Edward Jones's address book was full of impressive names. He arranged for some of the best Welsh preachers of the day to visit London. When they came, they filled their diaries with services at Wilderness Row and elsewhere. Crowds would move from chapel to chapel on a Sunday to listen to the latest pulpit celebrity. Those stars included Thomas Charles, whose links with Jones and Wilderness Row were severely strained by the episode involving the excommunicated Thomas brothers.

Charles and others were deeply embarrassed by Jones's actions: the brides were, after all, related to Daniel Rowland, the Methodist giant. But they found it very difficult to dislodge Jones, whose grip on Wilderness Row had strengthened: Daniel Jenkins complained in March 1800 that he was not to be allowed to preach there during Jones's visit to the Association (the crucial Methodist governing body) in Wales. It is said by Gomer Roberts in his official history of Jewin, *Y Ddinas Gadarn* (1974), that Jenkins and others were bent on retribution.

The opportunity presented itself on a spectacular scale. It centred on a high-profile court case heard by one of the country's most senior judges. The humiliating evidence and crushing verdict, widely reported in the press, would lead eventually to Jones's departure from Wilderness Row.

By 1799 Edward Jones had become a widower and in the process had lost the very sensible influence of his devout wife. A few months later he fell in love with a young woman 'of good family' but 'fallen on difficult times' as a 'maker of umbrellas' according to John Hughes in *Methodistiaeth Cymru (Cyfrol III)* (1856).

Jones sent her several letters following up on his marriage proposal which would prove both deeply damaging to him and uproariously funny to his enemies when presented in court. The nationwide press reports of the case brought by 'Miss Protheroe' and her supporters (Jenkins and others) dealt a crushing blow to the leading Welsh Methodist figure in London. This appeared in the *Bury and Norwich Post* on 4 February 1801:

> *An action was brought by a young lady of the age of 28 years, against the defendant, who was a methodist preacher, a publican, and a sinner, and who, at 60 years of age, had engaged [her] affections… and by his letters repeatedly had promised marriage. This was in the year 1799; in the spring of the year 1800 he had made a tour into Denbighshire… and while there, had written to Miss Protheroe, stating his determination to make her 'bone of his bone'; but when he did return, he found an excuse… being in debt… this was only a cloak to cover his hypocrisy, for soon after he united himself to a lady who had more substantial reasons for making the state of matrimony desirable, having £1000 to her fortune… the letters were then read; they were all written in the Welch language, and, on being interpreted, afforded much entertainment to the Court. The Jury, after retiring for near two hours, returned with a verdict for the plaintiff. Damages £50.*

It would be difficult to overstate the impact of this case. The London Welsh community was all agog, and reports of the case in Wales were eagerly devoured. It gave the satirist, Jac Glan-y-gors, and his friends at the Cymreigyddion and Gwyneddigion societies a source of whooping delight. They were firmly anti-Methodist in outlook and 'Ginshop Jones', in their view, had been justly poleaxed by Lord Kenyon and the Court of King's Bench.

More sensitive souls would have crept away quietly and lived the rest of their days in obscurity. But Edward Jones was not known for his sensitivity. He returned to Wilderness Row, despite all the ignominy, with the chapel keys and deeds still firmly in his possession. He had no plans to go quietly. It took the intervention of several powerful individuals to persuade him to change his mind.

Jones became increasingly bitter and withdrawn following the trial. The members of Wilderness Row sought guidance and leadership from the likes of Thomas Charles, John Elias (known in Wales as the 'Methodist Pope' because of his firm views), John Roberts and Ebenezer Morris. The guidance was not always clear and the leadership not always robust. The result was that Wilderness Row struggled for five years before resolving its problem. It is not difficult to imagine the dire effect on the cause.

When Roberts and Elias visited in 1802 they were appalled by the situation. It was much worse than they had imagined. Jones refused to budge and even challenged their right to intervene. Most of the congregation protested by moving to a rented room in Bunhill Row. Jones and his dozen supporters had become, in effect, squatters in their own chapel.

Morris and the elders took stock and decided to approach Jones once again in a spirit of compromise and Christian charity. This time, after prolonged bargaining, he reluctantly agreed to step aside.

No more preaching. No more running the show. No more sitting in judgement on others.

Edward Jones returned to Wales a few years later (by 1806 at the latest, according to several accounts) and spent the rest of his days in his native Denbighshire. Despite an unsourced suggestion in one account that Jones died in a workhouse in Greenwich, south-east London, Gomer Roberts asserts that he died at his Llansannan home, Llety Fforddolion, in 1816.

Original architect's drawing of Jewin Crescent (1823)
© The Goldsmiths' Company, photography by Richard Valencia

All of this meant a fresh start for the congregation of Wilderness Row. Jones's departure marked the beginning of a period of robust growth. John Elias encouraged the membership to submit to the full authority of the Calvinistic Methodists, and in return the denomination sent some of the best Welsh preachers to Wilderness Row. None was more popular than Elias himself. He would preach every day on his stays in London, and on Sundays would preach three times.

It is no wonder that John Elias preached the last sermon in the old chapel: the building was radically altered in 1806 to accommodate the rapidly-growing membership. John Thickens notes the early attempts to create a Sunday school in the same year; the start of an annual Easter preaching festival ('Cymanfa'r Pasg') in 1812; and the publication of a hymn book in 1816. John Foulk established a very successful Sunday school in 1821 which taught hundreds of children to read and write Welsh in the decades that followed.

The Easter meetings of 1822 were attended by huge crowds. They filled the big chapels of Spa Fields and Falcon Square and convinced the leaders of Wilderness Row that they needed a bigger home. In May of that year, Thomas Jones and Edward Cleaton reached agreement with the Goldsmiths' Company to lease a plot of land in Jewin Crescent on which they would build

James Hughes, 'Iago Trichrug' (1779–1844)
© National Library of Wales

a chapel and caretaker's house. The original lease was for 61 years at an annual rental charge of £30. The building costs were £3,200 which would correspond to £350,000 today (using a simple calculation based on the rise in the retail price index) or as much as £3,500,000 (using a calculation based on labour costs and income comparisons). Either way, it was a very big sum for a congregation of relatively poor workers. They performed miracles in paying off most of the debt within twelve years.

The new chapel, much more impressive than Wilderness Row, was opened for the Easter festival in March 1823. Rowland Hill of Surrey Chapel was one of the English guest preachers, along with some Welsh greats including John Elias. The line-up also included James Hughes, a blacksmith from south-east London, who became one of the most heroic figures in the entire story of the London Welsh chapels.

James Hughes, also known by his bardic name 'Iago Trichrug', was originally from Ciliau Aeron in Cardiganshire. He left for London in 1799 and settled in Deptford where there was plenty of work in the dockyards. For decades, he combined his work as a blacksmith with his duties as a chapel elder. He was a leading figure in a small Welsh cause in Deptford and later in Wilderness Row where he started preaching in 1810. He was ordained in 1816 and was appointed the first minister of Jewin Crescent in 1823 where he served until his death in 1844.

James Hughes's story, told in his own words in a series of articles, is moving and inspiring in equal measure. He was always short of money: the Welsh chapels could be exceptionally mean in their financial dealings with ministers. There have been some shocking examples of wealthy chapels paying starvation wages. Hughes suffered great poverty and struggled to provide for his big family. Despite all this he produced an impressive range of

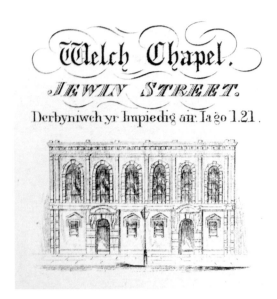

work, including hymns and poems, and a hugely popular Bible commentary, *Esboniad James Hughes*, which was still in use a century after his death. He was buried in London's Bunhill Fields, the Nonconformist burial ground opposite Wesley's Chapel, where he rests in the company of Richard Price, Daniel Williams, John Bunyan, William Blake, Isaac Watts and other major figures. He was one of the greatest Welshmen of his age and deserves more recognition.

His time at Jewin Crescent was marked by enthusiasm and consolidation. But the stability was seriously threatened by major disputes. One of the most damaging was caused by the process of Catholic emancipation, which involved removing many of the restrictions on Roman Catholics. The Sacramental Test Act of 1828 allowed Catholics to hold specified public offices, while the Roman Catholic Relief Act of 1829 allowed elected Catholics to take their parliamentary seats at Westminster.

The governing body of the Welsh Calvinistic Methodists was opposed to these reforms, but James Hughes's flock was divided on the issue. A small group, publicly identifying themselves as members of Jewin Crescent, petitioned both houses of Parliament in favour. They provoked a memorable storm. John Elias, in true 'papal' style, ordered their immediate excommunication. They included the artist, Hugh Hughes, who reacted furiously by publishing vitriolic attacks on John Elias and the Calvinistic Methodists, and the eminent lexicographer, Thomas Edwards ('Caerfallwch'). The episode turned Hugh Hughes into a blazing radical who also fought a protracted campaign against the Established Church.

There was worse to come. John Elias, in a new spasm of severity, urged the cause to exclude those (or at least refuse to christen the children of those) who worked on Sundays: 'breaking the Sabbath' had become the debate of the day. This was an early period of growth in the dairy business in London, a trade which provided work for many Welsh people. It would become a Welsh monopoly (in effect) by the end of the century. Preparation for the Monday morning milk rounds took place on Sunday evenings. There was no way around this. Loyal chapel members who worked in the trade were understandably affronted by the stiff-necked allies of John Elias. But 'Elias's Law' was nonetheless passed in 1835 or thereabouts. It pleased the purists, no doubt, but in splitting the cause and poisoning relations for decades it must be considered a catastrophic mistake.

James Hughes struggled to balance the demands of tyrannical elders with the more moderate instincts of the membership. He achieved remarkable success in tricky circumstances, siding with his members and backing their view that dairy workers and their families had every right to be full communicants. New elders, including the poet Robert Owen ('Eryron Gwyllt Walia') and Dr Edward Richards (brother of the pacifist and parliamentarian Henry Richard), did nothing, it seems, to ease the tensions. It is sad to note that James Hughes's death provided an opportunity for some to revive the 'dairy' argument, and sadder still to learn that the governing Associations of the denomination upheld 'Elias's Law'.

Everything changed in 1851 when Dr Owen Thomas, a preacher of rare ability, accepted a call to become pastor of Jewin Crescent. The church had spent seven years trying to find a replacement for James Hughes. The job was clearly not

Dr Owen Thomas (1812–91)
© National Library of Wales

Interior of Jewin Crescent chapel (1876)
© National Library of Wales

The congregation of Jewin Crescent chapel (1876)
© National Library of Wales

attractive to many. One of the greatest preachers in the history of Welsh Nonconformism, John Jones (Talysarn), turned down several invitations, as did Henry Rees, the man whose sublime preaching had convinced John Jones to enter the ministry.

Jewin Crescent, with 400 registered members, entered a new age under the energetic and powerful pastorate of Owen Thomas. The building was significantly altered and enhanced in 1858 at a cost of £900. An eye-witness at the re-opening described:

> *A noble new structure, extremely handsome… an imposing aspect… abundance of light is emitted to every nook and corner… there is a magnificent glass chandelier, suspended gracefully from the ornamented ceiling.*

Within two years, they had repaid as much as £551 of the debt. Later that year, the church called the Revd David Charles Davies of Newtown to serve the cause, and in 1861 the Revd John Mills was appointed to the team. They shared the city-wide pastoral work and sustained this effective arrangement until 1865 when Owen Thomas moved to Liverpool.

David Charles Davies was then asked to take charge of Jewin Crescent. He was a noted intellectual who turned down several academic posts in Wales before reluctantly deciding, in 1876, that his health would benefit by leaving his beloved London. Such was his popularity that he continued for six years to keep an eye on Jewin Crescent from his new home in Bangor, north Wales. It was an unusual arrangement but it worked.

The dates are significant because it was during this ministerial hiatus that the membership was forced to take the momentous decision to move home. In 1874 a new warehouse had been built next to the caretaker's home, casting shadows across the frontage. The chapel now had rather less of the 'abundance of light' celebrated in 1858. There followed two years of negotiation and bargaining with the Goldsmiths' Company. Hugh Owen (later Sir Hugh Owen, one of the foremost educationists of his day) was a member of the negotiating team, along with Abel Simner, a leading figure at Jewin for many years. Their work came to fruition in 1876 when the membership accepted an offer of £3,000 from the Goldsmiths' Company for the early surrender of the lease.

The last service at Jewin Crescent took place on 11 June 1876 when

NEW JEWIN WELSH CHAPEL,
BRIDGEWATER GARDENS.

You are earnestly requested to attend a

SOCIAL TEA & PUBLIC MEETING

Which will be held on

Tuesday Evening, Dec. 4th, 1877,

At

FALCON SQUARE CHAPEL,

(Kindly lent for the occasion.)

For the formation of a

NEW JEWIN WELSH CHAPEL BUILDING FUND.

T. J. THOMAS, ESQ., WILL PRESIDE.

The Rev. D. CHARLES DAVIES, M.A.,
The Rev. Mr. EVANS, Pastor of Falcon Square Chapel.
The Rev. G. DAVIES, Nassau Street,
The Rev. R. ROBERTS, Wilton Square,

Mr. Stephen Evans,   Mr. Morgan Jones,
   „ Hugh Owen,   „ Hugh Edwards,
   „ Abel Simner,   „ Hugh Lloyd Hughes,
   „ John James,   „ T. M. Williams, B.A.,

Will Address the Meeting.

Tea at 5.30.   Public Meeting at 7 p.m.

R. SAMUEL, Printer, 7, City Buildings, Cattle Market, N.

The Revd David Charles Davies (1826–91)   Poster for New Jewin fundraising event (1877)

the overflowing congregation heard a sermon by David Charles Davies. His theme, taken from Luke 21, could not have been more farsighted or judicious:

The days will come, in the which there shall not be left one stone upon another, that shall not be thrown down.

CHAPTER 4

JOURNEY TO JEWIN

The stones of Jewin Crescent would indeed be thrown down while the members were busy looking for a new home. During this time they rented various rooms to hold services and meetings, including the YMCA in Aldersgate Street, the Welsh Baptist chapel in Moorfields, the Congregational chapel in Falcon Square, and the Presbyterian chapel in Colebrook Row.

By 1877 the officers had found a plot of freehold land in Bridgewater Gardens, near Aldersgate Street, and they started fundraising. The cost of the land was around £5,000 and the building work would cost a similar sum. The chapel, which would take two years to complete, would have seats for 630 worshippers. David Davies MP, Llandinam, the coal magnate, set the foundation stone in May 1878 in a ceremony which also featured Henry Richard MP and J. H. Puleston MP. David Charles Davies remarked in the official appeal document in July 1878:

> *The congregation consists in great part of young men and women employed in various capacities in houses of business, or as artisans, or in domestic service, a large proportion of whom remain only for brief periods in London. The number of settled families is comparatively few. The parents of these young people who come up to London in increasing numbers every year, cannot fail to sympathise with this undertaking… to supply our young fellow-countrymen with a religious home… to preserve them from the sinful allurements of this great city.*

Davies was deploying an argument guaranteed to affect thousands of Welsh parents whose children were London-bound. Jewin and the other Welsh chapels provided an important base, a social centre and even a welfare network for those in need. The young men and women would often be met

Artist's impression of New Jewin (1879)
© National Library of Wales

on arrival at Paddington or Euston by a chapel representative (the minister at home would have written in advance requesting help), their lodgings would be arranged, and in many cases their work was also provided by a chapel contact.

The majestic structure of Jewin Newydd ('New Jewin') was ready by the winter of 1878, and the series of opening services began on 17 January 1879. The first meeting, at which Henry Richard MP presided, included no fewer than fourteen addresses. There followed a week of special services including one for young people. David Charles Davies supervised the church (from

David Davies, Llandinam, heads the list of contributors to the New Jewin building fund (1878)
© National Library of Wales

a distance) and took pride in its growth. It was already one of the strongest churches in the Association.

By 1886, the elders decided that they needed to call a full-time minister and (after a rather protracted process) they secured the services of the Revd J. E. Davies ('Rhuddwawr') of Siloh, Llanelli. He was the first of several Llanelli ministers who would serve the London Welsh churches for decades. The remarkable strength of Nonconformity in Llanelli meant that Rhuddwawr was considered a good bet for a bigger challenge.

Within a few years, he was facing a problem which today's ministers would welcome: his chapel was far too small for the membership. A warehouse next to the church was bought for £4,000 and this created the space for a new gallery, a new organ in its own recess, and an extended schoolroom, library and committee rooms underneath the chapel. There were seats for a thousand worshippers whose comfort was enhanced by central heating and electric lights. A more convenient entrance was built on Fann Street. The total cost (including the warehouse purchase) was almost £12,000 and the chapel re-opened in June 1898. Jewin was now among the grandest Nonconformist chapels in Britain with a surging membership (660 and counting) and a reputation to match.

For some, this reputation has always included an element of undisguised snobbery. The late Siân Busby, a Londoner whose maternal grandmother was from Cardiganshire, insisted her family's attitude to Jewin was typical of many:

They went to Holloway, their local chapel. It was nothing grand, quite homely and welcoming. I suppose it was similar to the kind of chapel you'd find in Cardiganshire. That was the secret of its success. They would never have dreamed of going to somewhere like Jewin. That was for wealthy people, or at least those who considered themselves socially superior. They never went there.

That view was supported to an extent by some of Jewin's own people. Myra Dawson (née James), who attended Jewin as a child in the 1950s and 1960s, said the chapel's reputation had become deeply ingrained:

There were two groups in Jewin chapel: people like my parents who'd come from Wales, who were considered to be peasants who spoke Welsh; and then the second generation of London Welsh who didn't want to admit they spoke Welsh. It was such a snobbish attitude. I was always aware of people looking down on my parents. The Welsh language had no official status in those days and I am so pleased that this has changed.

There is a supreme irony at work here. From the middle of the nineteenth century, the membership was dominated not by grasping parvenus but by

A rare image of the interior of New Jewin after the organ installation (1898)
© Eglwys Jewin

ordinary people, mostly dairy workers, whose simple lives were underpinned by the values of rural Wales. Jewin, the church which had approved and upheld 'Elias's Law', was now heavily dependent on the milk trade for members. As recently as 1879 Abel Simner had been objecting to 'the consecration of a milkman to the holy office of a Deacon'. His view that 'a milkman cannot be my Leader or any Driver in holy things' was clearly not shared by the majority who went on to elect dairymen as officers of the church.

There were milk carriers, shop workers, dairy negotiators, and even cowkeepers resident in Clerkenwell, Islington, and the surrounding areas. The hours were long and the work was unrelenting. The Welsh dairy shop was becoming a familiar sight throughout London, and the rattle of the milk carts with their measuring jugs was an equally familiar sound in the city's streets. The dairy trade was an overwhelmingly Welsh trade, and the dairy families were among the strongest supporters of the chapels in all parts of London.

It is clear that without the support (both financial and practical) of the people of the dairy trade, Jewin and other London Welsh chapels would not have thrived in the same way. Rhuddwawr certainly understood this and he encouraged the big dairy families to include their children in Jewin's life. There was a strong emphasis on provision for both children and young people. The church established Sunday school branches in Hackney Road and elsewhere, and the weekly schedule included Monday evening meetings for young people, with an additional education meeting on Thursday evenings. The young people also played an important part in the rich musical life of Jewin.

One of the most important ventures of Rhuddwawr's time was the project to replace Iago Trichrug's weather-worn gravestone in Bunhill Fields. This was eventually achieved with the generous support of Timothy Davies MP, the Liberal parliamentarian and close friend of David Lloyd George. In 1907 the old stone was put on display in Jewin (in the entrance hall) and an impressive marble and brass memorial was unveiled in Bunhill Fields at a cost of £100. It can still be seen today very near the entrance in City Road opposite Wesley's Chapel.

Rhuddwawr's initial ambition had been to serve Jewin for a decade, but when he finally resigned in September 1912 he had spent more than a quarter of a century in charge. His memoirs offer an intriguing glimpse of a

The Revd J. E. Davies ('Rhuddwawr') and officers of Jewin (1912)
© National Library of Wales

minister's busy life in London in the early-twentieth century. He found the
pastoral demands exhausting: visiting members in different parts of London
was a time-consuming, costly, tiring process. He received several requests
from Wales every week to visit people in London's hospitals. He spent many
hours on the road and rarely had a word of thanks for his efforts. The same
applied to the process of welcoming people (especially young people) at

Paddington or Euston. It was endless, thankless work. But he insisted that he found it rewarding, and was always grateful for the opportunity to help the vulnerable.

He left for Llandeilo with the deep gratitude of the elders and members of Jewin. His period in charge had seen the membership rise to 680, and the debt reduced by £2,000. He left behind a vibrant, active, confident church. It was a singular achievement given the transitional nature of the congregation.

His impressive record would take some beating. The elders might be forgiven a touch of superstition: they went back to Siloh, Llanelli, for Rhuddwawr's successor. It proved to be an inspired move. The Revd D. S. Owen arrived in London in the darkest days of the First World War when dozens of Jewin's young men were serving in the trenches. He had been advised not to accept the call: the London chapels, he was told, would all close within months. Here was a young man (he was 28) taking on one of the biggest Nonconformist churches in London. He clearly had courage and ambition, and he would need inexhaustible supplies of both in the decades to come.

'DS', as he was widely known, spent a herculean period of 45 years as minister of Jewin. His name is still mentioned with reverence today. What he achieved in that turbulent and crisis-ridden time between 1915 and 1959 is still a source of wonder. He managed a period of spectacular growth taking membership to record levels; he saw Jewin wrecked in the Blitz; and he spent the rest of his life rebuilding the cause he loved. It really is no exaggeration to say that without his heroic efforts, Jewin would have disappeared.

The Revd D. S. Owen (1887–1959),
minister of Jewin for 45 years
© National Library of Wales

His grandson, Geraint Pritchard, who spent a good deal of time in his company, remembered an impressive figure who commanded attention:

He was certainly highly respected, a gentle giant in some ways, but a very strong character. He could be slightly regal, but was a very caring and loving grandfather. He was fun, too, and loved pulling my leg. He had been an excellent footballer as a young man, he played golf, and loved Test cricket. His speaking voice was powerful and resoundingly clear. He could argue with force and fluency, and he would have made a very good barrister. He was an excellent Sunday school teacher and tutored us in public speaking and recitation.

It is true that the minister invested generously in Jewin's provision for children and young people. He created a new magazine *Y Wawr* ('The Dawn') in 1922 which featured competitions with prizes for the best writing. It is stunning to see the official roll of Jewin's children published in the magazine: there were 171 names in 1922, and 245 by 1939.

The year 1938–9 was also the high point of chapel membership: there were 1,148 adult members on the books in the year before the outbreak of war. These are truly remarkable statistics set in today's very different context. Even in those days they were impressive. When Jewin's destruction was reported in *The Times* on 14 September 1940, the prominent Welsh educationalist Sir Wynn Wheldon wrote to the editor:

It will, I think, surprise many who know the City of London well to learn that Jewin Chapel, where the services are conducted entirely in Welsh, is in number of members, the strongest Christian church within the City boundaries, with a membership of over 1,100. It has now no home, and its loss will be mourned by Welshmen everywhere, but more especially by its own members, many of them young men and women born and bred in Wales.

The decades of the 1920s and 1930s were punctuated by some major denominational events. The Southern Association held its annual meeting at Jewin on its first visit to London in October 1927. The presiding officer was Timothy Davies MP whose generosity in funding the creation of several London Welsh chapels will become more evident. Among those ordained into the ministry on that occasion was Dr Martyn Lloyd-Jones, who went on to be one of the most revered evangelists of the twentieth century. The

Northern Association paid its own visit in 1933, and two years later Jewin organised a series of major services to mark the bicentenary of the Methodist revival in Wales. There is wonderful image of the children who took part, posing for the camera on the steps of Jewin.

Jewin has been blessed and fortunate in its choice of officers and elders. There are far too many to mention, but among those elected in 1932 was Evan Evans, a remarkable and generous man who served the chapel and its denomination for decades. He was a native of Llangeitho who came to London in 1883. His business interests (hotels and travel) were hugely profitable (the coaches of 'Evan Evans Tours' are still familiar on London's roads) and he would even charter a private plane to take London Welsh people on day trips to agricultural shows in Cardiganshire. He was certainly the main 'go-to man' for a wise solution to any problem. His manifest readiness to help anyone earned him the respect of all. He served Jewin faithfully, including a long period as secretary, until his death in 1965. No one, with the sole exception of 'DS' himself, did more to ensure Jewin's survival and restoration.

Evan Evans was one of the minister's most dependable officers in the aftermath of the disaster of September 1940. From the outbreak of war in September 1939, D. S. Owen had feared the worst. The handbook for that year included a prominent reminder to members that they could find a robust air raid shelter within a three-minute walk from the chapel. Within weeks, the exodus was underway: hundreds of members, especially children and the elderly, left for Wales. At least four of the officers went with them. More than a hundred members joined the armed forces. But the church maintained an impressive range of weekly services.

These arrangements carried on until the fateful night of 9 September 1940, one of many terrible nights in the Blitz, when hundreds of German bombs were dropped over London. The firestorm which engulfed vast areas of Aldersgate and Cripplegate, not to mention the 'raging inferno' reported in eastern and southern areas of London, destroyed many valuable buildings, including Jewin.

The minister's home in Muswell Hill was badly damaged in an air raid later that month, but D. S. Owen showed exceptional leadership during this time. He sent a letter to all members and friends appealing for support, written in remarkably positive language and conveying a determined message.

Anniversary children's service, Jewin (1935)
© National Library of Wales

The minister declared that the disaster could yet be turned into a moment of greatness. His stated intention was to regroup and rebuild. It was, he said, 'the hour of our greatest opportunity, and a magnificent one'.

This letter, written in the darkest days of 1940, explains the troubled (and at times baffling) sequence of events which unfolded. Some of the other London Welsh chapels damaged in the Blitz would never re-open. Jewin was different. The church was homeless but at no time was there any serious plan to close or even to unite with any of the sister chapels. The minister commanded unqualified respect, a powerful factor in keeping the flock together.

Jewin was helped by the generosity of other churches, including the Welsh Independents at King's Cross, and the Anglican church of St Mary Aldermanbury. They also made use of the familiar YMCA hall in Aldersgate Street, and then settled more regularly at the London Welsh Centre in Gray's Inn Road. The building was new (it had opened in 1937 thanks to the generosity of the London Welsh businessman Sir Howell J. Williams) and the main hall was big enough to accommodate several hundred people. There was an excellent congregation there for the first service on 5 January 1941. Another London Welsh businessman, Sir David James, also made his Welsh

Club and cinema complex at Oxford Circus available on Sunday mornings for Jewin's services. The minister regularly paid tribute to the generosity of those who supported his work.

The end of the war brought hundreds of Welsh families back to London, and Jewin's services once again featured children's voices after 'years in

A wartime wedding in the ruins of Jewin (1943)
© Keystone Press Agency

the wilderness', in the minister's own words. The chapel funds were being replenished. Loyal members had even been paying fees for their non-existent chapel pews. The money would be needed if the minister's ambitious plans were to be realised.

Geraint Pritchard, now an elder at Jewin, recalled his years as a young member, and the lively atmosphere at his grandfather's home:

> *He loved company and conversation over dinner. His home on Highgate Hill was buzzing, especially on Sunday evenings after the service. Family and friends would congregate there for relaxation, including his great friend, the Revd Eliseus Howells of Lewisham. He was a virtual lodger there after his home had been destroyed. I remember spending many hours in his Austin travelling around London to various chapels. He taught me to play chess and took a great interest in his grandchildren's education.*

Throughout this time, D. S. Owen was leading the fight to rebuild. Permission had already been given for Jewin to construct a new home. A special fund was established, and contributions were sought in London and in Wales. There had been a distinct lack of sympathy and support, it seemed, from the denominational authorities in Wales, so Jewin's officers felt they had something to prove. (There is a deep irony here for today's members, acutely aware of the same authorities' interest in the big gains to be made from selling the chapel buildings.)

The first option was to rebuild on the Fann Street site. The City of London wanted to build new flats in the area, so the church was offered land near Holborn Viaduct, a more central location but not too far away from Fann Street. The plot was bought for £62,500 in 1948 and the plans for a new chapel were drawn up. The post-war planning process, however, became a major obstacle. The War Damage Commission agreed to compensate the church for the destruction of the Fann Street building, but the costs associated with Holborn Viaduct spiralled by the month. Building resources were scarce and getting permission to make a start proved impossible.

The architect's original estimate of the building costs was £117,000. It was a huge sum but the enthusiasm of the membership was undented. The estimate turned out to be hopelessly unrealistic: the tenders received were heading towards £200,000 with all related expenses included. This was far too big a sum to contemplate without massive external support. So in 1955 the Holborn Viaduct plans were dropped and a return to Fann Street was again on the cards.

There were more delays. The City authorities approved the Fann Street application, but the government minister with responsibility for planning intervened and insisted on having the final say. Interest rates were rising and the chapel's finances were being crippled by debt servicing charges. There was an agonising wait until February 1957 when final permission was given. The land at Holborn Viaduct was sold for a healthy £140,000 which eased the financial pressure considerably.

At this point the cause had been homeless for nearly two decades. It had been a long and exhausting journey for the members, who suffered a heavy blow when their beloved pastor D. S. Owen died on 26 March 1959. He was 72. He would never see his 'New Jewin' but he died knowing that his immense efforts had not been in vain. There were many impressive tributes paid at his funeral in Colwyn Bay. His fellow London minister, the Revd Denzil Harries of Walham Green, underlined his supreme qualities as a preacher but gave even greater prominence to his truly heroic pastoral achievement:

> *The temple had been destroyed, and for eighteen years he was deprived of a chapel, of a pulpit, of appropriate rooms in which to work, and the fact that there still exists a church of seven hundred members, full of hope and daring, is a miracle.*

D. S. Owen would have been happy with the speed at which matters progressed. On 31 March 1959 a special ceremony took place to lay the foundation stone of the new building. The Lady Mayoress of the City of London joined a big crowd of supporters who all went on to enjoy tea in Guildhall, the ancient home of the City of London Corporation. Within two years, the new chapel would be ready.

It is important at this stage to record a fateful missed opportunity to set the Welsh chapels of central London on stronger foundations for the challenges which clearly lay ahead. In the spring of 1959 the officers of the Welsh chapel in Charing Cross Road had suggested dropping the plans to rebuild in Fann Street, and to bring the two congregations together in the more central location. It was a very late bid, to put it mildly, though possibly a sensible one.

Evan Evans, secretary of Jewin (1961)
© National Library of Wales

Understandably, the officers of Jewin felt that they could not abandon nineteen years of hard work, endless fundraising, and relentless campaigning. Nor could they, within days of D. S. Owen's death, discard his vision.

Instead, they offered the members of Charing Cross Road a warm invitation to join them in the new building. This invitation was rejected. Without attaching blame, it has to be said in hindsight that the failure to come together (at either site) was a calamitous error. It diluted resources in the decades that followed and it made life much more difficult as the London Welsh chapels entered the 1970s.

The decision would not have been an easy one: the new building in Fann Street would have been much more user-friendly, comfortable and modern, but the Charing Cross Road location would have been more practical. The failure (or refusal) to see the bigger picture in 1959 would prove to be damaging and costly.

The new Jewin building, designed by Caroe and Partners, was one of the best chapel designs of the post-war period. Its light, airy interior delighted everyone. The excellent organ by John Compton (one of the company's last) impressed from the start. The quality of the carpentry (using a combination of mahogany and unpolished smoked American oak) was sublime. The stained glass windows by Carl Edwards were superb additions. One is dominated by Christ preaching God's word, but also includes scenes from the Blitz and is dedicated to those 34 members who lost their lives in two world wars. The other was installed in 1962 in memory of D. S. Owen.

The opening service on Thursday, 22 June 1961, was led by Evan Evans, Jewin's long-standing secretary and serving president of the Southern

Association. For him, and for hundreds of other loyal Jewin people, it was a day of joy, elation and deep gratitude. The guest preacher that evening was Dr Martyn Lloyd-Jones, and the following Sunday a thanksgiving service was led by the Revd Eliseus Howells, whose support in those dark years after 1940 had been inestimable.

Myra Dawson remembered all the excitement and bustle of the opening service. She was twelve years old, sitting with many other Sunday school members in the gallery. Her parents, who owned a dairy in Pollen Street near Oxford Circus, had married at Jewin in 1936 when they ran a dairy near the chapel in Bridgewater Square. They 'adored and deeply respected' their minister, D. S. Owen. Myra recalled a 'vestry packed with people after the service' and her mother 'serving gallons of tea with a team of other women in the brand-new kitchen'. There was a strong sense from her parents that this was a 'very important and significant occasion', underlined by the fact that her father had written to her headmistress asking for permission to leave school for the afternoon.

Myra remembered the new minister, the Revd Elfed G. Williams, who took over three months after the new building was opened:

> He had a relaxed manner, he was a really nice chap, and was quite academic in his preaching though this wasn't always apparent to people when they met him. His sermons were long, about 40 minutes, not fire and brimstone but quite reflective in style. I liked him.

This was a period of optimism and strength. Elsewhere, the 1960s brought a sharp decline in chapel membership, especially in the valleys of south Wales, and chapels were sometimes demolished within days of the closing service. London's chapels were certainly not immune to the same pressures, but they seemed more able to sustain their activities. It is remarkable to note that Jewin had 661 full members and 103 children on the register at the end of 1961.

Myra Dawson has vivid memories of one of the main annual events, *eisteddfod y plant*, the drama, writing, recitation and music competition for children and young people:

> This was a battle between all the Sunday schools in May every year. It was a very, very competitive event! The 'prelims' took place at Charing Cross chapel on Friday

night and then everyone would come to the London Welsh Centre the next day in a state of anticipation. You didn't know whether you'd been chosen to compete in the final round until the names were called. It went on for hours, starting at two o'clock and often not finishing until late at night. I have to say some of the mothers were very competitive, often much worse than the children… it meant a lot to some of them. Jewin used to come out on top most years. My mother was very keen on it, and even paid for a tutor to train me. But my father couldn't really care less!

The children were taught by energetic, able women (and some men) who formed part of the army of professional teachers from Wales who found work in London's schools in the 1950s and 1960s. The London County Council's chief education officer was once heard telling a group of teachers from Wales that the city's schools simply could not function without them. Every staff room, it seemed, had a Jones or Thomas or Williams or Jenkins among its members.

Despite this buzz, Jewin's report for 1965 set out the financial challenge and acknowledged that the church was simply not paying its way. It was relying heavily on interest from investments and receiving too few contributions. Gomer Roberts in *Y Ddinas Gadarn* provides some startling figures: receipts in 1938 had been £1,530 to cover expenditure of £1,400; by 1965 the receipts were £2,919 to meet expenditure of £4,308. Budget deficits of this order were impossible. Things had improved by 1967 but Jewin, despite outward appearances, was not a wealthy church by any means.

That situation has not changed. In the years since Elfed Williams retired in 1991, after a distinguished pastorate of 30 years, membership has slipped

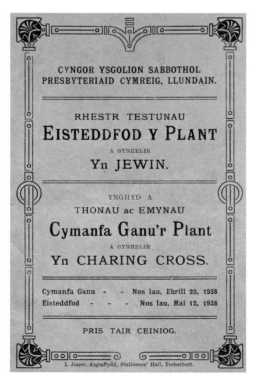

CYNGOR YSGOLION SABBOTHOL PRESBYTERIAID CYMREIG, LLUNDAIN.

RHESTR TESTUNAU
EISTEDDFOD Y PLANT
A GYNHELIR
Yn JEWIN.

YNGHYD A
THONAU ac EMYNAU
Cymanfa Ganu'r Plant
A GYNHELIR
Yn CHARING CROSS.

Cymanfa Ganu - - - Nos Iau, Ebrill 28, 1938
Eisteddfod - - - Nos Iau, Mai 12, 1938

PRIS TAIR CEINIOG.

I. Jones, Argraffydd, Stationers' Hall, Treherbert.

Programme for the children's eisteddfod (1938)
© Eglwys Jewin

Interior of Jewin (2014)
© Eglwys Jewin

and the burden has fallen on far fewer shoulders. This is not an unfamiliar story. But thanks to the efforts of dedicated ministers, elders and members, Jewin's doors are still open.

The past two decades have seen London-wide ministries led by the Revd Dafydd Owen and the Revd Anthony Williams, both of whom worked hard to establish different patterns of worship and new forms of cooperation. Their work has paid dividends. A period of regular shared services with the Welsh Baptist congregation in Eastcastle Street (now the Welsh Church of Central London) seemed to work well but was later abandoned, sadly. It is difficult to see a long-term future for either cause without the will to work together.

The current minister of Jewin, the Revd Richard Brunt, is a Somerset man who learned to speak Welsh as a student in Aberystwyth. He is responsible for all the London chapels within the Presbyterian Church of Wales. His dedication and leadership are already producing results and Jewin has embarked on a campaign to draw new members and plan for the future.

Jewin is an iconic church with a remarkable history. The story of Jewin is of paramount importance in the history of the Welsh in London. It is our cherished link with a distant past. By safeguarding Jewin's future we aim to protect a vital part of our Welsh culture. If the London Welsh are serious about their heritage, Jewin will be supported and preserved for years to come.

CHAPTER 5

FROM LAMBETH TO BOROUGH

The area of London south of the Thames is regarded as an exotic and rather sinister place by those who live elsewhere in the city. Paris is similar. Those who live on the right (or north) bank of the Seine tend to be disdainful of the louche types of the left (or south) bank. But it has to be said that Saint-Germain-des-Prés is rather more fashionable than most of Lambeth.

We have established that the Lambeth of the late-seventeenth and early-eighteenth centuries was a patchwork of farms, gardens and raised roads which reached all the way to the Thames at Lambeth Palace. The skyline was dominated by a few church spires and by windmills, vital sources of power in the pre-industrial world. In time, sawmills and boat-building firms appeared near the river, as did cramped rows of timber-framed hovels in narrow streets and alleyways. Later still came the potteries and their tall chimneys in a local industry dominated by the Royal Doulton company.

Lambeth became a thriving area which offered work to growing numbers of people, including significant groups of Welsh men and women. There are some interesting hints in various archives about the Welsh presence in this part of London. They were there in sufficient numbers in the first half of the eighteenth century to form a religious society, as suggested by Howell Harris's first visit in 1739.

The Welsh had a reputation for coarse, drunken behaviour in the fairs that took place from time to time in Lambeth. There are unconfirmed reports

Lambeth Fair, St David's Day (1850)
© Lambeth Archives

that Howell Harris, Daniel Rowland and other preachers were drawn to the Lambeth fairs because they were guaranteed big crowds with lots of potential converts. Harris's diary entry on 30 April 1749 records preaching to 'a great crowd of Welshmen' in Lambeth, which leads Meurig Owen in his excellent volume *Tros y Bont* (1989) to wonder whether this was indeed a fairground sermon.

The historian Thomas Allen explains in *The History and Antiquities of the Parish of Lambeth* (1826) that a particular fair near Lambeth Palace was linked to St David's Day:

> *In this street was held annually a fair on the first of March, until within a few years back. It was called 'Taffy's Fair,' from the number of Welsh who frequented it. Formerly there was a charter for a fair and a weekly market.*

The nineteenth-century Lambeth antiquarian, Charles Woolley, underlined the same theme in his description of buildings opposite the ancient parish church of St Mary-at-Lambeth:

Swan Yard was at one time largely a Welsh colony, and these people held annually a Welsh Fair on St David's Day in Lambeth Road, down to the Palace Yard.

The reference is to Lambeth Palace, and archives suggest that Swan Yard was a rather squalid jumble of buildings opposite the archbishop's residence. Its specific location is confirmed by John Lockie in his *Topography of London* (1810):

Swan-Yard, Church-Street, Lambeth, – a few doors on the R. from the Thames, and op. the church.

The church building, said to be the oldest structure in Lambeth, is still there today and houses the London Garden Museum. The Swan Inn, next to Swan Yard, was an ancient tavern first mentioned in records in 1463, according to Woolley. A modern block of flats occupies the spot where Swan Yard would have stood until the 1870s when the area began to change dramatically.

We know that the Lambeth meetings continued after Harris's last visit in 1767 because we have the 1772 letter sent to the Countess of Huntingdon asking for preachers to be sent to the 'many poor Welch siners' there. The letter was signed by Edward Jones and nine others. We now know that this was indeed the Edward 'Ginshop' Jones who was said to have built a network of Welsh worshippers in different parts of London. His work in Lambeth may even have started when he was an exhorter for Whitefield's congregation in Moorfields.

The Revd Ben Davies, writing in *Llawlyfr Cyfarfodydd Llundain* (1937), the handbook for the annual meetings of the Union of Welsh Independents held in London in 1937, asserts that Welsh preaching continued sporadically in Lambeth in the 1780s. An entry in the *Evangelical Magazine* (1801) sheds important light on what happened next. It starts by providing some useful context:

For many years Lambeth has been a place of public resort by Welsh people on the Sabbath Day; and the hours sacred to religious purposes have been devoted to those of amusement and dissipation. The reason assigned for this shameful practice has been their not understanding the language in which public worship is performed in this country.

Old Swan Yard,
Lambeth (1860)
© Lambeth Archives

So the Welsh tendency to enjoy the fair and shun the church is documented with clarity. The article is valuable because it was written within a decade of an event of prime importance in our story:

> *Therefore, in the year 1791, a few well-disposed persons rented a large room upon the spot, and met together every Sabbath Day to pray and read the Word of God in their own language, and were occasionally favoured with a Welsh sermon.*

Thus we have confirmation that the sporadic meetings of the 1780s have changed into weekly services. What happens next is the formation of a Welsh Independent congregation:

At length, the number being increased, they formed themselves into a Church, and
Divine worship is now regularly carried on twice every Lord's Day in the Ancient
British tongue in general, to as large an auditory as the place can contain, and,
there is reason to hope, not without success. The Congregation, however being poor,
consisting for the most part of hard-working people, are obliged to depend in great
measure upon the assistance of benevolent individuals.

Ben Davies makes the point that it became an Independent (not a Methodist) cause by virtue of the loyalties of its first minister, Edward Francis, who arrived in 1792. As it happened, he and the ultra-Methodist Edward Jones worked well together and Francis preached frequently in Wilderness Row. But within a few years there were questions about Francis's 'moral character' (no details are given): he left London in 1799, only to return a few years later in 1802. His second stint was unproductive, by all accounts, and he announced his intention to return to Monmouth in 1805. But evidence unearthed by the Revd Dr W. T. Owen (who served for decades as minister of King's Cross chapel) and Meurig Owen suggested that Francis never left Lambeth. They suspected that he preached in the area until his death.

That assumption was absolutely correct, we can now confirm. The final piece of the Francis jigsaw can be found in the burial records at the parish church of St Mary-at-Lambeth. They include an Edward Francis who died in 1830 at the age of 74. His address is given as Swan Yard, the site of the 'Welsh colony' described by Woolley. The dates fit perfectly and he is surely our man.

This makes much more sense when we consider the Lambeth entry in Manning and Bray's *History and Antiquities of the County of Surrey* (1814) which notes two Welsh causes in the area:

There are two [meeting houses] where Divine Service is performed in the Welsh
Language, furnishing an opportunity to the numerous labourers in the gardens in this
neighbourhood who annually come from the Principality, to hear Divine Service in
the only language they understand.

So we have two Welsh-speaking congregations, one a faction led by Francis, the other the original cause led by his successor. Francis's problems, not surprisingly, had badly damaged the Lambeth cause and he was shunned by his former collaborators. The 'large auditory' had dwindled. Francis's successor, the Revd Thomas Jones, a Llangeler man, was far more solid and serious. He had trained as a bookbinder, but started preaching under the guidance of his eminent brother-in-law, the Revd David Davies of Swansea, one of the ministers who frequently served the Welsh causes in London. The two men would preach together at the Whit Sunday meetings in Little Guildford Street, Borough, in 1809.

By 1826 we know that the Welsh occupied a small chapel (rented or bought) in Church Street, Lambeth, a short distance from the southern end of Lambeth Bridge and the archbishop's palace. Thomas Allen (1826) describes it as a 'Welsh Chapel, of small size and mean appearance'. It was clearly a modest building.

Bunyan's Hall ('TO LET' on the windows), Church Street, Lambeth (1865)
© Lambeth Archives

Images of Church Street in the mid-nineteenth century show a terrace of dilapidated buildings, one of which was called Bunyan's Hall. A press report in September 1888, at the time of the hall's demolition, said that 'during a long period the upper room of this old building was a Nonconformist meeting-place… for many years this old meeting-room contained the pulpit of John Bunyan'. The hall, on the first floor, was built over a passageway leading to Swan Yard, the old Welsh 'colony'. Given the descriptions of a Welsh meeting-room in the street opposite St Mary-at-Lambeth, Bunyan's Hall has to be a very good bet.

This Welsh congregation in Lambeth was, therefore, the first Welsh-speaking Independent cause in London. But we have no evidence that it produced branches which took root elsewhere, and its doors closed sometime after 1820. The precise date is unknown, sadly. So we must look elsewhere, but not too far away, for the 'mother-church' of the Welsh Independents in London.

The joint appearance by David Davies and Thomas Jones at Little Guildford Street in 1809 is a timely reminder of the significance of Borough, an ancient area of the city at the southern end of London Bridge, barely a mile and a half from Church Street, Lambeth. This is where the great network of London's Welsh-speaking Independent chapels really began.

We know that Thomas Thomas and Daniel Jenkins established a branch of Wilderness Row in Gravel Lane, Borough, sometime after 1788. Services were held there on Sunday mornings and afternoons, but on Sunday evenings all members were expected to make their way to Wilderness Row. There was clearly a growing demand for Welsh-language services in this populous part of south London which included significant river frontage with endless shipping business on the Thames.

The marriage dispute involving Thomas and his brother had soured relations with Edward Jones, and the result was a split with Wilderness Row. Gravel Lane became, in Ben Davies's words, 'thoroughly Independent' while Wilderness Row became 'thoroughly Methodist'. The Revd David Davies had been a major influence in encouraging Gravel Lane along the Independent path.

A small group of Methodist loyalists decided not to follow the crowd and stayed loyal to Wilderness Row. They worshipped in a small rented room, also in Gravel Lane, but closer to the river. Later they had their own chapel in Meeting House Walk, a narrow lane leading from Snowsfields, a street which still exists today on the southern flank of Guy's Hospital near London Bridge. It was at Snowsfields that the congregation of Wilderness Row would worship when their chapel was being rebuilt in 1806. Snowsfields chapel was at one time occupied by John Wesley before the flock decided he was no longer welcome, forcing him to find another chapel in Crosby Row, a stone's throw from Snowsfields. We shall have reason to return to Crosby Row later in our story.

All the while, the Independent bandwagon was rolling, and by 1806 the congregation decided to build its own chapel in Little Guildford Street, a short distance from Gravel Lane. It was opened on 5 January 1807. The Revd David Davies was among the preachers at the initial services. By 1811 the church had secured its first full-time minister, the Revd David Simon Davies, and he was responsible for setting good foundations during his fifteen-year pastorate.

We know that the Methodists of Wilderness Row suffered their share of scandal and division, but the Independents of Borough also had their own troubles to deal with in the early days. David Simon Davies was succeeded, in July 1831, by David Davies, a newly-ordained minister from Carmarthen College. He started well, and for many years was popular with the members. But history must record that David Davies did more harm than good to the cause. He started dabbling in business and commerce, and word spread (no doubt with his encouragement) that he'd been very successful and become a wealthy man. This wasn't true, and he eventually fled to the USA where his many creditors could not reach him.

All that would be bad enough, but David Davies also landed the cause in difficulty. Because of his arrogance and stupidity, the members found themselves without a chapel in 1866 when the lease expired. He had been asked many times to take action but had refused an offer to renew for £2,000 in 1864. The result was that the cause was homeless for seven years until a new chapel was opened in 1873. It is a remarkable tale of mulish incompetence, at the very least. But why did the members tolerate this conduct? Rees and Thomas in *Hanes Eglwysi Annibynnol Cymru* (1875 and 1891) claim that members were in awe of his apparent wealth. They suggest that a moneyless man would have been kicked out.

The chapel in Little Guildford Street opened in 1807
© London Metropolitan Archive

Davies survived for decades before his business debts forced him to flee. His record would take some beating: he had inherited a thriving congregation in a new building, and 35 years later left a much smaller gathering in a rented room in Newington Causeway. In many respects that is even worse than the misconduct of Edward 'Ginshop' Jones in Wilderness Row.

A big fundraising effort resulted in the purchase of the freehold of the site of the old chapel. The foundation stone of the new building, which would accommodate 500 people, was laid on 31 July 1872 by Samuel Morley MP, press baron and Gladstonian Liberal, an exceptionally generous supporter of Nonconformist causes including the London Welsh chapels. He contributed £500 to the initial fund, at least £40,000 in today's values (on a price comparison basis), and most of the building work was complete by the end of the year. The total cost of the new building, including demolishing the old chapel, was around £4,800, of which around £3,000 had already been raised.

The handsome building which opened on 23 February 1873 is the Borough chapel which still stands today on Southwark Bridge Road. The old chapel had faced Little Guildford Street, a 'narrow and dirty' road (according to Rees and Thomas) now merged into Great Guildford Street, whereas the new chapel building faced the 'wide and clean' Southwark Bridge Road, minutes away from Southwark Bridge which crosses the Thames near Shakespeare's Globe.

The first minister to be installed in the new building was the Revd Lewys Thomas of Llan-non, Carmarthenshire, in October 1875. He was popular with Welsh and English congregations and seemed destined for a very long pastorate at Borough. But after a decade his health failed and he died in January 1888 in Madeira where he had been recuperating.

Since Lewys Thomas's days, Borough has been noted for the quality of its ministry. That tradition was cemented by the remarkable 46-year pastorate of the Revd D. C. Jones who arrived from Merthyr Tydfil in August 1890. Borough chapel thrived under his leadership. A survey in *The Daily News* between December 1902 and August 1903 recorded attendance figures in all the London Welsh chapels: on 1 February 1903 there were 74 present at Borough for the morning service and 228 in the evening. In those days, Sunday evenings always drew the biggest chapel and church congregations. (The situation has now been reversed and few London chapels offer an evening service.) Membership rose sharply as Borough offered a wide range of social and cultural activity in addition to the full provision of religious services and meetings. The Borough Welsh Choir became famous by winning first prize at the National Eisteddfod and at competitions in London. It was energetically supported by the minister who believed strongly in the power of music to augment spiritual experience.

He was still at work when he died aged 84 in September 1936. His funeral drew more than a thousand mourners, many of whom also gathered later that day for the London Welsh tradition of escorting the coffin to Paddington station. They

Payment record for transporting a coffin from Paddington to Cardiganshire (1936)
© Beti Gwenfron Evans

stood on Platform 1 and sang the great hymn 'O fryniau Caersalem' as the train raised steam and puffed its way towards west Wales. There have been many similar accounts over the years. One of the most moving was provided by Beti Gwenfron Evans, describing events after her mother's early death which took place within months of D. C. Jones's passing in 1936:

> *My most vivid memory of the funeral was arriving at Paddington station on Sunday night. I had a white dress, black and white checked coat and black shoes. We came out of the car to a very crowded platform. The crowd made way for us, but all I could see were black coats, and the crowd closing behind us. We reached the carriage and opened our eyes wide. Not an ordinary railway carriage but a long room with a long, shiny table. There were two smaller carriages we could sit and lie in, and a place for the coffin and all the beautiful, sweet-smelling wreaths. Young as I was, I shall never forget Mother's final farewell to London. As the train started the whole crowd erupted into singing the Welsh funeral hymn, 'O fryniau Caersalem'. It was very emotional. Whenever I hear the hymn I'm reminded of Mam.*

The cost of transporting the coffin to the small station at Pont Llanio, near Llanddewi Brefi, on the former Carmarthen to Aberystwyth line, was £22.12s.3d. There are many who will recall the intense emotion of those farewells at Paddington and Euston stations over the years.

D. C. Jones, buried in Dinas, Pembrokeshire, was the man who guided Borough through the darkness of the Great War and built it into one of the liveliest Welsh chapels in London. His name is still cherished by members.

Membership peaked at 256 in 1938–9, on the eve of the Second World War, a pattern shared by most of the London Welsh chapels. Mr Jones's successor, the Revd Gwilym Bowyer, faced a challenging time during the early days of the conflict. He arrived in October 1939, but his ordination was delayed until March 1940 because of the chaos in London. His wife and son returned to the safety of rural Wales, as did so many London Welsh families, but he remained to arrange services and to offer help to as many members as possible. The circumstances were extremely difficult and life became almost impossible. In August 1943 he accepted a call from Ebeneser, Bangor, and remained there until 1946 when he became principal of Bala-Bangor College, the theological seminary of the Welsh Independents. He was in post when he died in 1965 at the age of 59. He is remembered as a superb public speaker, an incisive preacher and a talented broadcaster who made many appearances on Welsh radio and television.

Borough enjoyed the post-war boom experienced by most of the London Welsh chapels, but the arrival of the Revd Ifor M. Edwards in 1946 would prove to be an exceptional advantage. He was both a noted academic (his Ph.D. thesis was a study of 'The Moral and Religious Philosophy of Richard Price', the great Welsh thinker whose remarkable achievements deserve much wider recognition) as well as a noted action man: he took part in the Borough Drama Group; he was a footballer who played for local clubs; he was a good cricketer; and he sang with the Borough Choir.

His son, Huw, who won a famous parliamentary by-election in May 1991, serving two terms as Labour MP for Monmouth, provided revealing glimpses of his father's outlook:

> He didn't really like Welsh village life. He loved the anonymity of London but was also able to have a stimulating professional life – preaching, studying, teaching and lecturing. He regularly travelled to Wales for anniversary services and even for ordinary Sunday engagements – travelling home by train through the night on Sunday for college on a Monday, but also to avoid staying longer than necessary.

Dr Ifor Edwards enjoyed a 32-year pastorate at Borough. The members loved him and he served them with loyalty and distinction. It was a great time to be a member of a London Welsh chapel congregation, as Huw Edwards explained:

> The Boro' was a vibrant chapel in the 1950s and 1960s and played an important role in the social life of many Welsh people in London. There had been the Boro' Choir which had made its own recordings, and regular social events where individuals like Ryan Davies attended, and Welsh MPs would come to midweek meetings or 'brains trust'. For those of us who grew up as children of the Boro', there has been a lifelong bond. As I said in my maiden speech in the House of Commons: 'I grew up in a fine Welsh community – the Welsh community in London.' It gave us a richness of culture and purpose – and a strong sense, in my father's words, that we must bring 'honour to the family and honour to the chapel'.

The Revd Dr Ifor M. and
Mrs Esme Edwards in
1991
© Huw W. E. Edwards

As London's economy perked up after the war, the property market started to expand (though nowhere near the modern boom), allowing the chapels and their members to share in the new wealth created:

> There were families from Cardiganshire who owned dairy businesses, as well as City gents, given the closeness to the Square Mile. Single people came to the chapel, met and married. It was quite a wealthy chapel which owned the adjacent properties where the flats and businesses brought in regular rental income. Many of the families were quite well off and some of the ladies wore their mink coats to chapel. There would be dinners in prominent London hotels and a strong sense of 'only the best for the Borough'.

Dr Edwards believed in the highest standards and could be rather impatient when they slipped. Children not paying attention in chapel, deacons taking the collection or distributing the bread and wine in a 'slovenly' way, organists who dragged the hymns – any of these were causes for reprimand. His son added: 'You would not want to be the organist who started to play "Blaenwern", a tune my father hated, as you would be stopped and ordered to play "Hyfrydol"…'

Despite his manifest gifts, Dr Ifor Edwards was unable to reverse the downward trend in membership which affected all the London Welsh chapels. By 1951, after the chaos of wartime, there were 200 registered members, and the numbers dwindled in the decades that followed. Dr Edwards and his wife, Esme, retired to Neath in September 1978, where they both served the chapels of the Swansea Valley until their deaths, within days of each other, in March 2009.

After gaining significantly from two lengthy pastorates, Borough spent the rest of the twentieth century without a minister. It reflects well on the elders and members that they were able to keep going throughout this time, supported by many preachers including Richard Jones, Erasmus Jones, Roderick Lloyd, T. J. Morris, D. M. Thomas, and Arfon Jones.

From 1998, all the London Welsh Independent chapels became part of the pastorate of the Revd D. Gwylfa Evans. He had come from Llanelli to take charge of Harrow in 1978, then included Radnor Walk in 1983, and, finally, added King's Cross and Borough to his considerable workload in 1998. He retired as minister of Borough in 2007, but still serves the London Welsh chapels, regardless of denomination, with his customary generosity and dedication. The Welsh Nonconformist community in London owes him and Buddug, his wife, a big debt of gratitude for their 35 years of service.

There was a strong sense that if Borough was to lay solid foundations for the twenty-first century, in an age when far fewer men and women were being ordained, it needed to consider some radical options. Tegid Jones, the chapel secretary at the time, explained that Borough had faced the possibility of closure (with membership now at 58) but decided to explore new ways of reviving the cause. So the chapel broke new ground in 2010 when it invited Eiri Jones, a chief nurse by profession, to become church leader. She had trained in nearby Guy's Hospital and worked there for nearly two decades. Eiri became involved with the chapel through her parents, the aforementioned Revd T. Arfon and Enyd Jones, both Baptists who had developed strong links with Borough.

The chapel became one of the first in the Union of Welsh Independents to appoint a non-ordained, non-stipendiary church leader, a step copied by other Nonconformist churches since 2010. The new role had been created by the Union to lead worship and outreach, but not to undertake the kind of pastoral work expected of an ordained minister. Eiri's uncle, the Revd Gwilym Hughes, another Welsh Baptist minister, was present at the service.

Borough chapel opened in 1873 (2012)

The final prayer at the induction service was led by Simon Hughes, the local Liberal Democrat MP, who welcomed 'the resurrection of the mission of the Borough Welsh chapel'.

Eiri Jones explained the nature her mission at Borough:

Following in my parents' footsteps, leading a Welsh chapel, is a privilege. It also maintains my close connections with a part of London where I spent many happy years as a nurse. I feel that my mission at the Borough brings my role as a public servant full circle. I hope to be able to serve the Borough for many years to come as we rebuild the community element of the chapel's activity which reflects the work of earlier ministries.

A vital part of that mission has been to support local charities, and in key services collections are taken in aid of organisations such as Evelina London Children's Hospital and Great Ormond Street Hospital. Borough has also made an important contribution in the field of missionary work. Myfanwy Wood spent much of her life in Beijing teaching generations of students at Yenching University. She returned to Britain in 1942 but continued to further the work of the Christian Church in China.

The success of Borough chapel in the twentieth century has depended on many people, but there are a few whose records stand out. Ifor Davies served as treasurer for 46 years. His father had been treasurer before him. When he retired in 1997, tributes were paid to his exceptional contribution to Borough and to his work for the London Welsh Centre in Gray's Inn Road. Nellie Evans, a stalwart of the London Welsh community, was the mother of Dame Anne Evans, the opera star, and of John Evans, one of the founders of the Gwalia Male Voice Choir. Tegid and Margaret Jones have been tireless Borough workers in more recent times.

There is another name that cannot be ignored. E. B. Byron Jones devoted a lifetime's efforts to Borough and served many other London Welsh institutions, including the London Welsh Centre and the London Welsh Rugby Club, with distinction. His period as secretary of Borough spanned five decades, and when he died in 1993, 'Byron o'r Boro' was widely known for his commitment to Welsh culture (for which he received the OBE), as well as for his limitless supply of jokes.

Huw Edwards explained that his father and Byron Jones worked well together but did not share the same political or cultural outlook. This divided opinion is typical of the split personality of the London Welsh community:

> E. B. Byron Jones was a large man who came to chapel in a pinstriped suit and bowler hat. Byron and his wife Marjorie had a commanding presence in the chapel and within the London Welsh community. He was a prominent lawyer for the London County Council and acted as our family solicitor. Marjorie would coach the children in singing and recitation for the annual children's eisteddfod. She was a formidable personality and gave us all a great deal of confidence to face an audience and perform in public. Byron and my father respected each other but were different in many ways. They would argue bitterly in Sunday school – Byron being rather right-of-centre and seeing the world from the perspective of Cardiganshire – my father being rather left-of-centre having been brought up in Neath during the 1930s. He preached Christian Socialism openly and forcefully. Byron would shuffle uncomfortably in his narrow pew. They also disagreed over the language, Byron believing that the chapel should promote and teach Welsh, while my father argued we were there to 'worship a gospel not a language'.

But Byron Jones was not a man to be cowed. A prudent and clear-sighted article of his which appeared in the weekly newspaper of the Welsh

Independents, *Y Tyst*, in January 1986 also deserves mention. It is a significant but depressing piece which draws together major strands of London Welsh life from the perspective of someone who spent three-quarters of a century as a major participant. Byron Jones lamented the decline of Welsh cultural activity in London which he attributed to the fall in migration from Welsh-speaking Wales. He mourned the demise of the 'county societies' (he had been president of the Cardiganshire Society) and of the city's eisteddfodau. He criticised modern Welsh politicians, with a few notable exceptions, for their lack of interest in the chapels. He regretted the closure of Sunday schools, the dwindling popularity of the gymanfa ganu and preaching festivals, and the growing habit of using English in chapel services.

But his most telling point related to the future of the London chapels themselves. His frequent appeals for unification had been rejected, and he revealed his frustration at the 'failure to come together... setting aside and forgetting denominational differences... in one central tabernacle' to provide Welsh-speaking services for future generations of the London Welsh. The alternative, he warned, was that 'one by one, the remaining churches will fade and perish'. How right he was.

His comments were no doubt prompted by the closure of Charing Cross Road chapel in 1982, and that of Falmouth Road chapel, not far from Borough. Byron Jones admitted that his 'pleading' for London-wide unification had fallen on deaf ears. His frustration and regret were clearly conveyed. Others have made similar appeals in subsequent years but the response has been hostile and, it must be said, recklessly stubborn. Byron Jones's worst fears have now been realised: at least nine chapels have closed since those judicious comments were made in 1986.

Borough chapel, praise be, is not one of them. It has embarked on an innovative path, under enterprising leadership, supported by a committed congregation and trustees, seeking new members among the young Welsh families of south London, while offering bilingual services to widen its reach in the local area. It has, in a sense, reinvented itself to serve a modern, cosmopolitan community. It is not a straightforward process but there are some very encouraging signs.

Others would do well to follow Borough's example.

Byron Jones would certainly approve of that.

CHAPTER 6

DOCKERS

It was Henry VII, token Welshman and founder of the Tudor dynasty, who built the first royal dockyard at Portsmouth in 1496. But it was his son, Henry VIII, who established the two great dockyards on the River Thames, at Woolwich (1512) and nearby Deptford (1513), which rapidly became essential for national security. In the process, they created work for thousands of people, many Welsh among them.

By the mid-sixteenth century, Deptford had become the most important yard in England, surrounded by a network of immense storehouses to supply the vessels being built and maintained there. The operation was run by the Navy Board, created by Henry VIII, which was responsible for the building and maintenance of all naval warships.

Deptford and Woolwich declined in importance by the mid-nineteenth century for several reasons. Because of their location on the tidal section of the Thames, the docks gradually filled up with silt from the river. Thriving towns had grown around the royal dockyards, restricting the room for expansion. This is why Chatham and Plymouth became more natural choices for large-scale shipbuilding. But Deptford and Woolwich were still important for maintenance and repairs until they closed in 1869.

James Hughes ('Iago Trichrug'), the penniless blacksmith who came to London from Ciliau Aeron in 1799, was part of that army of workers drawn by the work opportunities offered by the royal dockyards. He provided a prized account of the origins of Welsh worship in Deptford in an article he published in *Goleuad Gwynedd* in May 1828. Hughes explains that the dockyards were booming when he arrived in the closing years of the eighteenth century, and that many Welsh people found work there. The harvest of 1798 in Wales had

A view of the royal dockyard at Deptford (Robert Dodd, 1789)
© London Metropolitan Archive

been exceptionally poor, driving many from Cardiganshire to seek work in Deptford and Woolwich. Some of them, according to Hughes, were people of faith. They would walk five miles to Wilderness Row to attend Edward Jones's services on Sundays, despite Hughes's view that Wilderness Row was 'not a thriving cause' at that time.

Hughes's account is important because it suggests he was among the small group of people ('several of us decided…') who came to the view that Welsh-language religious services were needed in Deptford. He noted that Edward Francis of Lambeth had made occasional visits to preach, as had Robert Roberts of Clynnog, but there was no regular supply and Deptford felt 'distant'. So they decided to take the initiative.

Early in 1799 they rented a room in Back Lane, opposite the Sheer Hulk public house, to hold prayer meetings on weekday evenings and occasional meetings on Sundays. They had to contend with open hostility not only from English neighbours but also from the Welsh licensees of the Sheer Hulk. Hughes directed his anger at the landlady, a Llanrwst woman, who mocked and taunted her compatriots without fail. Her main concern seemed to be that the pub's business might be affected by the prayer meetings. Despite her venom, those earliest days were the happiest, said James Hughes, because the society was a group of equals driven by 'pure brotherly love'. The real complications came later.

Sometime in the spring of 1799 the preacher Daniel Jenkins came to London and visited Deptford. This was the same Daniel Jenkins who, with Thomas Thomas, established a branch of Wilderness Row in Gravel Lane, Borough. His regular visits to Deptford were, for James Hughes, a cause of great joy. Numbers grew steadily, and the rented room was swapped for an old stable in Barnes Alley. It provided more space, but at a cost. Hughes described its location 'right behind the garden of the tavern' (the Sheer Hulk), with the 'landlord's pigsty leaning against our back wall'. It was 'very uncomfortable... with foul smells all around'. To cap it all, their meetings were disrupted 'almost all the time by bad English lads outside'. How they managed to stay there for three years is anyone's guess.

They were not supported at this stage by preachers sent from the Associations in Wales, so an offer of help from a Welsh-speaking Anglican clergyman in nearby Lewisham was warmly welcomed. The Revd Hugh Jones of St Mary's offered to administer Holy Communion to the group, through the medium of the Welsh language, believing them to be regular communicant members of the Church of England. The arrangement continued for some time until Jones discovered their denominational loyalties. He was unimpressed and terminated the deal. The story tells us something about the blurred dividing lines between Anglicans and some dissenting groups at that time.

James Hughes explained that more regular visits from Welsh preachers gave the cause in Deptford a significant boost. They were allowed to meet in a small chapel owned by English Nonconformists. This arrangement lasted up to three years, after which they held services in members' homes. Here, again, they suffered from a lack of space. So they moved again, this time to a bigger chapel being leased by the Welsh Independents who, by that time, had also settled in Deptford. It was a generous arrangement: they were able to use the chapel on Wednesday and Friday evenings, and on alternate Sunday mornings.

The arrangement worked for several years, but Hughes's frustration was clear. Not surprisingly, he and his Methodist group disliked being tenants and wanted a place of their own. They came close on two occasions to building a small chapel, but it never happened. So they carried on sharing premises with the Independents. Hughes stated bleakly that despite periods of 'joy and great blessings', the cause in Deptford never boasted more than 40 members. It was around 30 at the time of writing in 1828. Too many members were lacking in commitment, he said, but others had been able to restore their faith 'in this remote place'. This account, though 'stark and unembellished' in Hughes's estimation, is still an illuminating read nearly two centuries later.

James Hughes, elected an elder in Deptford around 1808, started to preach in 1811 and was ordained to the full-time ministry in 1816. But he carried on working as a blacksmith in the King's Yard until his appointment as minister of Jewin Crescent in 1823. His ministerial salary of £60 a year, though not lavish by any means, must have been a welcome boost after many years of struggling with debt. His strong link with the chapel in Deptford never weakened, and he supported the cause until his death in 1844. Without Hughes, the members struggled. The sparse records that remain include several appeals for ministerial support. The response was clearly inadequate: by Easter 1853, the Calvinistic Methodist cause in Deptford had ceased to exist. It would, however, resurface in nearby Lewisham some years later.

The 1851 Census of Religious Worship provided valuable evidence of Welsh religious activity in the Deptford area. It confirmed that there were two Welsh-speaking congregations, one Calvinistic Methodist, and one Independent, using the same place of worship. The address was given as Evelyn Street, which is now the busy A200 road leading from Rotherhithe to Greenwich.

Meurig Owen, in *The Welsh Church in Deptford 1800–66* (1979), asserted that Deptford was the story of two congregations whose lives overlapped. We know from the financial appeal published in 1806 by the Borough membership that the Independents had created branches in 'Deptford and Woolwich where a great number of the Welch reside'. In the *Evangelical Magazine* of the same year, another appeal mentioned Independent causes at 'Borough, Deptford and Woolwich'.

The chapel leased by the Independents in Deptford had been surrendered by a congregation of Wesleyan Methodists around 1803. It was located in Loving Edward's Lane (today's Edward Street), in the heart of Deptford, less than half a mile from the dockyards on the Thames. This was the chapel shared with James Hughes and the Welsh Calvinistic Methodists.

There is an obvious question to be asked. Why did this pair of Welsh-speaking congregations maintain separate causes in Deptford? The answer, it seems, lies in the original dispute between Edward Jones and Daniel Jenkins. The split which affected Gravel Lane also affected Deptford and Woolwich, creating a situation of sublime silliness: here were two, small, Welsh-speaking congregations in one part of London, sharing the same building, but unwilling to join forces. There was an important difference, however. The Methodist meetings of Deptford and Woolwich were 'branches' of Wilderness Row, while the Independent causes were truly independent.

The Revd David Morgan, a former Calvinistic Methodist, became minister of Deptford Welsh Independent chapel sometime after 1807 and served until his death in 1812. He was succeeded by the Revd Arthur Jones of Bangor, who was installed in 1814. It was during his ministry that the Welsh Independents built a chapel at Parson's Hill, Woolwich. Arthur Jones became a distinguished Independent minister, preaching in both Welsh and English throughout London, and publishing several books and sermons.

His pastorate ended when economic conditions worsened. The Napoleonic War (1803–15) had caused hardship, more expensive food, and lower wages. It is estimated that 300,000 men flooded back into society from the armed forces. The impact on areas such as Deptford and Woolwich was

The Welsh chapel, Parson's Hill, Woolwich, built c.1816

brutal. Arthur Jones returned to Bangor in 1823. His church went into decline, if we believe an account written by John James in 1837, but the Revd Job Thomas, a native of Llanarth, Cardiganshire, stepped in to take charge of Deptford and Woolwich for some 20 years until his death in 1857.

In his *Church History of Kent* (1859), the Revd Thomas Timpson noted that 'since 1836, they have assembled in a commodious school-room, in the Lower Road, Deptford; and their present minister is Mr. Flower'. Nathan Dews in his *History of Deptford* (1884) suggested that there may have been alternative English and Welsh services by that time. We know that the Revd Evan Evans also provided valuable leadership in the years after 1856, but Rees and Thomas in *Hanes Eglwysi Annibynnol Cymru* assert that the Independent Welsh church in Deptford had closed by 1866.

Woolwich is a rather different story. Much of this account is based on the valuable notes kindly provided by John Samuel, the former chapel secretary. The Welsh would continue to worship in Woolwich until 1981, before moving to Welling for a few years until the doors finally closed in 1983. It is an impressive tale of a small group of members demonstrating faith, hard work, and dedication in a challenging climate.

It should be clear by now that the stories of Welsh Calvinistic Methodists and Independents in both Deptford and Woolwich overlapped endlessly. It is sometimes impossible to tell who's in charge and when. The task is even more frustrating when we realise that here were four Welsh-speaking congregations all operating in a relatively small area of London, often sharing facilities, but never coming together.

In the section on Woolwich in his *Directory of Kent* (1847), Bagshaw mentioned the 'Welsh chapel, Parson's Hill… a small brick building erected 1816', and Timpson (1859) added that 'Woolwich has been visited by a considerable succession of natives of the principality of Wales… they have chiefly been Independents and Calvinistic Methodists… the congregation has always been small'. John Hughes in *Methodistiaeth Cymru* (1856) offered 1817 as the date of construction and drew the same conclusions about the weakness of the cause. There was a reference to 'ten or twelve members' in 1844, according to an account written by J. W. Jones of Jewin Crescent.

It is clear from the records of Jewin Crescent that the Calvinistic Methodists were paying the ground rent on Parson's Hill, and had been organising the supply of prominent preachers from the earliest days (including John Elias, Ebenezer Richard, and James Hughes). But, crucially, those records also show that Jewin Crescent was (from 1830 onwards) receiving quarterly rental income of £1 from the Welsh Independents for their use of the building. The religious census of 1851 confirmed the position: it recorded a building used by 'Calvin. Methodists and Independents, alternate Sundays' with a congregation of 20 people present on the morning of 30 March 1851. The entry was signed by David Lewis, a shipwright from Cardigan who made an exceptional contribution to the cause in Woolwich. He had been elected an elder in Wilderness Row in 1810 and looked after the affairs of Woolwich for decades. His trade fitted in perfectly with the local dockyard economy: the chapel register also included labourers, boilermakers, blacksmiths and joiners.

Parson's Hill was, therefore, a shared chapel building, but it soon became clear that the Independents were the stronger partner. In 1852, according to W. T. Vincent in *The Records of the Woolwich District* (1890), the chapel was offered to let, a clear hint of crisis. Arthur Rowlands, who worked as a missionary among Londoners, noted in 1854 that the cause was 'weak and listless', and Meurig Owen concluded that the Welsh Methodist cause ended 'in the early 1870s'.

The Independents had more staying power. Ministers David Morgan, Arthur Jones and Job Thomas had kept the cause in good health despite modest membership numbers. By 1874, they had taken over the lease of Parson's Hill from the Methodists of Jewin Crescent, making Woolwich a fully Independent cause.

The Revd Evan Evans, a tailor by trade, from Pennant in Cardiganshire, was ordained in Borough and took charge of Woolwich in 1856, leading the small church for 31 years until his death in 1887 at the age of 91. The records suggest he was paid a very small salary and lived very simply. The chapel was also supported in the last quarter of the nineteenth century by other visiting ministers, including David Harries, of the Southwark and Lambeth Mission in Westminster Bridge Road, who would also take charge of the Welsh causes in East Ham and Penge.

The lease on Parson's Hill expired in 1905, during the ministry of the Revd Llewelyn Bowyer (or 'Boyer' as he was later known) who had been installed in 1902. He was a coal miner's son from Rhosllanerchrugog, one of the strongholds of Welsh Nonconformist culture in north-east Wales, who must have felt at home in the working-class areas of East Ham (where he looked after the Welsh chapel in Sibley Grove) and Woolwich.

Thanks to his initiative, an appeal was made to other Welsh Independent churches to support a financial appeal. A plot of land was bought in Willenhall

Road, Woolwich, where a new chapel was built, called Bethel. The foundation stones laid by Mrs Benjamin Rees and W. R. Evans in June 1906 can still be seen on the site, though Bethel is sadly no longer there. The opening services were held on 25 November 1906, led by a galaxy of star preachers including Elvet Lewis ('Elfed'), Machreth Rees, and D. C. Jones of Borough.

Llewelyn Bowyer officiated at the last Welsh service in Parson's Hill on 28 October 1906, but he did not preside at the first service in Willenhall Road in early November: the evangelist, Rosina Davies, one of Evan Roberts's team of formidable female revivalists during the famous Welsh Revival of 1904–5, claimed that particular honour. She had been contracted by the Union of Welsh Independents to boost the young causes at Woolwich, East Ham, and Battersea, and to preach on weekdays at other Independent chapels. One report on the Woolwich experience describes 'excellent services… and the wonderful sight of an overflowing chapel… Miss Davies preached powerfully and sang very sweetly'.

Even today, with much better transport connections, it would be a challenge for a minister to look after two growing congregations in East Ham and Woolwich. Crossing the Thames in those days was more problematic, too. There were fewer tunnels and convenient routes. So it was decided that Llewelyn Bowyer would focus on East Ham, freeing Woolwich to find a new minister. The arrangement held for a few years until the Bowyer family returned to Wales in 1912, following a call from Dan-y-graig, Allt-wen, a newly-built chapel which would become one of the strongest in the Swansea Valley. There was a very practical reason for the move: the Bowyers had been dismayed by the failure of their children to speak Welsh fluently in London. There would be no such problems in the thoroughly Welsh-speaking district of Pontardawe where the Bowyers stayed until 1928.

The Revd R. Jones Mason was installed on 28 November 1909. By 1914 he had expanded his pastorate to cover Woolwich, East Ham, and Barrett's Grove, a chapel in Stoke Newington. This was a very considerable catchment area, far bigger than the one judged impractical for Llewelyn Bowyer. He served the three chapels for two years before heading in 1916 for the battlefields of Flanders as a YMCA chaplain. He survived the Great War and spent the rest of his ministry in Llansilin and Corwen.

Even in the dark days of the First World War, Bethel succeeded in

Bethel, Woolwich, built in 1906

finding a replacement within months. But the Revd Ishmael Lewis spent the briefest period in London before moving to Pembrokeshire and becoming an Anglican clergyman. These rapid changes destabilised the cause, and after the Armistice was signed in 1918 there was little sign of any revival. Indeed, there were serious concerns about the long-term future of Bethel. But thanks to the efforts of a small group of loyal members, including the secretary, Grier Thomas, and Cadwaladr Jones, the Sunday school organiser, things improved. Grier Thomas also served as chapel organist, proudly using the old Kelly harmonium donated by Fetter Lane Welsh chapel. This was the instrument played regularly by the great Welsh composer Joseph Parry when he was a member at Fetter Lane.

There were other notable figures whose contribution proved essential. The Revd Ben Davies, a coal miner who became one of the most respected Welsh preachers of his day, retired in 1927 from Pant-teg, Ystalyfera, after a 35-year pastorate, and made his way to London where his daughters lived. He served the city's small Welsh causes, including Woolwich, with energy and distinction until his death in 1937. He supplied several important essays on the history of the London chapels for the handbook given to those attending the Union of Welsh Independents' annual meetings held in London shortly after he died.

His family donated a Communion set, decorated with a silver plaque noting Ben Davies's years of service, which was used in Bethel until it closed, and is now kept at Borough. It is remarkable to think that Woolwich chapel, one of the smallest in the Union, had been led for so long by one of its biggest names. The Revd Ben Davies had served in effect as the chapel's minister, forging close links with the congregation which were maintained long after he'd stopped preaching.

Over the years, Woolwich secured the services of several ministers whose involvement seemed to come about almost by accident. The Revd Rees Richards settled in north-west London on his retirement in 1937 and became a member of King's Cross chapel. All the Independent Welsh chapels in London depended on his services during the Second World War, when most ministers had left the city, but he enjoyed a very close link with the Welsh congregation in Woolwich. He died in 1960 at the age of 90.

The flow of Welsh teachers into London's schools and colleges is a strong theme. The Revd Erasmus Jones spent many years as a teacher in Essex, became a member at Woolwich in 1961, and acted as unofficial minister until 1964. He then spent many years looking after the Welsh chapels in Slough and Leytonstone. The Revd Richard Jones, who taught in Newham, accepted the invitation to become minister of Woolwich in 1964. He stepped in to support Borough and Radnor Walk, Chelsea, on many occasions, and was greatly missed when he and his wife, Gracie, retired to Cwmgors in 1983. He died in 2010. The Revd Dr R. Leonard Hugh taught at Erith School, Kent, and became a member at Woolwich in 1966. He, too, served the London Welsh churches regularly until he moved to Llanelli Grammar School in 1974.

By the end of the 1970s, Woolwich was struggling to maintain its numbers, despite the involvement of some younger families. The chapel had been sustained over the years by the superhuman efforts of a small group of members: Mary Lewis, a native of Blaengarw who settled in London in the 1930s and whose unfailing loyalty led to Richard Jones describing her as 'the queen' of the Woolwich congregation; Emrys and Martha Ellis, veritable pillars of the cause for two decades until the mid-1960s; Tom and Annie Thomas, from Trimsaran, who came to London in the 1940s, where Tom served with great distinction as chapel secretary for decades until his death in 1972; Selwyn and Agnes Morgan, both from the Abertridwr area, who arrived in the 1950s when he gained work at the Woolwich Arsenal, and who became indispensable members. Their daughter, Dorothy, and son-in-law, Chris, also played their part in later years, as did John Samuel, secretary and organist, and his wife, Janice.

But by the 1970s, the powerful flow of people from Wales to London had become a trickle, chapel life was far less relevant or attractive to the majority, and there had been a significant change in the age profile of the congregations. Added to this was the familiar problem of vandalism, which started in Woolwich as early as the 1950s but became a much bigger issue in the 1960s and 1970s. The windows and rear garden were easy targets, but the area of land on the street side was also used as a rubbish dump by some locals. The cleaning and clearing involved many hours of voluntary effort by the officers and members.

A particularly bad spate of vandalism in Woolwich early in 1981, coupled with a leaking roof, not to mention the attempted theft of the Communion and baptism silverware, pushed the remaining 20 members towards a difficult decision. They would have to leave Bethel and seek refuge elsewhere. The Revd Richard Jones organised a room at the Methodist church in Welling. The final service at Bethel, Woolwich, took place on 17 October 1981, the seventeenth anniversary of Mr Jones's installation as minister, ending a 75-year chapter in the story of the London Welsh chapels.

The services at Welling continued until Richard Jones's move to Cwmgors in 1983. It no longer made sense to soldier on with so few members, so the officers decided to decommission the cause 'with dignity and thanks' in a service at Borough on 22 July 1983, led by the departing minister. It managed to be a celebration of Bethel's witness, not a lament for things lost.

The secretary, John Samuel, his wife, Janice, and two other members transferred their membership to Castle Street chapel near Oxford Circus, some eleven miles away, despite the existence of another Welsh chapel in south-east London. John explained that he had been brought up in the Baptist tradition, so Castle Street was a natural choice. That church is now the Welsh Church of Central London, a non-denominational organisation, which reminds us that denominational splits, so evident in the early life of the London Welsh chapels, have long become an irrelevance.

While John and his group opted for Castle Street, Ceridwen James preferred the shorter journey of four miles to Lewisham Welsh chapel, a small cause with a very interesting history.

This is where our story links up with the early Methodists of Deptford. We are back in the old territory of James Hughes and the dockyards of the Thames, less than two miles away to the north. The story of Lewisham, a relatively modern cause, is firmly rooted in the population movement of the late-eighteenth century.

As Meurig Owen noted, the Methodist cause in Deptford had closed by 1866. But within three decades, demand was once again exceeding supply. Towards the end of the nineteenth century, members of Falmouth Road chapel, which had opened in 1887 near the Elephant and Castle in south London, started organising a Sunday school in Harders Road, Peckham. Other members in Deptford and New Cross had also been holding services in their homes.

The result was that officers of the London Presbytery (the governing body of the Calvinistic Methodists in London) visited the area and decided to approve plans for expansion. A hall in New Cross (a district of Lewisham) was hired for a service on 9 October 1898. This proved a great success, so the hall was rented for a period of six months for regular services. The members decided in January 1899 to establish a church, and this was formalised on 12 February 1899 with 43 founding members. Its original name was Deptford Welsh (Calvinistic Methodist) Church.

The new church was led by a devout and strong-willed man, R. Vaughan Thomas, a recognised lay preacher at Falmouth Road. He was assisted by a team of elders which included William Jones, Griffith W. Jones, John Davies and Rees Davies. They worked well as a team, and by the end of 1900 the membership had reached 75, too many for the hall in New Cross. Thanks to a combination of fundraising and borrowing, they were able to purchase land in Undercliffe Road, Lewisham. The architect William A. Pike designed an unusual chapel (it looked like a detached house)

An early fundraising concert for
Lewisham chapel (1900)
© Eglwys Jewin

which opened on 15 December 1901. The change of location prompted a
change of name to Lewisham Welsh (Calvinistic Methodist) Church.

The chapel's first minister, the Revd R. Silyn Roberts, was an impressive
figure. He was a native of Llanllyfni, Caernarfonshire, who worked as a
quarryman before his ordination to the ministry. He was an accomplished
poet, winning the crown in the 1902 National Eisteddfod. He spent four very
successful years in Lewisham, leaving for Wales in 1905. Much of his life was
devoted to social reform (he was a prominent Labour Party figure) and adult
education. He went on to establish the North Wales District of the Workers'
Educational Association in 1925.

The church continued to flourish under the guidance of R. Vaughan
Thomas, helped by visiting ministers from Wales, and the initial building debt
of £6,800 was steadily reduced. By all accounts, the chapel in Undercliffe
Road was very basic, poorly heated, with uncomfortable benches for seating.
But there was plenty of activity for members, including the Sunday school,
and a lively literary society. The Sunday school tea became a fixed event and
remained so until the 1970s.

The proximity of Woolwich Barracks meant that many Welsh soldiers passed through the area during the Great War. For a period in 1917, the Revd D. W. Morgan came to Lewisham to minister to the soldiers in the area, and the female members visited many injured soldiers in local hospitals. The chapel lost two of its members in the First World War. Their names are engraved on a plaque which is now at Clapham Junction Welsh chapel.

It was already clear that a better building was needed. The chapel in Undercliffe Road was sold to a community of Plymouth Brethren in 1924 for £1,950. Thanks to the kindness of Sir Howell J. Williams, a wealthy businessman and an elder at Charing Cross Road, a piece of land and a house were bought in Lewisham Way, next to St John's Church, for £6,000. Sir Howell donated £1,000 to the cause, yet another example of his remarkable generosity to the London Welsh community. It was Sir Howell who financed the building of the London Welsh Centre on Gray's Inn Road in the 1930s.

Lewisham Way was a much more impressive complex than Undercliffe Road, with a lecture hall, an office for the minister, a caretaker's flat, a library, a billiard room, a table tennis room, and land including a tennis court at the

Original architect's drawings for the first Lewisham chapel (1901)
© Eglwys Jewin

rear. Lewisham was one of the best examples of a multi-purpose social and sports centre built around a chapel. The membership increased as families and young people came to the city to work. Not surprisingly, Lewisham chapel attracted Welsh people from all parts of south-east London.

Wyn Jones was born in Lewisham in 1925 and reckoned he was the first to be baptised in the new chapel. His father, William Henry Jones, a native of Llan Ffestiniog, had come to London in 1901 to work for the Peter Jones store in Chelsea. He went on to build a thriving drapery business, Beck-Jones, owning several stores in south-east London. William Jones was elected an elder at Lewisham in 1921, before the move to Lewisham Way.

Wyn recalled a 'great crowd in Lewisham in those days', when his father's services as a conductor and singer were in great demand. The chapel was moving towards its most vibrant period, with membership exceeding 200, thanks to the efforts of a new minister, the Revd Eliseus Howells, who arrived in 1931. He was one of the great characters in the history of the London Welsh chapels, a veteran of the First World War (he was badly injured in a gas attack), and a keen boxer in his youth.

Gomer Roberts, the preacher and historian, said Eliseus Howells was 'of unusual appearance, over six feet tall, with a rough, furrowed face, and he had an extraordinarily deep voice'. He was an 'original and popular preacher'. Wyn Jones, who formed a friendship with the minister's son, Marwood, said that Eliseus Howells was greatly loved by the London congregations who valued his wisdom and selfless service:

> Fair play to him, he stayed in London through the war, unlike many other ministers. They cleared off pretty quickly as soon as the bombs started, but maybe you can't blame them. Williams of Wilton Square did a bunk like lots of others. Mrs Howells and the two boys stayed with relatives in south Wales. My father owned the Lewisham manse in Wickham Gardens, but a big V2 rocket blew one side of the street to pieces. Eliseus lost everything, his library, his papers, everything. Luckily, he was out at the time, having supper with another Lewisham family. And he had to rough it, sleeping in the chapel basement. There were sleeping bags on the floor.

The church was not in a position to provide a new home for the minister after the war, so with sorrow the members agreed to his request to be released

Artist's impression of the new Lewisham chapel (1925)
© Eglwys Jewin

from his duties. Eliseus Howells moved back to his native Glamorganshire (to Hermon, Bridgend) in 1945, but he was a regular visitor to London until his death in 1969. His immense contribution was recognised by his election as moderator of the general assembly of the Presbyterian Church of Wales for the year 1963–4.

Lewisham was served by several ministers of the highest calibre: the Revd A. Tudno Williams, whose father had served as minister of Walham Green chapel in Fulham, was an excellent preacher and respected scholar. He was installed in 1951. Wyn Jones reckoned:

> He was more of a lecturer than a preacher, more of an academic, really, but he certainly had a very competitive side, especially when it came to tennis. We played on grass courts behind the chapel, and Mr Williams hated losing, I can tell you. My cousin Trevor Hughes would beat him for the hell of it. He was popular and a good visitor, but probably didn't have the following that Eliseus had. I knew his son, John Tudno, who became a very distinguished preacher, and his daughter, Mair, who married David Lloyd, one of the real pillars of Lewisham in later years.

During this time, the Sunday school and literary society flourished, the annual eisteddfod was buzzing, there were table tennis and billiards competitions, and the children's meetings were thriving. St David's Day dinners were held in the packed schoolroom next to the chapel.

The chapel developed an enviable musical tradition over the years, encouraged by a very musical Tudno Williams who enjoyed singing and performing. But the arrival of Geraint Evans (later Sir Geraint, the global opera star) and his family at Lewisham brought sparkle and world-class quality to the singing. He would perform in oratorios with the Lewisham choir, even after his stellar career had taken off.

By the time Arthur Tudno Williams left for Wales in 1968, his family had made a big mark on Lewisham and the other London Welsh chapels. His son, the Revd Professor John Tudno Williams, would later become principal of the United Theological College, Aberystwyth, while serving as moderator of the Free Churches Federal Council in 1990, and as moderator of the Presbyterian Church of Wales in 2006–7.

There had always been a strong bond between Falmouth Road and Lewisham, so it was a natural step for the Revd Glanville Davies, minister of Falmouth Road, to extend his pastorate by including Lewisham in July 1969. This was already a challenging period for the London chapels. Numbers were declining but Glanville Davies proved to be a good shepherd. Wyn Jones said he was a 'very caring visitor' and Meurig Owen noted that 'many blessings were received during his ministry, including a happy arrangement with the parish church of St John's next door'. There were combined Communion services at St John's, and in the chapel, with the vicar, the Revd David Howell, and the Revd Glanville Davies jointly officiating. This was indeed a very progressive initiative at that time. Glanville Davies retired to Llanelli in March 1980.

From then until 1998 Lewisham did not have the services of a minister, but the services and weekday meetings continued. One notable event was the 90th birthday party held in 1982 for Elsie McAuliffe, who had served with distinction for 35 years as a Presbyterian Church of Wales missionary in Habiganj, India. She returned to England in 1955, joining Lewisham chapel where she remained a loyal member until her death in 1987.

A small group of faithful, including Meurig Owen, Gwyndaf Evans, David and Mair Lloyd, and Ieuan and Jennie Jenkins, sustained the life of the church and took services when no preachers were available.

Professor Emrys Jones and Meurig Owen in their Gorsedd robes (2005)
© John Samuel

Meurig Owen really does merit a special mention. He was a native of
Llanrug who came to London in 1937 to work in the insurance business. After
wartime service in Italy, he returned to London and was elected an elder in
Lewisham in 1953, becoming secretary in 1961, a post later filled by Gwyndaf
Evans. Wyn Jones described him as 'one of the most important members in
the history of Lewisham', but in truth he deserves a much bigger tribute. It
is thanks to him that we have a trove of information on many of the London
Welsh chapels. All his chapel histories (including *Tros y Bont* and *Ymofyn am
yr Hen Lwybrau*) bear the hallmarks of meticulous research. His induction into
the Gorsedd of Bards in 2005, in recognition of his pioneering studies, gave
him genuine pleasure. But it is a matter of great regret that his admirable work
was not more widely recognised before his death.

The pattern of leadership changed in 1998 when the Revd Anthony
Williams became part-time minister. It was during his time that Lewisham
celebrated its centenary in memorable, well-attended services in April 1999.
The guest preacher was Dr John Tudno Williams, and a special centenary
booklet was produced by Meurig Owen.

A few years later, the church formed part of a London-wide pastorate

Special service at Lewisham to mark the publication of the New Welsh Bible (1988)

under the Revd Dafydd Owen and the Revd Anthony Williams. Thanks to Dafydd Owen's strategic vision, Lewisham became part of the newly-organised United Welsh Church of South London (Lewisham, Sutton and Clapham Junction), a re-organisation which would provide greater financial security in the years to come.

The city-wide ministry was continued under the Revd Richard Brunt, who took charge in October 2010 at a time when Lewisham's membership had dwindled to unsustainable levels. Under his guidance, the members took the difficult decision to close and to support other chapels in the London Welsh community. The final services were held on 13 September 2011, when Dr John Tudno Williams, his sister Mair, and their extended families shared their very happy memories of life in Lewisham.

I spent many hours in the Lewisham schoolroom sifting through the chapel's documents in the winter of 2011. Gwyndaf Evans, who had done so much to sustain the cause, provided tea and sandwiches and plenty of valuable anecdotes. We reflected on the courage, faith and dedication of previous generations, and we agreed on the vital importance of recording their achievements.

The Lewisham complex was sold for £1.3 million in 2013, a very healthy return on the original investment of a few thousand pounds. The

Interior of Lewisham chapel (2011)

highly-centralised culture of the Presbyterian Church of Wales decrees that the proceeds of sales revert to the church's central fund in Cardiff. This is increasingly controversial at a time when millions of pounds are being realised from the sale of buildings in cities such as London and Liverpool. There is a strong view that these funds should be dedicated to sustaining other causes in the same cities.

There have been some welcome developments in recent years. Because of the re-organisation instigated by the Revd Dafydd Owen over a decade ago, making Lewisham one part of a united church in south London, it became slightly easier (though not straightforward) for the sister chapels, Sutton and Clapham Junction, to claim some of the money to finance better facilities for the future.

In that important sense, we can at least say that the precious investment of the dockyard workers in still paying dividends.

CHAPTER 7

SERMONS FOR SAILORS

There is a romance and allure to the story of Falmouth Road which no other London Welsh chapel can match. We move from Welsh merchant vessels moored at Pickle Herring Stairs on the Thames, to an octagonal chapel once owned by John Wesley, to a small street off the New Kent Road beyond the Elephant and Castle. This is a journey around some of the oldest, murkiest parts of south London.

The Port of London Society for Promoting Religion Among Seamen had been formed in 1818 to promote the 'beneficial effects of inculcating a sense of religion among sailors'. Those sailors included hundreds from Wales whose boats regularly carried goods to and from London. The project involved organising religious services which would take place on board a specially-modified ship. *The Evangelical Magazine* (June 1818) provided important details:

> The ship fitted by this Society as a place of worship for seamen is moored near to the entrance of the London Docks. She was Newcastle-built; measures about 380 tons; and in the adaptation to the sacred purposes to which she was devoted on the 4th of May, there is a display of much ingenuity and propriety. The chapel has a gallery of three rows of seats on both sides, and four rows round the body, so that upwards of 700 hearers may at the same time be viewers of the officiating minister. The public services at the floating chapel will be on the Lord's day at half-past 10 o'clock in the morning, and half-past six in the evening. We understand that the attendance of seamen is very encouraging.

We also have an eyewitness account, by the Revd Ebenezer Richard of Tregaron, which described the opening services at the 'floating chapel' on

4 May 1818. He confirmed they were 'well attended' and that collections brought in a healthy £128. It was the success of this venture that prompted a group of Welsh captains to take their own initiative.

On 7 July 1820, Captain David Evans of Cardigan hosted a meeting with fellow skippers on board his ship, *Betsy*. Their aim was to provide a regular forum for worship for their Welsh-speaking crews on board one of the many Welsh vessels on the Thames. The 'floating chapel' at Blackwall was too far away from the meeting point of so many Welsh vessels at Pickle Herring Stairs, on the south bank of the Thames, almost directly opposite the Tower of London. HMS *Belfast* occupies that stretch of water today.

This meeting led to the founding of the 'Cambrian Union Society for Promoting Religion Among Welsh Seamen' in May 1820. There are numerous references in the press which shed light on the venture. *The Evangelical Magazine* (August 1820) mentioned the importance of catering for sailors who 'having been brought up in Wales, understand no other language than their own', and the same publication (December 1820) mentioned the presentation of a Welsh flag to be raised on board ship to attract worshippers:

> At a recent meeting, the Rev. G. C. Smith, of Penzance, offered to have a flag made, as a signal. On Sunday, Nov. 5th, Mr. Smith, accompanied by Captains and Seamen from different parts of the Thames, and members of the Bethel Union Society, attended on board the 'Hope', Capt. Jones, of Aberystwith, to present a Welsh Flag publicly, to their Brethren of the Principality. The 'Hope' lay in a tier of ships off Pickle Herring Stairs, opposite the Tower; her deck was crowded – several respectable females attended – the New Flag was very large; a blue ground, yellow star, and a dove, with an olive-branch in its mouth, and the words 'CYFARFOD GWEDDI', signifying prayer meetings, in large white letters, adorned the centre.

A separate report, concerning a different Welsh-owned ship, stated that 'the vessel appointed was distinguished by a red flag with the inscription PREGETH [sermon], hoisted at the mast-head from early morning'. The venture was a success, judging by accounts of the first anniversary in May 1821, when the *Chester Courant* provided some valuable details:

> There were always from 20 to 30 Welsh ships in the River Thames, most of the crews of which (from 200 to 300 persons) understood so little of the English, that instructions could not be received by them from public discourses in that language.

As ships arrive and become clear of their cargoes, it appears that the hold is swept,
and then, till she begins to load again, serves as a chapel, in which Welsh ministers
preach in the native tongue every sabbath. It was pleasant to hear the artless effusions
of the honest masters of vessels in pleading with the meeting for some assistance to aid
them in expenses.

It wasn't long before a campaign started to secure a permanent place of worship for the Welsh sailors. There was even talk of establishing a kind of 'Welsh Ark' on the Thames, similar to the vessel at Blackwall. But that was soon abandoned: *The Evangelical Magazine* (November 1820) mentions the search 'to procure a place of worship in or near Tooley-street, as a Sailor's Tabernacle, as many seamen are found loitering about in that neighbourhood'.

The Cambrian Union Society Chapel for Seamen opened in Fair Street, Horsleydown, off Tooley Street, on 6 November 1821. The building, originally a wool warehouse, had been used as a Quakers' meeting house for several years. The 'Cambrian', as it was widely known, would also share its premises with the Bethel Union Society, an English organisation devoted to the religious welfare of seamen.

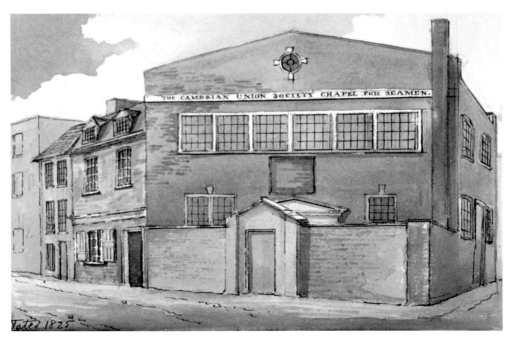

The Cambrian Union Society (1825)
© London Metropolitan Archive

It is important to note that the Cambrian was not tied to any denomination, though Independents and Baptists tended to be more prominent. The Revd David Davies of Borough, and the Revd Evan Evans for the Baptists, officiated regularly. The trustees included six businessmen and three ships' masters, including Captain Edward Humphreys, whose vessel *New Harmony* (built in Barmouth) made regular trips to London. He played a leading part in the Cambrian for many years.

Things changed following the deaths of the two ministers, and by 1830 the arrangements for Sunday worship were in the hands of the Calvinistic Methodists of Jewin Crescent. Financial control was also transferred: the Cambrian accounts were always included in the financial statement for Jewin Crescent.

A Sunday school was established in 1830. One of the teachers was Hugh Owen (later Sir Hugh Owen, the Welsh education pioneer) who had joined the cause at Jewin Crescent on arriving in London in 1825. The Cambrian did not experience any big surges in membership, and the character of the congregation changed in the mid-nineteenth century. There were fewer sailors, and more people who worked in the factories and shops of Horsleydown, the area of the south bank which stretches from London Bridge to Tower Bridge. By 1853 there were 35 members, and 54 in the Sunday school.

There is fascinating detail available about the kind of people who attended the Cambrian. The baptism register noted the trade or profession of the father: tanner, carpenter, clerk, warehouseman, lead smelter, gold refiner, brewery servant, sailor, eating house keeper, cowkeeper, dairyman. Many of these were typical of the local industries of Southwark and Bermondsey at that time. The numbers of dairymen and cowkeepers would surge in the second half of the century.

The religious census of 1851 provided more information, recording a congregation of 40 at the morning Sunday school, a hundred for the afternoon sermon, and 60 at the evening service. The seating capacity was given as a hundred. The Jewin Crescent elder, Robert Owen ('Eryron Gwyllt Walia'), explained in a separate entry that 'a part only of the building (the floor above) being rented by the Denomination, and this not being a properly constructed Chapel, the sittings chiefly consist of mere Benches or Forms'.

The Cambrian became a church in its own right in 1854, with 51

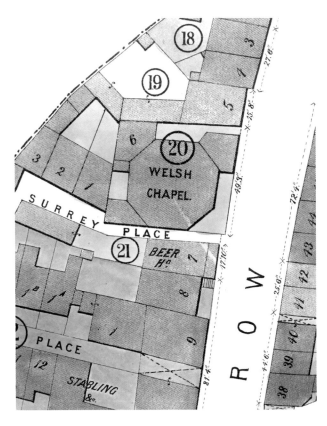

Part of the sale documents for
Crosby Row chapel (1879)
© London Metropolitan Archive

LOT 20.
(Colored Green on Plan.)

A FREEHOLD PROPERTY,

Situate in CROSBY ROW, adjoining the preceding lot, and comprising

A LARGE OCTAGONAL BUILDING,

Occupied as a

WELSH CHAPEL

With Minister's Room adjoining, and

A Dwelling House, No. 6 Crosby Row,

Containing three Rooms, with small Wash-house and Yard, let to Mr. Lewis, at a Rental of

£45 PER ANNUM,

Tenant paying rates and taxes.

A Cellar extending under the Chapel,

Let to Mr. Kipps (Builder), at a Rent of

£10 PER ANNUM;

Tenant paying Rates and Taxes. And

THREE DWELLING HOUSES

failed to impress. There are contemporary reports of a 'small chapel lit by a row of oil lamps in the centre, with the congregation seated at the sides in the shadows'. Two candles were set each side of the small harmonium to improve the organist's vision. They certainly liked singing, judging by the many references to rehearsals and chapel concerts.

It was claimed that the tradition of 'penny readings' among the London Welsh started in Crosby Row. The readings, as originally devised, were meant to draw people away from the evils of the public house by giving them an alternative form of entertainment. By the second half of the nineteenth century, the readings had become synonymous with the small eisteddfod, a competitive gathering where prizes were awarded for reciting and singing. There are several hilarious episodes related by the Revd J. D. Evans about these gatherings in Crosby Row. He recalled old Job Rees of Pontrhydygroes opening his address with these immortal words: 'Dewi Sant started preaching not long after the Apostle Paul had left Cardiganshire.'

From September 1880, tea was provided after Sunday school to encourage 'young people who live too far away' to stay for the evening service. It worked. Other chapels offered the same provision, and the Sunday tea became a vital tradition in most of the London Welsh chapels, where it was not practical for members to travel great distances twice or three times for Sunday services.

The weekly programme for 1888 reflects the buzz and energy of Crosby Row. On Sundays, the prayer meeting at ten in the morning was followed by a service at 10.45, then Sunday school at 2.30, and evening service at 6.30. There were reading classes on Monday nights, in addition to missionary prayer meetings once a month. The church meeting took place on Thursday nights, temperance fellowship on Fridays, and a literary society on Saturdays.

But it's worth noting that Crosby Row was in a rough area of south London. The local press frequently carried reports of crime in the surrounding area of Long Lane and Borough. Meurig Owen quoted Mrs D. R. Hughes, a Falmouth Road stalwart who attended Crosby Row as a girl, describing how a policeman would stand guard at the chapel door to allow the service to go ahead undisturbed.

It was this combination of unappealing surroundings and a lack of space which eventually prompted the search for new premises. On 21 July 1885, members voted to explore the options but the matter was delayed, possibly

Falmouth Road chapel
opened in 1889
© National Library of Wales

because of the slim majority of fourteen in favour. By 11 May 1886, after a lively debate, a big majority declared in favour of building a new chapel. There was general agreement that the area of the Elephant and Castle, towards the New Kent Road, would provide the best opportunities for the church.

After a search in the streets lying east of the Elephant, they found a substantial plot of land in Falmouth Road. With guidance from the Welsh entrepreneur and Conservative politician, Sir John Puleston, it was bought for £1,000 in October 1887. Contracts with the builders, Richard and Edward Evans of Peckham, and with the architect, Charles Evans-Vaughan of Westminster, were signed on 3 November 1887. Evans-Vaughan's masterpiece would be the opulent Finsbury Town Hall, one of modern London's hidden treasures. His flamboyant style was certainly applied to Falmouth Road, which English Heritage has described as 'a combination of different features and materials calculated to produce a most variable and

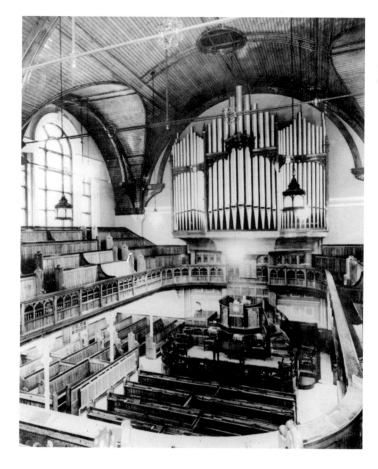

Interior of Falmouth
Road chapel after the
organ installation (1906)
© National Library of Wales

picturesque composition… an early instance of the Queen Anne manner
applied to a church or chapel'.

The construction work began three days before Christmas of that year.
Among those who contributed to the building fund was William Carnell,
licensee of the County Terrace public house on the corner of Falmouth Road
and the New Kent Road. It is said that he placed a gold sovereign coin on the
first clod dug that day. His presence would have horrified the vast majority of
Calvinistic Methodists in Wales, but London was a different world. Carnell
was a neighbour in the tough, working-class area of the New Kent Road. His
cooperation would have been valued.

The foundation stones were laid on 16 March 1888 by Sir John Puleston
and a representative of the Davies family of Llandinam. David Davies,
the coal baron, founder of the Ocean Coal Company, was an influential
Calvinistic Methodist who funded the building of New Jewin and numerous

other chapels. The day ended with a tea party and public meeting at the Metropolitan Tabernacle, Elephant and Castle, the Baptist church where the famous Charles Spurgeon spent 38 years as pastor. At that time it was the biggest Nonconformist church in Britain.

Falmouth Road chapel cost £7,220 to build, £2,056 of which had already been collected by the time the building was ready. The chapel opened with a long series of meetings in January 1889, starring some of the denomination's biggest names, including Thomas Charles Edwards, one of the leading preachers of his generation and the first principal of University College of Wales, Aberystwyth. He was assisted by Dr David Saunders of Swansea and others.

The *Cambrian News* carried a detailed report of the services on 25 January 1889:

> *The Calvinistic Methodist Church and congregation, formerly assembling in the old Crosby Row Chapel, have built a commodious and attractive new chapel in Falmouth Road, adjacent to Spurgeon's Tabernacle. At the opening services, the last and the previous week, the Reverends Dr Saunders, Principal Edwards, W. Jones and Hugh Jones, Liverpool, officiated. The edifice reflects great credit upon the architect and builders, the prevalent opinion being greatly in favor of the type of architecture.*

It was certainly an attractive building, boasting carpentry of the highest quality, stained glass windows, and excellent facilities in the hall and rooms on the lower-ground floor. This was one of the best-appointed Welsh chapels in London, with a price tag to match. Despite the generous contributions, some added costs meant that the debt stood at £5,656 at the end of 1889. Crosby Row, rather surprisingly, was still unsold and carried a debt of £495. The officers were convinced that the chapel and houses on the plot would bring in useful rental income. This turned out to be a poor decision: the rents received were modest, and the building was not sold until May 1905.

The gleaming new chapel in Falmouth Road had no difficulty expanding its membership: there were 306 members in 1887; 325 in 1888, and by 1891 there were 395, with 137 children on the Sunday school roll. The 1890s were a period of unchecked growth, thanks to the efforts of the minister and his officers. One of them was R. Vaughan Thomas, a construction foreman by day, who devoted most of his evenings to Falmouth Road and became a registered local preacher. He left in 1899 to establish the cause in Lewisham.

Falmouth Road was a hive of cultural activity even by the impressive standards of the London Welsh chapels. Indeed, there is a credible case for stating that Falmouth Road made a greater impact in this field than any other Welsh place of worship in the capital. This claim is not made on the basis of its extensive programme of public lectures, though the appearance of speakers such as 'Cranogwen' (Sarah Jane Rees, the poet and temperance campaigner) and 'Mabon' (William Abraham, the prominent trade unionist) underlined the quality of this provision. The claim is more firmly based on the eisteddfodic tradition fostered by the men, women and children of Falmouth Road.

The man whose ambition and supreme organisational skills propelled a local chapel eisteddfod to 'semi-national' status was David Rowland Hughes, a native of Treffynnon who came to London in 1894 and became a member at Falmouth Road. In the long story of the Welsh in London, there are very few men or women who can match his list of herculean achievements. His work at Falmouth Road (where he served as secretary), his promotion and editorship of *Y Ddolen* (the London Welsh periodical), his leadership of the Caernarfonshire and Denbighshire Historical Societies, his constant support for Welsh publishers – all these added up to an exceptional contribution.

For all that, his greatest achievement was in relation to the eisteddfod. He would serve as secretary of the National Eisteddfod of Wales in the 1930s and 1940s, ensuring its survival during the Second World War. But his lion-hearted efforts on behalf of the Falmouth Road eisteddfod deserve a special mention. This event became one of the prime cultural institutions of the Welsh in London, drawing the best poets and musicians to compete for its prizes.

It started with the tradition of competitive 'penny readings' at Crosby Row and by 1890 the eisteddfod model (of organised, programme-based competition) had been adopted. These meetings were held in the chapel but a spot of bother in 1893 encouraged a change of plan. There was an oblique reference in the *Cardiff Times* on 21 October of that year:

> The Rev. R. H. Morgan, M.A., of Menai Bridge, who conducted, was justifiably severe on the noisy youths who have made the meetings at Falmouth-road a bye-word.

'Noisy' was probably not the best adjective to use. The youths in question had let off a stink-bomb in the gallery, and followed this up with a second downstairs. The eisteddfod was suspended for several hours, and there was talk of moving the event elsewhere. But it stayed at Falmouth Road in 1894 (a policeman was present to keep order) and eventually moved to Shoreditch Town Hall in 1895. D. R. Hughes, the organiser, also acted as compere.

The eisteddfod moved to Lambeth Baths in 1900, the Royal Victoria Hall (today's 'Old Vic') in 1901, and the Exeter Hall in 1902, when the event's status was enhanced by the calibre of the competitors, who included Ben Bowen, the national chaired bard. The following year, the venue changed to the Queen's Hall, when it was chaired by D. H. Evans, the Llanelli man whose vast department store would become an Oxford Street landmark. They stayed at the Queen's Hall in 1904, when the revivalist preacher, Nantlais, won the chair. The Rhos choir won the male voice prize. The eminent composer and choirmaster, Caradog Roberts, was the eisteddfod accompanist. By any standards, this was an impressive line-up.

The next step was much more daring. D. R. Hughes and his colleagues decided that their venue for 1905 would be the Royal Albert Hall. The sweep of their ambition was thrilling. They would take a chapel eisteddfod to one of the biggest venues in Europe and confidently sell tickets for almost five thousand seats. Adverts were displayed throughout London, especially in underground stations, and the *Daily Mail* (yes, really) publicised the valuable prizes on offer. The eisteddfod, chaired by the Lord Mayor of London, was a runaway success. No event in the history of the London Welsh chapels, before or since, has matched the eisteddfod of 1905 for sheer scale and scope.

There is no doubt that the success of 1905 helped D. R. Hughes make the case for holding the National Eisteddfod of Wales at the Albert Hall in 1909. Its previous visit in 1887 had been a royal shindig of epic proportions, thanks to the presence of Prince Albert Edward, the Prince of Wales. But 1909 would be remembered for rather different reasons. One of the guest speakers was Herbert Asquith, the prime minister. His speech was interrupted by suffragettes who grasped an opportunity to publicise their campaign for the right to vote. The archdruid ('Dyfed'), representing the eisteddfod in all its patriarchal pomp, condemned their 'audacity' in disrupting the bards' fun.

By 1911, having demonstrated its pulling power, the Falmouth Road

Programme of the penultimate Falmouth Road eisteddfod (1959)
© Eglwys Jewin

eisteddfod returned to the Queen's Hall. It moved again in 1913 to Methodist Central Hall, Westminster, and that is where it remained until the final event was held in 1960. Eisteddfod programmes for the 1920s, dotted with many adverts for London Welsh dairies and other businesses, list dozens of competitions, reflecting the event's continuing popularity between the wars. It was a different story after 1945. It took five years for the eisteddfod to restart, but the first post-war event in May 1950 was evidently successful. New choral competitions were introduced which boosted competitors' numbers, and new prizes were offered by the businessman and philanthropist, Sir David James, whose James Pantyfedwen Foundation is still making a major contribution to Welsh life.

Sadly, the writing was on the wall. The last Falmouth Road 'semi-national' eisteddfod was held at Methodist Central Hall on 25 April 1959. The programme included a summary of the event's history, on which much of this account is based.

It would be a mistake, however, to assume that Falmouth Road's ministers were all fans of the big eisteddfod venture. This should come as no surprise: the endless reports, never failing to underline the 'semi-national' status of the event, suggest a rather obsessive attitude. The Revd Samuel E. Prytherch, who came from the Welsh chapel in Stepney, in London's East End, in 1897, clearly thought his members' priorities were wrong. This was a message delivered to a full congregation on a Sunday evening:

You speak repeatedly of the eisteddfod, indeed, the eisteddfod, but why not learn a few oratorios just in case a few of you make it to heaven?

Samuel Prytherch, never one to mince his words, enjoyed a busy period at Falmouth Road: societies flourished, weekday meetings were popular, and a major fundraising campaign led to the installation of an excellent pipe organ in November 1906. The cost was £981 for a powerful three-manual instrument built by the famous firm of Norman and Beard. Despite all this activity, it is interesting to note that the minister did not preside over steady growth in membership. There were 404 members (and 118 children) when he arrived, but when he left in 1910, there were 373 adults (and 127 children). The real growth would come under his successor. Samuel Prytherch spent six years in Wales and emigrated to the United States in 1916 where he took charge of several Welsh churches, the last of which was Cambria, Wisconsin. He died there in 1941.

His successor, the Revd Morgan Henry Edwards, arrived from Siloh, Llanelli, in 1913. It is worth underlining again the strong link between Siloh and the London Welsh chapels: this was the Revd J. E. Davies's base before his call to Jewin in 1886, and also the Revd D. S. Owen's before his call to Jewin in 1916.

Within days of his installation, Mr Edwards was plunged into a funding crisis. The entire network of London Welsh chapels was drowning in debt:

The Revd M. H. Edwards and elders of Falmouth Road in the 1920s
© National Library of Wales

the total owed, after the building boom of the previous decade, was £45,915 – which corresponds to £4.7 million today. This burden led to the creation of a debt-reduction strategy whose main architect was Timothy Davies, the Liberal MP and businessman, a member of Walham Green chapel in Fulham. The ruling committee was chaired by the businessman Sir E. Vincent Evans, a Jewin grandee, pillar of the National Eisteddfod Association and the Honourable Society of Cymmrodorion, close friend of David Lloyd George, and without question one of the most influential Welshmen of his generation. He served Jewin with distinction for half a century.

A grand bazaar held at Caxton Hall in June 1912, sponsored by Margaret Lloyd George, who worshipped at Clapham Junction chapel, raised valuable funds. The plan was to raise a central fund of £10,000 to be shared between those churches whose debts amounted to more than £5 per member. The fundraising prospectus includes a table which shows that Falmouth Road was among the least indebted at £7 per member. Top of the table was Lewisham at £43 per member, followed by Mile End, Hammersmith, Walham Green, Stratford, and Willesden Green – all in excess of £20 per member. The chapel with the smallest debt per member (£2) was Charing Cross Road, where the high membership (753) meant a much lower debt-per-head figure. The scheme was a remarkable success. Falmouth Road's debt was reduced from £2,800 to £1,900. The entire sum would be cleared by 1926.

There should have been a collective celebration. Instead, the Welsh churches watched as dozens of young men and women signed up at the outbreak of war in 1914. By 1917 there were 81 men and five women from Falmouth Road serving in the armed forces. Ten of the men did not return. Many others were badly injured. One of the young women, Katie Jones, was killed in a Zeppelin attack on south London.

The years after the war were a time of recovery and rebuilding. A new organist was appointed, J. Islwyn Lewis, whose term would span four decades. He was a talented musician who gave instrumental tuition at many London schools and who created an enviable musical tradition at Falmouth Road. The number of members reached 517 in 1934 (with 170 on the Sunday school register), with high levels of participation in the eisteddfod, the literary society, Welsh language lessons, the branch of Urdd Gobaith Cymru (The Welsh League of Youth), and the children's choir.

It is revealing, therefore, to read the repeated appeals by the minister for more loyalty to the Sunday morning service, to the Sunday school, and to the weekday prayer meetings. He raised difficult questions, too, about the language of services:

> As the Welsh language disappears from our homes, what will become of our children? What will be the story of our Welsh churches in twenty years' time? Most important of all, if the language is lost, and if no provision is made in English, what will happen to our children in churches where they understand not a word that is uttered?

The minister was asking those questions before the Second World War. We now have the answers, painful as they are.

It is a difficult balance to strike: loyal members attend their chapel to worship in the Welsh language. That is the whole point. There are plenty of (frequently more convenient) places offering worship in English. To attend a Welsh-speaking chapel is to affirm one's faith and identity, to enjoy the warmth and companionship of a Welsh community, and to celebrate a shared culture in the world's most diverse city. Offering a mix of language can certainly work in certain services. Children from homes where Welsh is not the main language (by far the most common pattern in the London Welsh community) can happily take part in services where both languages are used. They also become familiar with the form of the service, the wording of prayers, and the most popular hymns. Most of the London Welsh chapels have shown flexibility in the use of language: there is no other alternative if young Londoners are to feel included.

The 50th anniversary of the opening was celebrated on 11 May 1939. One of the main speakers was D. R. Hughes, who delighted everyone with an entertaining talk on the history of the cause. It was one if his last public meetings at Falmouth Road. After retiring from his work as an executive of United Dairies, he, his wife, Maggie, and daughter, Dilys, settled in Old Colwyn. All three had made a very significant contribution to Falmouth Road.

When war was declared in September 1939, dozens of the chapel's men and women joined the armed forces, and many members left the dangers of London for the peace of rural Wales. The minister remained, and published this moving but defiant statement in the annual report at the end of the year:

Many of us refused to believe, after the bitter experiences of 1914–1918, that Europe would be mad enough to start another war. But the storm is upon us. We shall not know the cost until the calm arrives. The lights have been dimmed, but nothing will dim the light of faith and Christian witness. The actions of a senseless dictator can destroy a church building and scatter its members, but cannot defeat God's Church. Believe this, and take comfort. We shall do our best, though the night is dark.

Mr Edwards had already celebrated his quarter-century in February 1937. He was now leading a London church in wartime, an onerous task for a fit, healthy man, but the minister was showing signs of serious illness. He soldiered on, despite having to move out of his bomb-damaged home, and did his best to look after those members still in London. The Revd M. H. Edwards died on 5 October 1942. The tributes paid by fellow ministers and officers spoke of a scholar, a gentleman, and a preacher of rare quality. He was deeply loved by the people of Falmouth Road.

The Revd Eliseus Howells of Lewisham agreed to look after the church until a new minister was appointed. This happened when the Revd Daniel Lodwig Jones of Cross Inn was installed on 16 May 1946. He was a native of Bwlch-llan, Cardiganshire, whose long career in the ministry included periods at some of the strongest churches in Wales, including Crwys and Pembroke Terrace, Cardiff, and Siloh, Llanbedr Pont Steffan (Lampeter).

Lodwig Jones was already an immensely popular preacher when he arrived at Falmouth Road. His immediate task was to rebuild the cause after the ravages of wartime. It was a time of hope and confidence: despite the upheaval, there were still 390 members and 90 children on the books. And yet the minister had to repeat the appeals of his predecessor for more loyalty to Sunday morning services and to the Sunday school. The monthly children's service was restarted in 1948, thanks to the efforts of the organist, Islwyn Lewis.

After seven industrious years, Lodwig Jones announced his decision to accept a call to Crwys Road, Cardiff, in July 1953. He had been a great addition to the ministerial team in London, where his lively preaching style brought him many fans, but he also made frequent visits to preach at special services throughout Wales. He was released from Falmouth Road

The Revd Glanville Davies (1910–99)
© National Library of Wales

on 25 June 1953, where a crowded chapel heard tributes and messages from fellow ministers and officers. Mr Jones died in December 2012 at the age of 95.

This is where our Llanelli link emerges once again. The Revd Glanville Davies, a son of Glenalla chapel, Llanelli, accepted the invitation to become minister of Falmouth Road in March 1954. He and his wife, Elizabeth, and their six-year-old daughter, Catrin, arrived in July of that year. Catrin shed light on the minister's lot at that time:

> *Dad didn't have a car for some years after we arrived, and as our house wasn't near the chapel, we got to know the underground Northern Line very well, emerging at the Elephant and Castle to what was still in the 1950s an old bombsite near Spurgeon's Tabernacle. Dad travelled on the Tube for all his pastoral visits, and had been helpfully given a map of London with all the members' locations, so that he could link visits together if he was in a particular area. I still have this map and it's interesting to see how dispersed the membership was even at that time. There were many family groups in most of the London chapels, and as members married and moved around the city they still tended to worship at the chapel where they'd been brought up. Looking back, I smile when I think of how we used to differentiate between all the Maries and Joneses by adding the street or area where people lived. I remember Marie Archway, and Mrs Edwards Old Kent Road, and my mother was always known as Mrs Glan! There was always an air of informality in Falmouth Road, although they took their religion and devotion very seriously.*

Indeed, Falmouth Road was known for the friendliness of its welcome and its refreshing lack of pomposity. Catrin described the warmth of the company throughout her time, and the way in which the chapel interacted with the local community:

The Sunday evening service was very well attended, and was a social event as much as a time of worship, with tea and biscuits in the vestry at the end of the service. The chapel was very much a community, and members were always willing to take part and help with the numerous events, too many to mention. We had a marvellous Christmas party each year. Some of the members were as proud of their genuine Cockney roots as they were of their Welsh ones, leading to some spirited renditions of the 'Lambeth Walk' and old music hall songs. We also held regular jumble sales which became notorious in the area with queues around the block. Some of the locals attended regularly, and the banter between them and the Falmouth Road ladies who had been brought up in similar localities was like being in a street market. The annual Whitsun coach outing was for several years to the 'country' in Rickmansworth. We then branched out to the coast and one memorable trip to Brighton in the 1960s when the mods and rockers rioted in the town...

The challenge outlined by the Revd M. H. Edwards of maintaining the Welsh language in services and activities was even more pronounced in the 1950s:

The Sunday school was well attended, even up to my teenage years, and we took the annual scripture tests and the Welsh language tests that were circulated around the London Welsh Presbytery. But in Falmouth Road many spoke English, though there was a core of older members who had arrived from Wales in their youth, whose first language was Welsh. But the majority were London-born and mainly English-speaking, many of whom had retained some understanding of the Welsh language having heard it spoken at home as children. I attended the local primary school in Clapham and quickly learned English from my fellow pupils, so to this day I speak English with a south London accent, much as I've heard immigrant children in Cardiff talk English with a Welsh accent. My parents wanted me to maintain my Welsh language and so at home we'd inevitably talk Welsh. My father was determined that the chapel should be relevant to non-Welsh speakers, the younger members, and those who'd married into Welsh families and were very loyal and active members. He included some English in his sermons and instigated a regular English service with the blessing and cooperation of the deacons. The young people of Falmouth Road continued to be loyal, but in the end it wasn't the language that reduced the membership, it was changing society. Family groups linked to specific chapels dispersed further afield, with the older generation either moving back to Wales or outside London. My generation moved away to college, married non-Welsh men and women, got more involved in social networks linked to our working lives, and increasingly young Welsh people arriving in London weren't drawn to a religious environment for their social connections.

One of Catrin's contemporaries was David Williams, now a leading baritone with the London Welsh Male Voice Choir, who had been christened at Falmouth Road in 1951 by the Revd Lodwig Jones. David was introduced to the choir in 1969 by the chapel's organist, Tudor Davies. David's parents, William David and Elizabeth Ann, were both from Bronant, Cardiganshire. They ran a dairy in Auckland Street, Vauxhall, and later at Thorne Road, south Lambeth, before retiring to Bronant in 1970. They were all members at Falmouth Road.

David recalled a busy, friendly chapel where the young people would sit together on the gallery for the evening service. This habit ended when the congregation dwindled as more people (his parents included) moved back to Wales. There were plays produced in the vestry by Reginald Evans (who also staged plays at the London Welsh Centre in Gray's Inn Road) and featured talented actors from Falmouth Road, including Marie Vaughan Jones, D. R. Daniel, and Gwynne Powell. There were regular table tennis competitions on Friday nights which brought together lots of young people from different chapels.

David's most vivid recollections will strike a chord with many chapel members from that time: he described the notoriously-competitive children's eisteddfod, which provoked a form of warfare between the chapels. He remembered the 'prelims' on a Friday evening in the basement of Charing Cross Road chapel, when the teenagers would be allowed to congregate in the Wimpy Bar next door after competing. He still remembers his 'fiercest rivals', including Lisa Morgan of Willesden Green, and Delyth Jones and Ann Beynon of Shirland Road. The final rounds would be held the following day at the London Welsh Centre.

But Catrin Unwin's recollection of the children's eisteddfod was rather less rosy:

'Eisteddfod y plant' was not one of my happier memories, it filled me with dread each year. My mother was a singer, but I certainly wasn't, and being shy I hated going on stage. I remember the 'prelims' in Charing Cross chapel with some of us

sneaking out one night into Soho and very quickly being stopped by a policeman who told us to turn around! It would have been inconceivable at that time to see Charing Cross becoming part of the Soho scene as a nightclub.

This was a remarkably rich period for the Welsh in London, with strong links between the chapels and a very active London Welsh Association in Gray's Inn Road. Strange as it may seem today, those links were certainly strained when the club was granted a drinks licence! But it was still possible at this time for the London Welsh community to come together to fill the Royal Albert Hall for a hymn singing festival and St David's Day concerts.

Falmouth Road chapel was served by a succession of talented officers. D. R. Daniel, one of the real mainstays, was a wonderfully eccentric figure who for five decades ran a dairy in Moreton Terrace, Pimlico, not far from Victoria station. He was an entertaining reciter of verse, and a colourful storyteller. There is a superb image of him, in his silk topper, delivering milk to the grand homes of Belgrave Road.

D. R. Daniel delivering milk in Belgrave Road, Pimlico
© National Library of Wales

No less important were the women of Falmouth Road. They rarely found themselves elected to the elders' 'big seat', but it was their hard work and unfailing support which kept many chapels open. Mrs Charlotte Williams led a formidable team of women who often provided meals for hundreds of people in the vestry. Catrin Unwin recalled that in the 1950s and 1960s, the 'chapel ladies' would treat themselves to a trip abroad, to Italy, Majorca, and other exotic destinations, for a week's holiday. Catrin's mother would often go with them.

This was the busy church that Catrin's father, the Revd Glanville Davies, inherited in 1954. His 28-year ministry in London was a happy and successful one, but in some ways it was also a stark illustration of the fate of the city's Welsh chapels in the late-twentieth century.

When he began his ministry in July 1954, there were nineteen Welsh chapels in the city. The total number of communicant members was 4,164. There were 871 children on the chapels' books. There were 1,189 adult and child members of the Sunday schools. The average attendance on Sundays was 670. The chapels collected £14,377 in the collection boxes. Total contributions reached £35,984. The chapels' debts were £47,755. To our eyes, these are astonishing figures.

As Glanville Davies approached the end of his ministry in 1981, those figures had changed drastically. There were thirteen chapels, 1,374 communicant members, 264 children, and average attendance was 118. Collections amounted to £31,766, with total contributions at £88,314. The chapels' debts totalled £5,160.

Catrin Unwin explained how her father, always a realist, tried to manage the evident decline:

> He eventually took over the ministries of Lewisham and Sutton, but it was clear that time was not on the side of Falmouth Road. Dad could see that the financial situation was worsening, and thought that by giving up the ministry it might help the chapel's finances. He felt that the deacons, some of whose links to the chapel went back generations, would be more free to make decisions about the fabric of the building.

It was very clear which way things were going. The membership peak of 514 at Falmouth Road was achieved in 1938, on the eve of the Second World

Ladies of Falmouth Road and other chapels enjoy a break in Majorca (1966)
© Catrin Unwin

War. By the end of 1981 the number was 99, most of whom lived quite a distance from the chapel. There was one Sunday morning service, drawing a congregation of around 20 people.

Mr Davies expressed his dismay and frustration in a paper presented towards the end of his ministry at Falmouth Road:

> *Several times in a Presbytery meeting or Sasiwn I would hear someone asking what was the meaning of an 'unnecessary chapel'. Here is a good example of this. The chapel was a large one, able to seat 850 to 900 people comfortably, and the service was assisted by the sound of a pipe organ of the best sort. With the decline of the membership, the upkeep of the building became a burden. By the end, the task fell to two deacons, T. Ivor Williams who had been the treasurer for 41 years, and D. R. Daniel, who had been the secretary since 1955. They maintained the ministry admirably, but it was the upkeep of the vast building that beat them in the end. I can only praise the loyalty of the remaining few who carried on to the bitter end.*

The closing service was held on the evening of Wednesday, 15 June 1982. Taking part were the Revd H. Llewelyn Jones of Holloway, the Revd Elfed G. Williams of Jewin, and the Revd Geraint Thomas of Shirland Road, chairman of the London Presbytery, who celebrated Holy Communion. The Revd Glanville Davies, who outlined the history of the cause, was presented

The former Falmouth Road chapel, now the Church of the Brotherhood of the Cross and Star (2012)

with the minister's chair from the pulpit. The chair is still in his daughter's possession.

Most of the remaining members transferred to Jewin, the mother church, where the Falmouth Road story had started in the late-eighteenth century.

The admired D. R. Hughes once described Falmouth Road as 'a friendly, welcoming Welsh chapel with not an ounce of snobbery attached to it'.

Many years later, his endorsement has lost none of its power.

It is good to note that the building is still a centre of worship. The Brotherhood of the Cross and Star, founded in Nigeria in 1956, maintains a quasi-Christian tradition which differs significantly from the beliefs of the founders of Falmouth Road. But the sight of hundreds of Brotherhood members, in their gleaming white robes, congregating outside the chapel building on Sundays, is truly impressive.

An African religion has found a Welsh home in London.

CHAPTER 8

EAST ENDERS

Jenkin Edwards, the ancestor of mine who settled in London's East End in the early years of the twentieth century, joined the army of Welsh traders who dominated the city's dairy business. He was already in London in 1901, working as a dairyman's assistant in King's Cross, but by 1905 had moved to Camberwell, where he married Mary Jones, a native of Tregaron.

A few years later, they left south London and bought a shop in Cadogan Terrace, Victoria Park, an area in the heart of east London flanking parts of Bethnal Green, Hackney, and Bow. Their children were young when Mary died of 'exhaustion', at the age of 29, in 1911. Jenkin remarried, and the family moved to a bigger shop in Mape Street, Bethnal Green, barely a mile from the Welsh chapel in Mile End Road.

When Jenkin died in November 1935, the *Welsh Gazette* carried a report which underlined his links with the chapel:

On Thursday afternoon, the 15th inst., the remains of Mr. Jenkin Edwards, 5, Mape-street, Bethnal Green, were interred at the City of London Cemetery, Ilford. Although the weather was boisterous, there was a large gathering of friends and sympathisers. Deceased was of a genial and kind disposition, and exceedingly popular among the Welsh community in London. The services were conducted by his pastor, the Rev. W. R. Williams, Mile End-road, where the deceased had been a member for a great number of years. Mr Edwards, with the assistance of his family, built up a very successful dairy business at Mape-street. He died at the age of 53, and deep sympathy is extended to the family. A memorial service at Mile End chapel on Sunday evening was conducted by the Rev. W. R. Williams, and was attended by a large number of relatives and friends from all over London.

Jenkin Edwards at his shop in Cadogan Terrace

Jenkin's grave, in the City of London Cemetery, lies in a secluded section which contains numerous Welsh headstones. They include ministers, elders and members of the chapels of Mile End Road and Stratford. There are several Edwards stones. A few years after Jenkin's death, the chapel report for 1938 listed contributions from no fewer than seven members of the Edwards family of Mape Street.

Jenkin's granddaughter, Mary Green, whose father was raised in east London but later moved to Hertfordshire, explained that Mile End chapel was the centre of the family's life in the East End:

Jewin was where they went mainly for special occasions, the Mile End Road chapel was nearer so they went there regularly. Chapel obviously played a large part in their lives but maybe more for social than religious reasons! My father in his letters to his brother writes of the social committee, the teas and whist drives, and dances. That was in 1935–6.

Jenkin was said to be 'fond of a drink' so the chapel's eventual fate might not have upset him quite as much as it did others. It is now a pub, The Half Moon, where the main bar retains part of the old chapel gallery. There is an engraving on display in the foyer outlining the history of the building, which stands a few yards from Stepney Green underground station.

On a Sunday morning in March 2014, Eirlys Bebb, a prominent member of the Welsh community in London, came with me to visit Mile End chapel for the first time since she was christened there 80 years ago. She was one of three children raised in the East End, where her parents ran a dairy until they moved to north London and joined the Welsh chapel in Holloway. Studying the engraving in the pub, Eirlys was struck by how little the exterior had changed, and how the bar area was strangely familiar, with its church-like roof lantern, and a choir gallery above the entrance. The stairways to the gallery, on each side of the main doors, are still there.

Mile End chapel closed in 1959 and was used for some years by the University of London. It later fell into disrepair before being saved in 1979 by the Half Moon Theatre Company, which installed fixed seating around a central performance area. The theatre opened with a dramatic adaptation of Robert Tressell's novel *The Ragged-Trousered Philanthropists* (1914), a classic of working-class literature which depicts the social, political and economic life of Britain in the early-twentieth century. It was a fitting choice: the work was written when the working-class Welsh of London were living and working in wretched conditions, some of them collecting funds for their new chapel on the Mile End Road.

Just as hundreds of Welsh had been drawn to the dockyards of Woolwich and Deptford, many others found work, north of the Thames, in the vast yards of the West and East India docks. In the 1840s and 1850s, demand surged for blacksmiths, carpenters and shipbuilders in the areas of Millwall and Poplar. The arrival of a significant number of Welsh speakers, including sailors whose ships docked around the Isle of Dogs, created demand for a Sunday school in Poplar.

There were 40 members on the books in 1853, according to the official statistics. By 1855, regular services were being held under the leadership of the Revd Owen Thomas of Jewin Crescent, and a new church was formed later that year. Meurig Owen in *Ymofyn Am Yr Hen Lwybrau* (2001), an indispensable

The Half Moon (formerly Mile End chapel) in 2014

The roof lantern and part of the old chapel gallery

history of seven extinct London Welsh religious causes, suggested that the services were held in Brunswick Hall, a mission hall in Brunswick Road, Poplar. The date is problematic: the hall did not exist in 1855, according to *Edward Stanford's Library Map of London and its Suburbs* (1862), so the original meeting place must have been elsewhere. But the congregation was evidently meeting at the hall in later years and held services there until 1884. The Revd John Mills had taken charge in 1864, supported by David Williams of the London City Mission. There was a long period of cooperation with Crosby Row in organising visits by preachers from Wales.

By the 1880s it was felt that a 'more convenient' location would help. Brunswick Road, near the East India docks, lay roughly where the modern A12 approaches the northern end of the Blackwall Tunnel, one of London's prime traffic horrors. The more convenient location turned out to be White Horse Street, Stepney, an area of huge population growth in the second half of the nineteenth century. White Horse Street had been the main street of the medieval village of Stepney, centred around St Dunstan's church, but its importance as a thoroughfare had been diminished by the building of Mile End Road and Commercial Road.

A run-down building, owned by a sect of English Baptists, called Cave of Adullam, was sold to the Welsh Calvinistic Methodists in 1884. We can pinpoint its location, thanks to the census of 1901, between numbers 108 and 108B White Horse Street. Not everyone was happy with the move: in the classic tradition of the Welsh chapels, a small group decided to break away and sought the assistance of the Revd John Evans, Eglwysbach, one of the leading Wesleyan Methodist preachers of the day, then minister of City Road chapel in the City of London. They opened their own chapel in Duff Street, off East India Dock Road, in December 1887. They would move eastwards to Cumberland Road, Canning Town, in 1915.

Despite the split, the move to White Horse Street proved to be beneficial. New members joined, including some Jewin families who found the location far more convenient. Membership exceeded a hundred for the first time. Both Sunday school and literary society flourished, a successful annual concert and an eisteddfod were established, and some of the best Welsh preachers accepted invitations to preach. The records show three services on Sundays, a church meeting on Tuesday evenings, a children's meeting on Thursday evenings, prayer and choral meetings on Thursdays, and Bible class on Friday nights. All of these activities were conducted in Welsh.

The location presented challenges, nonetheless. There were persistent problems with smashed windows, and frequent mentions in the minutes of vandalism (by local youths) which led to the expense of fitting wire grilles to the windows. By 1890, the elders came to the view that the area had become too bothersome and that Mile End Road would provide a much better environment.

In November 1890 a group of elders and members visited a vacant chapel near the famous Great Assembly Hall in Mile End Road, and decided to explore the options. Nothing came of the venture, so they decided to redecorate White Horse Street and stay there until a better solution emerged. Such was their confidence that they appointed a full-time minister. The Revd Samuel E. Prytherch, Carmarthen, who started his ministry in Stepney in December 1895, received a welcome gift of a 'purse filled with £25'. He moved into a house off Mile End Road and soon became a big hit with the London Welsh chapel community, despite his tendency to speak his mind. It came as a blow, but no great surprise, to the Stepney members when he was poached by (the much bigger and richer) Falmouth Road chapel in 1897. There were rumours that he disliked the Stepney building, and that 'individual persons' made his life difficult.

Samuel Prytherch's abrupt departure poisoned the well: he was told not to return to preach in Stepney (a remarkably un-Christian response) and the matter was referred to the denominational *cyfarfod misol* ('monthly meeting') of the Calvinistic Methodists in London. But the tensions eased by degrees, and he did officiate at Stepney in the years that followed. It has to be said that Falmouth Road enjoyed a very successful period under his leadership.

The Stepney elders achieved their goal of moving to Mile End in 1898 when they bought a rank of three shops (numbers 213–217 Mile End Road) near Stepney Green station. The building fund was boosted early on by pledges of £600. Meurig Owen revealed that most of the members at that time were involved in the dairy business, and they remained 'the backbone of the cause' until the days of the Second World War.

This was a time of soaring hope. As work on the new chapel started in

1899, the members showed great faith by calling a new pastor. And it took a rather confident man to accept the challenge. The Revd David Oliver of Twyncarno was installed in a service at Stepney in November 1899, taking charge of a relatively small church (160 members, 67 in the Sunday school) with a projected building debt of £9,000. This would correspond to at least £900,000 today by the most conservative (purchasing power) comparison. A comparison based on labour costs would suggest £3.2 million.

The foundation stones were laid on 5 April 1900 and the chapel was ready six months later. The opening services were held on 20–22 October 1900, drawing big congregations and significant financial contributions. More than £2,000 was collected by the end of the year, but it still left a very high level of borrowing. Mile End's debt (calculated per member) was among the highest of the London chapels.

Selling the old chapel in White Horse Street would have made a lot of sense, but early attempts to sell it for £2,200 came to nothing. The price was eventually reduced to £1,200. Even at that level it remained unsold. Incredibly, the Stepney building was retained by Mile End Road for another quarter-century. There are clear parallels with Crosby Row, which remained unsold for years after the move to Falmouth Road.

Mile End Road was growing under a dynamic young minister. Membership rose to 194 (plus 53 children) in 1901. It is often said of the chapels that they spent far too much time studying the figures, and planning new buildings, and far too little time investing in the spiritual health of the cause. This cannot be said of Mile End in the early years of the twentieth century. Yes, there was an unavoidable focus on money, but the spiritual life of the church was given a huge boost by the religious revival of 1904–5, led by the charismatic Welsh evangelist, Evan Roberts.

The revival transformed David Oliver's preaching, with the result that the chapel was often filled for services lasting several hours. Membership rose to 238 (with 107 children) in 1905. Many new members stayed loyal, supporting the minister in his work, and by 1911 the debt had been reduced to £6,040. The debt-reduction scheme championed by Timothy Davies, the Welsh businessman and politician from Fulham, led to a further reduction to £3,980. It is remarkable to note that in the four years to 1912, the Welsh Calvinistic Methodist chapels repaid some £15,000 of debt and saved around

£5,000 in interest payments. This was a prodigious fundraising exercise by any standards.

That exercise was backed by a full programme of events, including regular concerts, cementing the chapel's strong musical tradition. The children's choir established a very good reputation. In 1913, the Benjamin family of Commercial Road donated an organ for use in chapel services. The instrument was 'opened' on 19 June 1913 by the well-known organ scholar, E. T. Davies of Dowlais. The choice was perhaps not surprising: in 1909, at the National Eisteddfod held in the Royal Albert Hall, Davies had accompanied the victorious Dowlais Male Voice Choir, and won the top composition prize for *Ynys y Plant*, a ghastly but nonetheless popular number about an eternal paradise for children. Davies was said to have inaugurated more than a hundred new organs in England and Wales.

Thirty young men from the chapel joined the armed forces in the First World War, one of whom lost his life. The minister and many of the chapel's women visited injured soldiers in local hospitals, providing support and gifts, and they joined in the efforts to find accommodation for Belgian refugees. The soldiers injured on the Somme included one of the minister's sons, Thomas Charles Oliver, who spent three years recovering from his wounds. He later qualified as a doctor, spending many years in practice in Old Colwyn.

The new life and energy experienced by the chapel after the war, including major contributions to the building fund in 1919, were badly affected by the sudden death of the Revd David Oliver in May 1920. His 21-year pastorate had been an unqualified success, and his contribution to the London Welsh chapels was a significant one. A huge crowd attended his funeral on 25 May 1920 at the City of London Cemetery, Manor Park.

The Revd John Thickens of Willesden led a service of remembrance at Mile End that evening, and later published a warm tribute:

> *We shall not look upon his like again. When he accepted the call from Mile End Road, he knew the scale of the challenge. This was a small church, deep in debt, in the heart of the East End. We shall never know to what extent the strain of carrying this burden shortened his life. His last initiative was to collect the enormous sum of £1,660 by knocking on hundreds of doors and asking for support. His plan was to eliminate the debt by the end of 1920. He was a caring shepherd and the most loyal of friends. His watchwords were 'prayer', 'faith', and 'revival', and he burned with*

intense desire for revival within the church and within society. He left a widow and four children: his two boys are medical students at the London Hospital, his elder daughter is a teacher, the younger is but eight years old. He gave his all to the cause.

The church took some time to come to terms with the loss, but by April 1922 the elders decided to ask the authorities for permission to call a new minister. The Revd W. R. Williams, an Anglesey man based in Newtown, accepted the call and started his ministry in November 1923.

W. R. Williams was a very different kind of preacher: where David Oliver had been fiery and combative, his successor was quiet, calm, and rather slow in his delivery. This did not seem to harm the cause: the 1920s were a period of unchecked growth for Mile End. The old chapel building in White Horse Street was sold for £1,050 in 1926, but the accounts showed a credit for £1,497 after taking into account all rental income and costs since 1900. This was seen as a very positive outcome. But it has to be said that significant interest payments would have been saved had the original sale gone through a quarter-century earlier, and the proceeds credited to the building account.

Such was the level of confidence (or was it vainglory?) that the elders even considered taking on more debt by purchasing a bigger chapel in Harley Grove, Bow. The prominent businessman and Calvinistic Methodist grandee, Sir Howell J. Williams, was firmly in favour and advised Mile End to buy the old English Congregational chapel which had been offered for sale at a 'reasonable price'. The plans came to nothing: the minutes provide no further information about the Harley Grove project. The chapel would become the Mile End and Bow District Synagogue in 1929, changing in 1977 to a Sikh temple. The building can still be seen today, and it is easy to imagine it as a rather grand Welsh chapel. But the decision not to take on a new burden, whatever the reason, was probably the right one.

Accounts of the weekly activities speak for themselves. Sundays were astonishingly busy: a service at 11 a.m., Sunday school at 3 p.m., Sunday school debate at 4 p.m., the hugely-popular tea at 5 p.m., hymn-singing rehearsal until the evening service at 6.30 p.m., then choral rehearsal at 8 p.m. There would be intensive preparations for the annual children's eisteddfod at the Kingsway Hall or at Jewin. D. R. Lloyd, who owned a thriving slate business in Bow, would spend many hours preparing the children for the big event, which always drew a huge crowd.

There were many reports of sharply-competitive parents going to extreme lengths to push their child to victory. On Tuesday evenings, young people aged 11–16 would be tutored for the denominational examinations. Mile End's children were known for their ability to answer all questions in Welsh, unlike the children of some other chapels. The literary society would meet on Wednesdays, organising debates, presenting papers on current affairs, staging plays and organising concerts. On Thursdays, the Band of Hope met, and Welsh language classes were held for children and young people – these were well attended. There were more Welsh classes on Fridays, as well as tuition in the widely-used Tonic Sol-fa musical notation system.

Mile End passed a significant milestone in April 1929 when the chapel finally cleared its debt, thanks to a decade-long programme of fundraising concerts, lectures and financial appeals. One report describes the celebrated mezzo-soprano, Leila Megàne, singing to a packed crowd at a concert in the chapel.

There were around 200 members on the books at this time, with new members stepping forward to take on the duties of the older generation. J. E. Booley moved to Birkenhead after 45 years of service, including periods as precentor and secretary. In the winter of 1929, the long-serving treasurer, Evan Evans, returned to Wales after four decades at Mile End, 24 of them as an officer. He was described as a 'big man, his legs bent with arthritis, regularly seen with his horse and cart carrying brewers' grains through Bethnal Green'. There is a moving account of his experience in the 1904 religious revival, discarding his walking sticks as he walked into chapel, shouting: 'Lord, I can walk!' Sadly, the sticks were back within weeks. He died within a year of his move back to Wales.

Owen Williams was another pillar of the cause: he owned a thriving drapery business in Stratford, and lived in a big house in Buckhurst Hill, Essex. Unfortunately, his accountant let him down and he lost everything in a bankruptcy action. He was remembered in chapel for his dapper style, and for his habit of placing his hand on the Bible and exclaiming: 'Read this, dear friends, read this!'

D. R. Lloyd, the slate merchant, had two sons who enjoyed distinguished careers as ministers. The Revd R. Glynne Lloyd was an able scholar who spent decades as a minister in the USA. His younger brother, the Revd John

Meirion Lloyd, spent many years as a missionary and headteacher in Mizoram, India. He died in 1998. His recollections of childhood in Mile End shed more light on the life of the church:

> Mile End was among the smallest of the London Welsh chapels. This is where I was accepted as a full member, and this is where I started my journey to the ministry. The first members were labourers in the Poplar district, but by our time, everyone seemed to be from Cardiganshire, most of them from Tregaron. The members were in the dairy trade, and most of them were related to each other in some way.

Everything changed during the Second World War: the Mile End area was heavily bombed by German planes aiming for the dockyard areas of the Thames. The chapel was damaged on several occasions, but the homes and businesses of members suffered far greater destruction. Mr and Mrs Jones of Bow Dairy were killed in one of the air raids, while 20 chapel families lost their properties and possessions.

On the eve of war in 1939, the number of members stood at 215 (with 39 children). By 1945 this had reduced dramatically to 137. The abrupt resignation of the minister in September 1940 had clearly weakened the cause. He was said to have left 'because of the extensive damage done to the eastern parts of London', and because his health was not robust. The Revd W. R. Williams had spent seventeen years at Mile End. He moved to Rhyd-ddu, a village in Snowdonia, where he died in November 1943.

It is sad to say that things never fully recovered after the war. There were five elders leading the cause, without the guidance of a pastor, including the veteran Owen Williams, who had been elected in Stepney in 1885. He died, in great hardship, at the age of 92. His fellow elders had extended regular financial support over the years. Owen Williams spent a remarkable 63 years as an elder, and his passing marked the end of an era.

Despite the arrival of the Revd Michael Parry, the dynamic young minister of Walthamstow, as caretaker pastor in 1949, the decline had set in. There were fewer members to pay for expensive repairs to the building, including a leaking roof. In the minutes for 1950 there was a hint of things to come: the elders noted that the cause was to carry on, despite the problems. It was the first admission that closure might be an option.

The chapel was reopened after repair work in November 1950, amid

Kenneth and Ann Evans's wedding at Mile End chapel (1953)
© Halifax Photos Ltd

talk of setting new foundations for the decades to come. New elders were elected in 1953, but the cause suffered a heavy blow when David Edwards, a servant of Mile End for the past half-century, died in 1954. W. H. Williams, the long-serving secretary, retired the following year.

By 1955 the number of members had reduced to 97, with 20 children on the books. By May 1956 the elders decided to explore all options for the future of Mile End. There was a sense of crisis, according to the minutes, as the numbers attending services fell and the cause lost its vitality. There was concern that the enthusiasm expressed in 1950, when money was collected for major repairs, had not been justified. A special meeting in December 1958, attended by 30 members, voted unanimously to end the cause.

The vote was considered by the denominational monthly meeting held at Charing Cross Road chapel in January 1959. It was explained that the families of Mile End had suffered more than those of any other chapel during the war years. Members were scattered throughout east London and beyond, and the flow of Welsh people to the East End had stopped.

Sadder still were the final statistics: 62 adult members, not a single child, an average attendance of twelve on Sundays, and no meetings held during the week. The contrast with the days of David Oliver and W. R. Williams was painful. On Sunday evening, 18 January 1959, an official delegation visited the church to canvass opinion among the members. There were 25 in favour of closure, with four against. Mile End chapel was deconsecrated in a special service on 15 April 1959.

Meurig Owen noted that a motion was passed to safeguard Mile End's records and registers by handing them to London Presbytery officials, but this was not done. Some documents were found, years later, at Leytonstone chapel. Sadly, this is typical of the appalling carelessness of many Welsh chapel officers and members over the years. Valuable documents have been discarded with shocking regularity.

The Mile End Road building was sold for £6,000 to Queen Mary College, University of London, in December 1959. Some of the money was used to reduce the debts of Leytonstone, the new chapel which opened in 1958 in Leytonstone High Road, some five miles away from Mile End.

Leytonstone chapel, which sits on a multi-million pound site in north-east London, is, sad to say, something of a hidden gem these days. Few are aware of its existence, fewer still of its intriguing history. It forms part of Eglwys-y-Drindod, the united Welsh church in north London. Members of the old causes at Wood Green and Holloway now meet regularly at their chapel in Cockfosters, while holding a few services every year in Leytonstone.

The Leytonstone story cannot be properly understood without taking into account what happened in the wider region of east and north-east London. The economists would say that it suffered from an excess of supply for Welsh-speaking worshippers. A ludicrous excess, as it turned out. At one stage, there were three Calvinistic Methodist causes, one Independent, one Wesleyan Methodist, and one Anglican – all within a tight radius. The result was that every cause was weakened by this over-supply.

The Leytonstone cause originated in Walthamstow, the borough which lies at the end of the underground Victoria Line, not far from the Essex county boundary. The history of Walthamstow chapel overlapped with that of Stratford, as we shall see, and their congregations gradually combined with that of Mile End to form the new cause at Leytonstone.

A visitor to Stratford these days will be struck by the vast Westfield shopping centre, next to a modern transport interchange, the main London hub built for the 2012 Olympic Games, and the huge sporting venues which dominate the urban landscape in this part of east London. It is no exaggeration to say that the Stratford area, known for decades as one of the shabbiest parts of London, was transformed by Olympic investment. It is now linked by high-speed rail to St Pancras International, and boasts no fewer than nine overground and underground connections, along with dozens of bus services. Property prices have boomed. Stratford is without question a desirable location nowadays. No other part of London has changed so much in recent years.

Compare this to the area which drew so many Welsh workers and their families a century ago: they came to a community very much on the outskirts of London, further east than Mile End, just a few miles from the Essex town of Ilford. The journey to central London could be slow and troublesome. Indeed, just getting as far as Stepney every Sunday for chapel services in White Horse Street could be tiring.

This was why members decided to rent a room in Stratford in 1890 to start their own religious meetings. There is some confusion about the date of formation of a new church: it seems this happened in 1892, but there is no specific reference in the denominational papers or in the regular press. The records show 42 registered members, with twelve children at Sunday school, at the end of 1892. In July of that year, the elders had started looking for a permanent home. They found a 'convenient chapel in a central location', available for purchase or rental, but nothing came of the plan.

It is astonishing to note that with relatively few members (72 in 1894, with 37 children), and no permanent home, this church moved quickly to appoint its first minister. Robert Parry, an Oxford graduate, was a member of the Welsh chapel at Holloway who'd started preaching in 1890. Meurig Owen searched high and low for a reference to Robert Parry's installation as minister of Stratford: I found one small reference in the *Western Mail* on 17 July 1894 which noted that 'the Rev Robert Parry has undertaken the pastorate of the recently-formed Welsh Presbyterian Church at Stratford, Essex'.

His brief stay (just three years) included the great venture of building a new chapel. A plot of land on the junction of Tavistock Road and Romford Road was bought for £500, and the trust deeds were signed on 17 July 1894, a few days after Robert Parry's appointment. There are very few details available about the new building and its cost. We know that the local authority (West Ham) had given permission for the building work on 10 April 1894, and that the foundation stone was laid on 10 October 1894, but we have no account of the opening of the chapel. This is highly unusual. The opening services

A rare image of Stratford Welsh chapel
© National Library of Wales

of any new chapel were normally reported in full in the denominational press. We have to assume that the chapel probably opened in early 1895 as there are press references to meetings of the 'Forward Movement at Romford-road Chapel, Stratford' in June 1895.

The Revd Robert Parry took charge of a church with 94 members, 41 children, and 162 'listeners' (non-members who attended regularly). The chapel's debts in that first year of his ministry were £2,450. This was a heavy burden for such a small church and would remain a headache for decades to come.

Robert Parry left Stratford for Llanrug, in north Wales, in 1898. He was an energetic young minister whose services were already in great demand in London. His departure was a heavy blow for the new cause at Stratford, but he left behind a growing church with good prospects. Sadly, Robert Parry's fragile health led to his early death at the age of 50, and he was buried at Llanrug, on his birthday, in 1909. Tributes were paid to his gifts as a preacher, poet and playwright. His English translations of popular revival hymns, including 'Dyma gariad fel y moroedd', are still popular.

Time and again, Stratford struggled with money. The Forward Movement agreed to contribute an annual sum of £50 to the church until 1908. The main denominational fund also committed to pay £200 to the London chapels to help expand the network. Seven new causes were established between 1896 and 1907. By 1899, Stratford's debt had been reduced to £2,450.

Robert Parry's successor was the Revd J. Wilson Roberts, a native of Y Felinheli (Port Dinorwic), who arrived in Stratford at the turn of the century. His appointment prompted a burst of new activity: membership rose to 140 (with 44 children) and a new team of elders helped the minister in his work, which included sponsoring meetings in Walthamstow in 1901. Those meetings would lead to the formation of a new cause in 1903.

The buzz in Stratford was underlined by the long list of services and meetings for 1902: three Sunday services (11 a.m., 2.45 p.m., 6.30 p.m.); a prayer meeting (7.30 p.m.) and reading/literary club (9.30 p.m.) on Mondays; a second literary club (7.45 p.m.) on Wednesdays; a children's meeting (6.30 p.m.) and members' meeting (7.30 p.m.) on Thursdays.

For a young church with modest membership numbers, this was an impressively full week. Extra events including concerts and bazaars helped reduce the debt to £2,000 by 1904, when the religious revival in Wales took hold and boosted attendance to new levels, despite the loss of some members to the new chapel in Walthamstow. Revivalist meetings were still being held in Stratford in May 1905, long after things had calmed down elsewhere.

There is a brief reference, in a published history of Walthamstow chapel, to attempts to unite the Walthamstow and Stratford causes sometime in 1906. This attempt failed, and it may have been a factor in J. Wilson Roberts's decision in 1908 to leave for Ynyshir, Rhondda. He spent 23 years in south Wales before returning to Dyffryn, Meirionnydd, where he died in 1939.

There could have been another reason for his departure. There was a sharp fall of 32 in Stratford's membership in 1908, leaving 76 members and 33 children. Meurig Owen noted that 20 had transferred their membership to other churches (including more to Walthamstow), but fifteen left without their 'transfer tickets'. This was a constant problem for the London Welsh chapels. The numbers coming and going every year meant it was very difficult for officers to keep tabs on everyone. Over the years, thousands of lapsed members simply lost contact with the London chapels and never returned.

As the people of Ynyshir prepared to welcome a former London minister, they said farewell to one of their own, the Revd D. Glyn Jones, who moved to the capital in 1911 to look after both Stratford and Walthamstow. This joint venture was to be his first pastorate. He proved to be a decent, hard-working, conscientious minister, but his time in London was marred by constant anxieties about the finances. This wasn't helped by the departure of some key personnel.

It is a fact that some of the more upwardly-mobile or ambitious London Welsh were drawn to English-speaking Nonconformist causes, or even to Anglican ones. Owen Thomas, an experienced elder who left Stratford, is a good example. A press report on his death in 1912 said:

He joined an English-speaking church in Willesden, north London. Many wealthy Welshmen did this kind of thing late in life. When young, he played a prominent part in Welsh societies in London, but in later years his main interests were in English circles.

Having said that, Owen Thomas had been a loyal and generous servant of Stratford chapel. His business partner was Owen Williams of Mile End, and their clothing business, Williams and Thomas of Stratford, was well known in the area. He had served as treasurer for a decade and presided over a sharp fall in the debt to £1,830 in 1911. A significant contribution from the central fund in 1912 cut this further to £1,108.

By 1914, on the eve of the Great War, Stratford was in better shape. The minister was allowed to focus entirely on Stratford, freed from his responsibility for Walthamstow, where there were growing concerns for the future of the cause. Those concerns spread to Stratford as the First World War progressed. Three young men lost their lives, serving in the armed forces, and it is regrettable that the marble memorial bearing their names disappeared after the chapel closed.

Among those who enlisted was John Oliver Francis, a gifted musician who had become the organist at Stratford in 1907 at the age of fourteen. He was presented with a framed illuminated address by the chapel in 1914 when he joined the Royal Welch Fusiliers. The Francis family were veritable pillars of the cause: Hugh Richard, a deacon and precentor, and his wife, Laura, were tireless workers. They would all serve the chapel loyally until the outbreak of the Second World War.

Stratford emerged from the war with significant problems. There were just a hundred members in 1919, struggling with a debt of £1,075, having to make special appeals to the central fund to boost the minister's salary. It was a very sorry situation. D. Glyn Jones tendered his resignation in 1919, an honourable move on his part as he considered this a helpful gesture. A temporary measure allowed him to remain until December 1920 on a salary of £250. By the time he left, the debt had been reduced to £705, but membership had slipped to 93 (with 23 children).

D. Glyn Jones was appointed a teacher at a local school and became a member at Mile End Road. In the years that followed, he preached regularly at Stratford (and other London Welsh chapels) and proved to be a wise counsellor. He left London in 1927 to become minister of the Welsh church in Melbourne, Australia, where he died in 1945.

It is a sad fact that while the 1930s were years of powerful growth for most of the London Welsh causes, it was a decade of unrelenting struggle for Stratford. The members rejected several formal attempts to unite with Walthamstow, stubbornly insisting on the right to call their own minister. But the finances simply did not justify this ambition: any spare cash was spent on maintaining the building, and there were serious doubts about the chapel's ability to pay for a full-time pastor. It was all too easy to predict the constant need for handouts from the central denominational funds.

Fundraising concerts were organised at Stratford Town Hall, starring Welsh singers and well-known London entertainers, and one of the biggest was planned for the evening of 16 November 1939, when the line-up was to include the popular Cockney comedian Arthur Askey.

The concert never took place: it was cancelled following the outbreak of the Second World War in September. The Revd W. R. Williams of Mile End agreed to supervise Stratford in 1939 and this arrangement persisted until the dreadful events of the following year.

Stratford chapel was badly damaged in an air raid in April 1940, and the decision was taken to close the building for the duration of the war. The 95 members and fifteen children were urged to attend services at Mile End Road. The Stratford area was heavily bombed throughout this time, and in 1941 the chapel suffered more damage. The adjoining chapel house was repaired and re-let in 1942, but in 1944 more damage was caused by German rockets.

At the end of the war, a panel led by Professor David Hughes Parry recommended the closure of Stratford. They argued that the state of the building, and the difficulty of reuniting the members, meant that closure was the best option. This recommendation was accepted and the buildings were finally sold in 1949, becoming part of a carpet and bedding factory.

There is an easy conclusion to be drawn from the Stratford story: this was a chapel that never really found its feet; it always struggled financially; it was opened in a part of London already rich in Welsh-speaking causes; it should, therefore, never have been built; so it was a foolish venture.

There is a good deal of truth in those assertions. But to embrace them is to cheapen the reputation of all the good people who worked so hard to sustain Stratford over the years. They are to be respected and admired for their faith and loyalty. This was a very transient membership: some were in settled businesses, but many were young workers spending brief periods in this part of London, especially between the wars. The addresses in the members' register include Nurses' Home, West Ham Hospital, Fever Hospital, and Village Homes (Dr Barnardo), where many young Welsh women worked as nurses and assistants.

These young workers became chapel members to make contact with other Welsh people, but many of them soon lost contact with the chapel community. Keeping tabs on this ever-changing crowd was impossible. Despite that, for half a century Stratford provided a valued spiritual home for thousands of Welsh people. And that's how it should be remembered.

There is a comforting link between Stratford and Leytonstone. The Daniel family played a big part in Stratford and they left their impressive mark on Leytonstone, too. Captain and Mrs Daniel of Ilford, Essex, were pillars of the cause in Stratford for many years. Their son, T. Llewelyn Daniel, a Stratford member, was the architect who designed Leytonstone chapel. He was in business with his son, Hugh Llewelyn Daniel. His daughter, the

EGLWYS BRESBYTERAIDD CYMRU

Trefn Gwasanaeth Cysegru

EGLWYS MOREIA
HIGH ROAD
LEYTONSTONE LLUNDAIN

PNAWN IAU EBRILL 17, 1958
am 4 o'r gloch

Artist's impression of Leytonstone chapel (1957) and the official programme for the opening services (1958)
© Eglwys Jewin

Interior of Leytonstone chapel (2014)

artist Dilys Mary Daniel, created a superb mural, depicting stories from the Mabinogion, which hangs in the Leytonstone vestry.

The Leytonstone complex is something to behold: it is such a strong expression of the confidence which still existed in parts of London in the 1950s, despite the closure of Mile End and the weakening of other causes. The chapel itself is airy and modern, the quality of the building hugely impressive, the design a far cry from the gloomy Victorian sheds in other parts of London. The raked seating affords worshippers an unobstructed view of the pulpit and stained glass windows. The chapel is surrounded by several meeting rooms, a big vestry with stage and theatre lighting, a kitchen and classroom, a car park – all built on a wide plot of land which at one time included a tennis court. The chapel's property portfolio also includes a row of shops on Leytonstone High Road. In all probability, it is (with the possible exception of Jewin) the most valuable property asset owned by the Presbyterian Church of Wales.

Leytonstone chapel opened in 1958, thanks to the efforts of its young minister, the Revd Michael Parry, and a group of enthusiastic members, chief among them the singularly generous Alban Davies family. David Alban Davies and his son, Jenkin, were both powerful figures in the London dairy trade. Jenkin was the man who drove the efforts to find a modern new home for the Walthamstow congregation. They had been worshipping in a small chapel – funded, notably, by David Alban Davies – for the previous half-century.

Walthamstow, like Stratford, is a story of constant hardship and struggle. But, unlike Stratford, Walthamstow survived the Second World War and flourished.

Oswald Rees Owen, in *Moreia Walthamstow: Hanes yr Achos* (1953), his booklet on the history of Walthamstow chapel, noted that the economic crisis in rural Wales at the end of the nineteenth century drove many to north-east London. Walthamstow was growing rapidly, thanks to the new rail link to Liverpool Street station, and thousands of new homes were being built on the Warner and other big council estates. The busy high street included several shops (drapers and dairies) owned by Welsh people.

The first Welsh-language services in the area were held in January 1901, in a room above a restaurant in St Mary's Road. Before long they moved to a commercial school in Grove Road, owned by a Welshman, J. O. Davies. There were around 20 regular worshippers of all denominations. This changed when members had to choose a hymn book for regular use. Their choice of the Calvinistic Methodist selection meant that some enthusiastic Baptists abandoned the cause.

Under the guidance of the Revd J. Wilson Roberts of Stratford, and later the Revd J. Garmon Owen, a City of London missionary, the Walthamstow meeting grew in strength. On 15 March 1903 a new church was formed with 55 members (and eighteen children in Sunday school). They still worshipped in rented rooms. The Revd Llewelyn Edwards took charge for a year, at the end of which there were 61 members. It is significant that there were attempts as early as 1905 to unite Walthamstow with Welsh causes in Tottenham and Wood Green. We know that a similar attempt to join with Stratford in 1906 also failed. There were concerns even in those days that these individual causes were simply too small to be viable. But common sense was defeated by territorial and tribal impulse, as it was across London and in so many towns and villages in Wales.

The first elders were elected in 1907. They included the secretary, J. O. Davies (of Grove Road), who still provided accommodation for the church, and the treasurer, a young David Alban Davies, already a very successful businessman. The social mix among the officers was typical of

Moriah chapel, Walthamstow, built in 1933

The interior of Moriah chapel, Walthamstow

the era. Enoch Morgan, the secretary from 1908, was a road sweeper. His fellow elder, Dr Stanley Owen, secretary of the building fund, was a respected local physician and elected councillor. Dr Owen would organise sessions of clay-pigeon shooting for chapel members: they would meet at Green Pond Farm, a 200-acre site on the outskirts of Walthamstow, owned by the Alban Davies family. This was also the location for many Sunday school outings.

In the midst of all this social jollity, there was a membership crisis. Numbers fell from 50 in 1910, to 41 in 1911, and then a sharp drop to 34 in 1913. Forming a joint cause with Stratford in 1911 clearly did not help. Sunday morning services were abandoned. An appeal for financial help from central funds was unsuccessful. Membership stood at 30 in 1914. The future looked very bleak at a time when many other London Welsh churches were flourishing. A proposal to close the doors by August 1914 was defeated, but the authorities were unconvinced by the enthusiasm and determination of David Alban Davies, who led the campaign to stay open.

It is a miracle that the church survived the years of the First World War. It was a monumental struggle to keep things going. The Revd David Oliver of Mile End provided regular support, celebrating Holy Communion and preparing young people for full membership of the church. Despite the addition of young members, the membership statistics for the years after the war were dire: 26 in 1920; 22 in 1921; 23 in 1923. It is no surprise to learn that the denominational authorities felt this was a lost cause. They urged Walthamstow to join forces with another congregation. But David Alban Davies had other ideas. He fought 'like a lion', according to Oswald Rees Owen, and provided essential financial support during those very dark days.

Things moved quickly in 1927: the rented schoolroom was no longer available so services were held in the vestry of Pembroke Road Independent chapel. David Alban Davies urged the members to buy or build their own chapel. It was, to put it mildly, a very bold move given the fragility of the cause. The Revd David Owen, Cilfynydd, carried out his own investigation in September 1928, and after several local appeals, membership rose to 41. On this basis, they moved in 1929 to new accommodation at the YMCA on Church Hill. But membership slipped again: 37 in 1929; 27 in 1930; and 23 in 1931.

David Alban Davies was convinced that the main obstacle was the lack of an appropriate place of worship. When the YMCA property was offered for sale in 1932, he bought the buildings and the surrounding land. He then paid for a small chapel to be built at a cost of £1,491 and in 1933 he transferred the ownership to the London Presbytery, the local governing body of the Presbyterian Church of Wales (which had by then changed its name from the Calvinistic Methodist Church). Wisely, he inserted a condition into the contract stipulating that the London Presbytery owed him £1,000 for the property. He wanted to make it as difficult as possible for the denominational authorities to close the chapel.

The new chapel, called 'Moreia', drew new members. There were 44 on the books in 1934, and 66 by the following year. The prospects had been transformed. Another attempt to unite the cause with Stratford in 1934 came to nothing, and in February 1935 Walthamstow secured the services of its first minister, the Revd Victor Thomas of Cerrigydrudion. He moved into a house on Church Hill bought, it goes without saying, by the Alban Davies family.

Later in 1934, David Alban Davies and his wife moved back to Wales, to Bryn Awelon, a grand residence on the main road approaching Llanrhystud from Llan-non. His extensive London dairy business was transferred to his sons, Jenkin and David Harold, who built it into an even bigger empire in the years that followed. David Alban Davies showed titanic generosity throughout his life to a wide range of Welsh causes. Very few people in Wales can match his impact and influence. He even presented a 200-acre site at Penglais, Aberystwyth, to the University of Wales, to save it from building development. He died at Bryn Awelon in 1951. It is good to be able to pay tribute, over 60 years after his death, to this exceptional man.

Fortunately for Walthamstow chapel, Jenkin Alban Davies was as committed and as generous as his father. He supported the new minister in his work and took pride in the remarkable range of activity in the church. Sunday school was restarted with 37 members, there were prayer and literary meetings, and by 1939 the young people's meeting was one of the liveliest in London. The Moreia children were notably successful in the competitions

London Welsh ministers in 1960: (back, left to right) Michael Parry (Leytonstone), Alun Richards (Clapham), Geraint Thomas (Shirland Road), Denzil Harries (Walham Green), W. T. Phillips (Hammersmith), Richard Jones (Charing Cross); (seated) Richard Williams (Willesden), Huw Llewelyn Hughes (Dr Barnardo's), W. Lloyd Price (Holloway), A. Tudno Williams (Lewisham)

at the annual eisteddfod. The church also became the focal point of Welsh life in the Walthamstow area, just as David Alban Davies had predicted when he insisted on building the new chapel.

Membership surged to 101 in 1936 and to 165 in 1939. These numbers would have seemed totally unrealistic a decade earlier. D. R. Lloyd and his family moved to the area from Mile End Road, and he became secretary at this exciting time. But the onset of war scattered the membership, the minister resigned and moved to Newquay, and those members in the armed forces were kept up to date by means of the *Moreia Messenger*, edited by Dewi F. Lloyd, which included all kinds of Walthamstow news.

Walthamstow did not experience the wartime damage suffered by Stratford. Indeed, it emerged with a strong sense of purpose, confidently calling a new minister. The Revd Michael Parry of Capel Curig arrived in October 1945. Membership stood at a respectable 124 in that year.

Michael Parry's daughter, Bethan, was born in Hackney in 1949. She explained that by the early 1950s, it was felt that Moreia was no longer big enough to house the congregation. A plot of land was bought in Leytonstone, and plans were made for the new chapel where she would be married in

1972. She shared her memories of her childhood as a minister's daughter in London:

> *It was a very lively time in Walthamstow: the children's eisteddfod at Jewin, the 'prelims' in Charing Cross Road, lots of children competing, five shillings for the winners, and a new outfit for the big day! Exams in Biblical knowledge, exams in the Welsh language, a children's 'cymanfa ganu' in June, Welsh lessons at the London Welsh Centre on Saturday mornings. Will Price, the Holloway minister, would be there to have tea and a cigarette with my father.*

The move to Leytonstone took place in 1958, after a big fundraising campaign, and generous support, once again, from the Alban Davies family:

> *The original chapel in Church Hill, Walthamstow, is still there. I think it now belongs to the evangelical Church of the Nazarene. We still lived in Walthamstow after the chapel moved to Leytonstone, and we could hear the Nazarene congregation singing joyfully during the summer months when all the chapel windows were open. One of the motives in building a new chapel was catering for the army of young Welsh teachers who came to work in Essex and Hertfordshire.*

Bethan sheds light on her father's appointment, and on the role played by Jenkin Alban Davies:

> *I have a copy of the letter sent by Jenkin Davies to my father outlining the terms of the offer. It's in English, of course, and offers a salary of £350 a year ('I trust you will find this acceptable') and promises that he will not use his influence to undermine the minister's work. He adds that he does not consider the minister to be his 'personal chaplain'. Make of that what you will!*

The design of the new chapel, pioneering in its day, was indeed a talking point:

> *Leytonstone is a lovely chapel, unusual in design, not like a traditional chapel at all. A big plot, with modern facilities. Exceptional, really. The effect on the church was dramatic. Attendance increased and it was usual to see at least 30 in the morning, and 40 in the evening, many of them young teachers. The main 'sponsor' was Jenkin Alban Davies, who employed hundreds of men in his dairy business, and who was incredibly generous to the London chapels, especially ours. Despite*

his wealth, he was not a snob. He had no time for some of the 'nouveaux riches'
among the London Welsh. He paid for some beautiful stained glass windows at
Leytonstone, in memory of his parents, and they are to be moved to Llan-non if
Leytonstone ever closes.

The quality of these facilities meant that local groups and societies were
keen to use them: nursery schools and playgroups have been a familiar feature,
along with drama clubs and dancing schools, and political parties have held
many meetings in the hall. These days, Forest Baptist Church uses several
rooms for services every Sunday.

Above all, Meic Parry (as he was affectionately known) and his family
loved London life. His wife taught in local schools and they stayed in the
capital until his retirement in 1972. There were a few tricky moments along
the way: Meic Parry was a hugely popular eisteddfod compere, performer,
and broadcaster, and was understandably keen not to lose this work when he
came to London. He managed to juggle all these demands, but there were
times when some of his elders made their reservations known. He and his wife

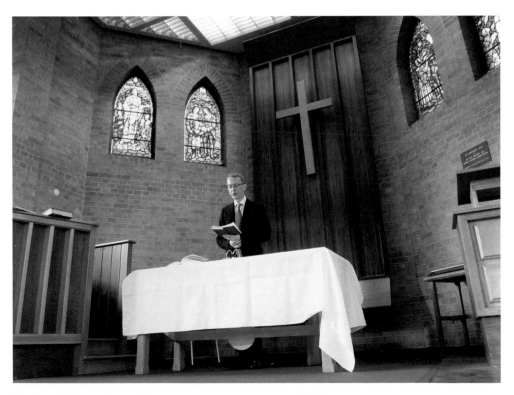

The Revd Richard Brunt officiating at Leytonstone chapel (2014)

enjoyed seven years of happy retirement in Rhyl until his death in 1979. He is still mentioned fondly by chapel members today.

Things were never the same after Meic Parry's departure, despite the heroic efforts of several ministers and loyal members. Leytonstone became linked with Holloway and Wood Green chapels in a new pastorate under the Revd Huw Llewelyn Jones. This lasted until 1992. A retired minister and local teacher, the late Revd John Erasmus Jones, generously offered his services to the chapel over many years. His widow, Elvira, is still a member. At the turn of the millennium, the Revd Dafydd H. Owen and the Revd Anthony Williams took charge of all the Presbyterian Church of Wales chapels in London, a responsibility now borne by the Revd Richard Brunt.

Tony Platt has done more than anyone to keep the Leytonstone doors open in recent years. He was a member of Jewin for many years before moving to Leytonstone in the mid-1990s. His father, T. R. Platt, was treasurer of the new buildings fund in the 1950s and 1960s, and Tony remembers coming with him to Leytonstone after the opening services in 1958. It was a time of great enthusiasm and confidence, boosted by the energy of the secretary, Dafydd Rees Owen, son of Oswald Rees Owen, and the treasurer, Jimmy James. But when they moved back to Wales in retirement, as so many London chapel people did, Tony took on their roles until the merger which created Eglwys-y-Drindod. Given Leytonstone's extensive assets, Tony says his job as treasurer 'is more akin to being a property manager!'.

Leytonstone's future is very uncertain, but Tony offers one encouraging signal: 'These days it is interesting that the majority of those who attend have found out about us on the internet.' The use of social media platforms – to promote awareness and reach out to people of all ages – has the potential to transform the situation for the Welsh chapels in London.

But will there be a Welsh chapel for the East Enders of the future?

On current form, sad to say, it's unlikely.

CHAPTER 9

ELFED'S KINGDOM

Few parts of London have changed as dramatically as the King's Cross district in recent decades. During the 1970s and 1980s, it was notorious as a centre of prostitution and drug abuse, hardly the kind of neighbourhood associated with respectable chapel people. After the war, this busy industrial area, dominated by the railway terminus and hundreds of working-class terraces in Camden and Islington, had gone into steep decline. But the rapid regeneration which started in the 1990s has propelled King's Cross into a new league. This is now the prestigious home of the Eurostar international rail service, and the site of King's Cross Central, the huge redevelopment to the north, with its hotels, restaurants, cultural venues, and residential accommodation.

A four-minute walk eastwards from King's Cross station, along the Pentonville Road, leads us to one of the biggest Welsh landmarks in London, the great Victorian rockpile of the Tabernacle, a Welsh Independent chapel sold to the Ethiopian Christian Fellowship Church in 2009. Its remaining members joined forces with Radnor Walk and Eastcastle Street chapels to form Eglwys Gymraeg Canol Llundain, the Welsh Church of Central London.

When people pass the distinctive building today – there is a better view of its scale and structure from King's Cross Road – it is worth remembering that during the first half of the twentieth century, the 'Welsh Tabernacle' (as it was usually called in the London press) was one of the most dynamic and powerful churches anywhere in the country. For many years, as membership numbers exceeded one thousand, its minister occupied a prominent place on the national stage. The Revd Howell Elvet Lewis (known universally by his bardic name, 'Elfed') was the supreme example of a pragmatic Welshman

The Revd H. Elvet Lewis, 'Elfed' (1860–1953)
© National Library of Wales

who thrived at the heart of the British establishment. King George VI made Elfed a Companion of Honour in 1948, in recognition of his 'outstanding achievements' as a poet and preacher.

Elfed was a man who added sparkle to so many aspects of London Welsh life in the twentieth century. He spent 36 years as minister of the Tabernacle, King's Cross, during which time it became one of the most prominent causes in the history of Welsh Nonconformist worship. Such was the minister's hold that the chapel was frequently referred to as 'Capel Elfed'. Tourists from Wales would add the Tabernacle to Buckingham Palace, Westminster Abbey, and the Houses of Parliament on their list of 'must-see' attractions. These days, a visit to the colossal Westfield shopping centre would be a safer bet.

No account of Welsh life in the capital would be complete without an expansive reference to Elfed's achievements. He was one of the giants of Liberal, Welsh-speaking Wales; a preacher, poet, hymnwriter, lecturer, author, archdruid, freemason, all-purpose bigwig and celebrity. He was one of the brightest stars of his generation, a preacher at ease in both Welsh and English, a polished littérateur, and a skilled networker with finely-tuned political antennae.

It would be quite wrong, however, to suggest that the story of King's Cross chapel was all about Elfed. Indeed, it could be argued that one of his successors did even more to sustain the cause. And it is certainly true that the foundations of the success he enjoyed were laid by others, in the middle of the previous century.

After much debate, some members of Borough chapel decided to rent

An artist's impression of King's Cross chapel (1889)
© National Library of Wales

a room in Snow Hill, Holborn, in September 1847. They were people who lived north of the Thames and wanted a far more convenient place to worship. This branch of Borough chapel was opened by the Revd John Thomas, Bwlchnewydd, later to become Dr John Thomas, Liverpool, one of the great Welsh Nonconformist leaders of the past two centuries. His prodigiously gifted brother, Dr Owen Thomas, would become minister of Jewin chapel a few years later.

The growing congregation soon moved to a bigger room in Neville's Court, an alleyway off Fetter Lane, the narrow street which snakes from Fleet Street to Holborn. This proved to be a useful move, as the members spotted a plot of land in nearby Bartlett's Passage which would easily accommodate a small chapel. It was bought for £700, and the foundation stone was laid on St David's Day in 1850.

Fetter Lane, mentioned in the city's records as early as the fourteenth century, was already known for its dissenting congregations. Oliver Cromwell's chaplain, Thomas Goodwin, had preached at Fetter Lane Independent Church between 1660 and 1680. The Moravians, a reforming Protestant sect that had come to England from Bohemia in the early-eighteenth century, opened a chapel there in 1738: the Fetter Lane Society met for prayer and fellowship, involving prominent Anglicans such as John Wesley, Charles Wesley, George Whitefield, and Howell Harris.

This, then, was the neighbourhood in which the Welsh Independents built Ebenezer, their new chapel in Bartlett's Passage, Fetter Lane, which opened on 1 December 1850. The total cost, including the land, was £3,000. The Revd Caleb Morris, a Welshman from Pembrokeshire, one of London's most popular preachers and veteran minister of Fetter Lane Independent Church, took part in the inaugural services, as did the Revd David Rees of Capel Als, Llanelli, one of the undisputed Welsh radicals of the age.

At around the same time, the congregation was formed into a new Independent cause, consisting of 90 members, under the leadership of the Revd David Davies of Borough. The church started life with a heavy debt of £2,000. He remained in charge until 1856, by which time the debt had been cut to £1,000 and the membership had risen to 140. He handed over to the Revd Owen Evans, Maentwrog, whose ministry, divided into two periods (1856–63 and 1881–1901), with spells in Wrexham and Llanbrynmair in between, would span six momentous decades.

View of Ebenezer Chapel in Bartlett's Passage, off Fetter Lane (J. Appleton, c.1890)
© London Metropolitan Archive

There are some wonderful accounts of Fetter Lane in *Hanes Eglwys y Tabernacl, King's Cross, Llundain 1847–1947* (1947), the chapel history edited by the Revd Llywelyn Williams. Mrs Wilfred Rowlands described it as 'a very pretty little chapel, with a decorated iron gallery, and seats for around 400 people who would fill it on Sunday evenings'. Mrs R. P. Jones praised the 'remarkably quiet location, near busy Holborn Circus, a convenient spot to meet friends on a Sunday'. She remembered the half-hour walk from her home (there were no buses) and the 'warm, friendly atmosphere' of the chapel. But it can't have been that friendly for the 'sinners' (non-members) who had to sit in the rearmost pews, closest to the exit, as she recalled.

It is hardly surprising that fundraising was a major activity. Tea meetings and excursions were all part of church life. This was before the time when such innocent pastimes were regarded by cranky ministers as frivolous or even sacrilegious. The expanding membership was drawn from a wide area which extended as far as Hornsey, Kentish Town and Westminster. Owen Evans left behind a thriving church with fewer debts when he moved, because of his family's health problems, to north Wales in 1863.

The period of stellar growth started under his mercurial successor, the Revd Rowland Williams, one of the great personalities of nineteenth-century Wales, better known by his weird bardic alias, 'Hwfa Môn': the clue lies in the name of the Anglesey village where he lived as a boy – Rhostrehwfa, Ynys Môn.

Let it be said right away that Hwfa (sounds not unlike the well-known vacuum cleaner) Môn was an appalling windbag. His interminable sermons broke all records, and it is a miracle that the congregation grew under his stewardship. Mrs Rowlands admitted that his pulsating performances were lost on younger listeners. But he was a very big character and enjoyed a terrific reputation as a champion poet. He won a long list of eisteddfod prizes, including the national chair and crown, and proved to be a powerful, reforming archdruid.

Hwfa was responsible for starting the literary society at Fetter Lane in 1876, which would be a success for over a century to come. Eminent speakers drew big crowds, and the society was praised for the valuable opening it gave young people to develop their public speaking skills or to perform as

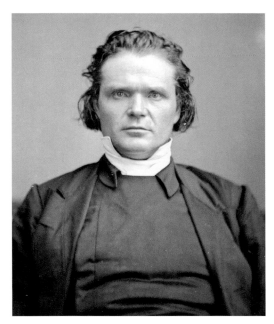

The Revd Rowland Williams, 'Hwfa Môn' (1823–1905)   The Revd Dr Owen Evans (1829–1920)
© National Library of Wales   © National Library of Wales

musicians and actors. Many prominent politicians, ministers, teachers, actors, and singers would pay tribute to the chapels for the early opportunities they were given.

Hwfa's fourteen-year ministry at Fetter Lane, which started in December 1867, was certainly eventful. The chapel debts were cleared, and the building was refurbished and extended at a cost of £2,200. The need for this work was outlined in a report in 1869: 'The chapel is well filled on Sunday evenings, and in the summer time the place becomes almost unbearably hot and oppressive… we must have a larger chapel, the health of our dear pastor and the comfort of the congregation demand it.' This, apparently, was an oblique reference to Hwfa's tendency to perspire torrentially during his theatricals. Mrs Rowlands gave a very funny account of the children's obsession with his high collar, which gradually became soaked in sweat and, at a climactic moment in the sermon, would collapse.

The musical tradition of the church, always a source of pride in the century to come, was established by a certain Joseph Parry, a student at the Royal Academy of Music between 1868 and 1871. The future famous Welsh composer did much to encourage the highest standards of congregational and choral singing. His harmonium organ later found its way to Woolwich chapel, and later still to the Welsh chapel in Slough.

By the time Hwfa Môn returned to Llanerchymedd, in his native Anglesey, in 1881, there were moves to recall the ever-popular Owen Evans to London. This was highly unusual: Welsh chapels rarely recalled a minister, even a very popular one, to avoid the risk of disappointment. But Owen Evans agreed, and was re-installed as minister in October of that year, when the membership stood at 329. It was a rather different Owen Evans who returned, a much more experienced and confident preacher, soon to be awarded a doctorate for his many publications on theology and biblical studies. His status was confirmed by his election to the chair of the Union of Welsh Independents in 1886.

Fetter Lane now entered a new phase: a report in 1887 noted the advantages of its central location, but underlined the need for 'a Commodious Central Tabernacle for the Welsh Independents of London'. The church had no debts, so it was free to explore all options. A search for suitable plots of land in central London drew a blank, until the London Congregational Union offered for sale a building in Pentonville Road.

The vacant chapel, built in 1854, had been known as Battle Bridge Congregational Chapel, and then Pentonville Road Chapel. It was built during a time of rapid expansion for the London Congregationalists (essentially the same denomination as the Welsh Independents) in this working-class area. The architect was Henry Hodge, and the cost of the building was a hefty £5,000. The church struggled to prosper, not least because of the heavy debt, and the congregation of Fetter Lane provided an ideal solution. They completed the purchase in 1889.

It is fair to say that King's Cross chapel, though imposing in size and form, was far more impressive inside than out. The building was conceived in a simple Gothic style, set at an awkward angle to the surrounding streets, its Pentonville Road side partly hidden by houses, its King's Cross Road flank more attractive and fully visible. Internally, it was a very different story, a prime example of Victorian Nonconformist chapel design, with a vast, wooden roof, high galleries with pews running around three sides, while the organ dominated the fourth, its pipes raked to allow light in from the rose window.

Interior of King's Cross chapel (1947)
© National Library of Wales

This, then, was the iconic building occupied by a Welsh Independent congregation from 1889 to 2006. It was bought for £4,000 and they spent another £3,000 on changes before they moved in. Fetter Lane was sold for £1,800, a rather disappointing sum, but it is worth noting that the entire debt was settled within eight years.

The opening services took place in September 1889, starring Dr Herber Evans of Caernarfon and Dr John Thomas of Liverpool, two of the biggest names in Welsh preaching, and the crowds were so big that hundreds stood in the street outside, unable to find seats in the chapel or the large vestry.

This was the start of a period of heart-stirring growth and activity for King's Cross. It became one of the biggest and busiest churches in London, known for the warmth of its welcome, the unstuffy nature of its community, the quality of its religious services and music, and the impressive range of meetings held throughout the week.

The half-century jubilee meetings were held in 1897, though it might be argued that 1900 would have been more accurate given the precise date (1850) when Fetter Lane was established as an independent cause. Dr Owen Evans was by now affectionately referred to as 'the Welsh bishop of London', and by others as 'a king among his people', so high was his standing in the capital. His reputation meant that he could get away with saying things which today's ministers would consider reckless. When he retired in 1901, he used his valedictory to rebuke those members whose attendance and contributions he found unsatisfactory. He even questioned their faith and their motives. These days, pastors understandably wish to avoid upsetting the few members still on the books.

The Revd Llywelyn Williams, writing in 1947, remarked that the twentieth century presented immense challenges to King's Cross and all the London Welsh chapels: just imagine his reflections on the situation today! In his day, London was growing ever busier, transport developments made King's Cross supremely accessible, and the chapel's membership would peak at a whopping 1,043 in 1931. But the lives of millions, King's Cross members among them, would be ruptured by two world wars, and by the economic hardship of the 1920s and 1930s.

This was the half-century dominated by Elfed, who arrived in April 1904 (after much persuasion, it seems) from Harecourt Congregational Church in north London. It seems incredible that this giant of Welsh culture was embarking on his first Welsh-language pastorate at the age of 44. All his previous churches in Buckley, Hull, Llanelli and Canonbury had been English-speaking. Much has been written about Elfed's apparent desire to be acceptable to the English. It has also been suggested that he was daunted by the challenge of taking on the Welsh-speaking citadel of King's Cross, a claim which seems laughable when we consider Elfed's magisterial authority and supreme gift as a preacher and public speaker.

Elfed was already a celebrated preacher-poet when he arrived at Harecourt in 1898. He had so dominated the National Eisteddfod in Wrexham in 1888 that it became known as 'Eisteddfod Elfed'. His free-verse poem 'Y Saboth yng Nghymru' won the crown, and his love poem 'Llyn y Morwynion' was widely acclaimed. He wrote dozens of popular hymns, including the patriotic 'Cofia'n gwlad, Benllywydd tirion', often referred to as the second national anthem of Wales. There are no fewer than 44 of his hymns in the current Welsh hymnal, *Caneuon Ffydd*, a number beaten by only one other, the incomparable William Williams, Pantycelyn.

He lived a remarkable life. This son of a farmhand, born in the hamlet of Blaen-y-coed, Carmarthenshire, rose to become one of the most prominent and respected Welshmen of his age. He is said to have learned the alphabet by studying the capital letters in his father's Bible. His parents sacrificed a great deal to send him to the grammar school at Newcastle Emlyn when he was fourteen. This was when he started to preach and became known as the 'boy preacher'. He excelled at Carmarthen Presbyterian College, where he won every prize going, and in 1880 accepted an invitation to become minister of St John's English Congregational Church, Buckley, Flintshire. Given the nature of his upbringing in the depths of rural Carmarthenshire, the decision to take charge of an English-speaking church puzzled many. Four years later, he left Wales and accepted a call to Fish Street Congregational Church, Hull. It is possible that immersion in a very English world may have triggered his desire to embrace Wales and Welsh culture more fully: this is when his literary skills were sharpened, and the eisteddfod prizes started to pile up.

After his period in Hull, Elfed spent seven years at Park Congregational Church, Llanelli, winning the bardic chair at the National Eisteddfod of 1894, and boosting his status as a literary man. There are thrilling accounts of his triumphant return to Llanelli as the bands and crowds greeted him at the railway station. He published *Caniadau Elfed*, and three years later *Plannu Coed*, a popular volume of sermons. He left Llanelli for London in 1898, after accepting a call from Harecourt, a church famous for its ancient connections with Cromwell.

But the big move came in 1904 when Elfed was prevailed upon to become minister of the Tabernacle, King's Cross. This would be his powerbase until 1940 when he moved to Cardiff. His contribution to Wales and Welsh culture was immense, and included a period as archdruid. Among other important positions he held were: chairman of the Congregational Union of England and Wales; chairman of the Free Church Council of England; chairman of the Union of Welsh Independents, and chairman of the London Missionary Society. He was also an eager freemason, having been a founder member of London's Dewi Sant Lodge in 1925.

His sermons and devotional poems, full of rich imagery, influenced a generation of Welsh preachers. It comes as no surprise that Elfed's church was chosen for the first ever broadcast of a religious service in Welsh on St David's Day, 1925. It was the first of many. Elfed was a seductive communicator, and to listen to archive recordings of his sermons is to be charmed and mesmerised. He died in January 1953, at the age of 93, and his ashes were buried at Blaen-y-coed.

It has been suggested that Elfed's ministry at King's Cross was divided into three periods: the age of revival and growth in the early years of the century; the fallow years after the First World War; and the dynamic decade of the 1930s, when thousands left the economic hardship of south Wales, converging on London, relying on the chapel network in the search for jobs and accommodation.

Elfed managed to resist the more excitable effects of the revival of 1904–5, and this might account for the fact that King's Cross held on to a respectable percentage of the new members who came. Many other churches, especially in south Wales, experienced a tide which ebbed rather quickly after the initial rise.

On the eve of the First World War, membership was heading for 800, and the church was in a strong position. More than a hundred of the chapel's young men and women joined the armed forces and nursing units, while the minister led a network of workers providing support and comfort (including food and accommodation) to those in need. Elfed instigated a 'silent covenant', urging members to pray every evening (between 7 and 8 o'clock) for peace and understanding among the nations of the world.

The years following the war, such a difficult period for many of the churches in Wales, were years of growth and expansion in London. From the early 1920s, an army of thousands of Welsh men and women were driven from home by high unemployment and poverty. London (and other English cities, especially Liverpool, Bristol, Manchester and Birmingham) offered unmatched opportunities.

Caradoc Evans, in *Nothing to Pay* (1930), his biting satire on the London Welsh scene, tears into Amos Morgan, the chapel-going draper's assistant whose parsimony and greed reach epic levels. But Amos, despite his many unappealing traits, nonetheless represents the impressive work ethic of so many

Welsh people who came to London with nothing and worked interminably to make something of their lives. Caradoc Evans, in all his toxic self-hatred, can never disguise that.

This, then, was the period in which the chapels emerged as the most important city-wide network for the London Welsh. Faith and worship were still the main business, naturally, but they became job centres, welfare centres, and social centres. They provided a network of contacts and support. It is no exaggeration to say that without the chapels, many of the young Welsh arriving in London would have been homeless and jobless. These services are conveniently forgotten by those determined to dismiss the chapels as mean, grim places. The truth is that the chapel network, acting on the best Christian principles, reached out to thousands in need, and helped them. That help was not confined to the Welsh community: the local poor and homeless in London, and wartime refugees from other countries, all received generous support from the chapels.

One of the high points of Elfed's period at King's Cross was the decision to host the annual meeting of the Union of Welsh Independents in London in 1937. This involved a major series of public meetings and services: the crowds

Elfed and officers of the 1937 annual meeting of the Union of Welsh Independents ('JR' is second from left, back row)
© National Library of Wales

were so big that Whitefield's Tabernacle in Tottenham Court Road was borrowed for the main sessions. King's Cross was far too small! Elfed and his team, including the indefatigable J. R. Thomas, the chapel secretary, worked hard to make the event a success. Given the strength of all this activity, it is no surprise that three new churches were established during the 1930s, at Harrow, Luton and Slough.

John Rowland Thomas is without question a commanding presence in the 250-year story of the London Welsh chapels. He was a world-famous specialist in silk (first at Harrods, then as chief silk buyer and, later, a director of the John Lewis Partnership) and recognised as a first-rate businessman. But he also achieved truly great things in the world of the London Welsh. He was a member of King's Cross from 1902 to 1965, a deacon from 1921, and chapel secretary from 1940 to 1953. He edited the chapel's quarterly newsletter, *Lamp y Tabernacl*, from its launch in 1932, and he instigated the campaign to build more chapels in the London suburbs.

He was, let it be said, the original 'JR' (forget Larry Hagman in *Dallas*) and without his support, the cause in Harrow would not have opened in 1937. Under his leadership, the new church quickly grew to 200 members. His national status was recognised by his election as president of the Union of Welsh Independents in 1949. He generously promoted countless Welsh causes, including Urdd Gobaith Cymru, the Welsh League of Youth.

One minister described JR's home, 'Y Nant', in Dollis Hill, as 'an open door for a host of Welsh people, especially ministers of the Gospel'. One of his three capable daughters, Morfudd, married the first minister of Harrow, the Revd J. Idris Jenkins. Morfudd, who collaborated closely with Meurig Owen in researching the story of London's chapels, left a valuable collection of notes which have been an important source for this book.

Morfudd Jenkins explained that while King's Cross and other London chapels had managed to come through the First World War, and in most cases had rebuilt and thrived, they found the seismic changes of the Second World War too much to overcome. Worship in London during the war was described by one minister as 'an act of courage in a city where Sundays were not special, and where the bombing was merciless'. The chapel was damaged in several raids, but for a long period, King's Cross was the only Welsh chapel holding Sunday evening services during the war. The members of Barrett's

Grove chapel, in north London, joined King's Cross in 1941 when their own chapel was closed because of bomb damage.

Would anyone be able to fill the great Elfed's shoes? That was the biggest question at the end of the war. The awkward answer came soon enough: his successor did not stay long enough for people to form a view. The Revd Llywelyn Williams, a native of Llanelli, one of the rising stars of the denomination, was one of four very talented children, including his sister, Olwen, who pioneered Welsh-medium education as headteacher of Ysgol Dewi Sant, Llanelli. The family were all members of Capel Als, one of the leading Nonconformist causes in Wales. He was ordained in Bethesda, Arfon, and moved after six years to an English church in Abertillery, an industrial town where the minister felt very much at home, and to which he would return some years later in rather unexpected circumstances.

In a whirl of post-war elation, Llywelyn Williams was installed as minister of King's Cross in January 1946 and, supported by Elsie, his accomplished wife, set to work immediately on rebuilding. More than 120 members returned from the armed forces, boosting the membership to more than 700, with an average of 50 new members joining annually between 1945 and 1950. Morfudd Jenkins, writing in *Capel Elfed* (1989), describes it as a

The Revd Llywelyn Williams and elders of King's Cross (1947)
© National Library of Wales

'young church, with an active Sunday school, and high attendance on Sunday evenings', literary meetings and theatre visits during the week, and plenty of fun at the chapel's sports ground in Cricklewood at weekends.

The minister took over the editorship of *Lamp y Tabernacl*, one of the most successful publications of its kind, appearing without fail for six decades until the chapel closed. *Lamp y Tabernacl* had been an important means of communicating with members (including soldiers and nurses) throughout the war. It was now filled with notices of meetings and events, and many forthcoming weddings: the chapels were the prime matchmaking centres of the London Welsh.

This was such a stimulating time to be a member of the capital's Welsh chapels: membership was growing, new ministers were keen to come to London, cooperation between chapels was effective, and joint events were remarkably well attended. The King's Cross annual hymn-singing festival on Good Friday was an evident highlight, the children's eisteddfod was a hugely competitive affair, and the all-London gymanfa ganu at Westminster Chapel (where the noted evangelical preacher Dr Martyn Lloyd-Jones held sway) was attended by up to 2,000 people.

King's Cross celebrated its centenary in September 1947 (three years early, as previously hinted) with a range of special services starring Elfed and other leading figures. Every hymn and tune sung at these services had a King's Cross link: words by Elfed, Hwfa Môn, Eliza Evans and Ben Davies, and tunes by Joseph Parry, W. J. Evans and David Richards.

The musical tradition of the chapel, with its grand concerts, oratorios, and congregational singing, was always praised. The organist and composer, David Richards ARCO, served heroically for nearly half a century, from 1905 to 1950. He was one of the best-known accompanists of his day, a gifted musician with a swaggering flair for making events special. He was succeeded by the equally-gifted Cyril Anthony FRCO, a musician who dominated the London Welsh scene for decades and played at the Albert Hall and Westminster Chapel festivals. His deputy was Dr Dewi Lewis FRCO, who served the chapel for many years before moving to Cardiff in retirement. This line-up of highly-qualified organists, spanning an entire century, had to be one of the most impressive of any Welsh chapel. The three-manual Norman and Beard organ, installed in 1904 and rebuilt in 1970, when the console was moved from the gallery to ground level, was a superb instrument which greatly enhanced the worshipper's experience.

But what of the enigmatic Llywelyn Williams? He seemed destined for a long, distinguished ministry at King's Cross, but shocked and dismayed the church in November 1950 by announcing his candidacy in a parliamentary by-election. He became Labour MP for Abertillery, resigning his pastorate barely five years after he'd started. The members were deeply disappointed; some of them clearly felt let down by his decision, and could not understand how a man with such a powerful sense of Christian mission could opt for a new career. They had lost an excellent preacher, pastor and leader. But the voters of Abertillery gained a hard-working MP, devoted to the causes of social justice and world peace. He was an outstanding public speaker and delivered some memorable speeches in the House of Commons. After fifteen years in parliament, he died suddenly in 1965 at the relatively young age of 53.

By the time of Llywelyn Williams's death, his successor had already spent fourteen years at King's Cross. The Revd Dr W. T. Owen arrived from Swansea in October 1951, at the start of a hugely successful 30-year ministry. It could certainly be argued that his leadership of the church, in a much more challenging period than Elfed's, was the most impressive in the King's Cross story. Managing gradual decline is much more difficult than managing wild success.

Dr Owen inherited an active, lively church, and realised in the first weeks that regular visits to his 650 members across London would be impossible. He tried to prioritise hospital visits, youth work and preparation for Sunday sermons. It was a very full week. His elders were deputed to look after their own 'sections' of London, drawing the minister's attention to those members in need.

There were many high points during his three decades in charge: Dr Owen listed many events in *Capel Elfed*, including Coronation services in 1953, several BBC radio and television broadcasts recorded at King's Cross, events to raise significant funds for the Welsh chapels in Luton and Harrow, installing a stained glass window in memory of Elfed, officiating at the funeral of Sir Rhys Hopkin Morris KC MP, the respected politician and broadcast executive who died in 1956, and welcoming the Revd Llywelyn Williams

Detail of Elfed's memorial window at King's Cross
© Rita Clark

back to preach at King's Cross, after much persuasion, in 1957. Dr Owen wrote in the warmest terms about his friendship with his predecessor.

By the end of his first decade, Dr Owen reflected on the fact that membership had fallen by more than a hundred since his arrival, despite the active and healthy life of the church. His analysis was typically perceptive and insightful:

> *Migration from Wales to London was falling from year to year, and those who came tended to represent the spiritual condition of Wales. It was this realisation which encouraged some of us to try to unite Radnor Walk, Borough and King's Cross, in the belief that unity based on relative strength would be better than uniting in weakness… but at that time, attachment to the local chapel was too strong for us to succeed.*

Underlining the trend, the first post-war chapel closures were taking place: the small chapel in Battersea Rise, in south London, closed in 1960, and the chapels in Woolwich and Slough needed extra help.

But the 1960s also brought days of happiness and celebration. One of the King's Cross members, the author and poet, Caradog Prichard, won the chair at the 1962 National Eisteddfod in Llanelli, cementing his reputation as one of the most gifted writers of his generation. He used his long night-shifts as a *Daily Telegraph* journalist to write a range of works, including his great novel

Un Nos Ola Leuad (1961). Prichard's Llanelli bardic chair is on display at the London Welsh Centre in Gray's Inn Road.

There were other prominent public figures on the membership list during that time. Dr Ben G. Jones was a solicitor and Liberal politician who would serve as chairman of the Council on the Welsh Language, president of the Honourable Society of Cymmrodorion, a member of the BBC General Advisory Council of Great Britain, and vice-president of the University College of Wales, Aberystwyth.

Another who would serve on the Council on the Welsh Language was Emrys Evans, the King's Cross treasurer for a period, and one of the great Welsh philanthropists and networkers of his day. 'Emrys y Midland Bank' worked hard for many charities, and his commitment led to his appointments as treasurer and president of the Union of Welsh Independents. He and the minister, Dr Owen, were great Spurs supporters and attended most home games together on Saturday afternoons. They would park outside Wil Harris's dairy in Lordship Lane (near the White Hart Lane stadium) and after the match would spend hours chatting and enjoying Annie Harris's famously good apple tart and 'teisen lap'. The Harris family were stalwarts of King's Cross chapel.

Arthur Rocyn-Jones was an eminent orthopaedic surgeon who would rush from his Harley Street consulting rooms on a Wednesday evening to attend the prayer meeting at King's Cross. Dr Idris Jones, after a brilliant academic career as a chemist, served as director-general of research for the National Coal Board. He was a Welsh international rugby player and a great supporter of London Welsh organisations. His brother, Lord Elwyn-Jones, became Lord Chancellor in the Labour government of 1974–9.

There were many more, whose names were less prominent, who

The Revd Dr W. T. Owen (1914–2001)
© National Library of Wales

contributed so much to the success of King's Cross. Dr Owen mentions them in *Capel Elfed*, the chapel history he edited in 1989, and pays particular attention to the work of the many women whose efforts enriched all areas of chapel life. This was true of all the Welsh chapels. It is a fact that the chapels were rather slow (as was the rest of society) to apply principles of equality: very few women were elected to the elders' 'big seat', or indeed to hold senior posts. But it is vital to underline the part women played in keeping many causes open. This was especially true in the decades after the war, when membership started to fall and many London Welsh people returned to Wales to enjoy their retirement.

Mrs Ann Thomas was singled out by Dr Owen for special praise. She and her husband, Glynne, an elder since 1934, were mainstays of the cause at King's Cross for many years until they moved to Llwyngwril, near Barmouth, in the late 1960s. They were part of a great exodus between 1960 and 1980. Dr Owen lamented the failure to keep officers in post for sustained periods. The other stalwarts at that time included the hard-working secretary, John Williams, and his wife, Gwen. John seemed to have limitless supplies of energy, especially in the inter-chapels eisteddfodau. Gwilym Parry Griffiths also did valuable work with young people, and his reminiscences about life in his parents' dairy business in Southgate Road were a fascinating insight into a lost world. At the end of 1970, membership had fallen sharply to 380. The trend was clear, but too many chapel members lacked the vision, the will, and the courage to embrace change. This failure would carry a deadly price in the years to come.

Retirement wasn't the only reason for moving to Wales: Emrys Evans and his family left London in 1972 when he accepted a new post with the Midland Bank. His departure was certainly a blow for the minister, but also for King's Cross. He had first known the chapel as a young Royal Navy radio operator passing through London during the war, but wasn't to become a member until 1957. His introduction to *Capel Elfed* exudes warmth and gratitude: he celebrates the friendliness of King's Cross, the generosity of its welcome, the extraordinary work of the chapel's women, the high quality of its services and of its music.

But Emrys Evans makes one curious assertion which many of today's London Welsh would question:

The number of members has decreased for reasons we should welcome, as young
Welsh people are no longer obliged to come to London to be educated and employed.

With respect to Emrys, that assertion is surely wrong in several ways. London is still the biggest employment magnet in the United Kingdom, and its superb range of higher education institutions is the envy of many of the world's greatest cities. The attraction is as powerful as ever, even if the flow of people has dwindled. And while some Welsh people certainly felt 'obliged' to head for London, many more were positively keen to embrace the infinite opportunities it offered.

The reasons for the decrease in chapel membership could certainly be linked to a reduced flow, but far more relevant was the changing attitude of society to faith, values, and organised worship. Tied in with this, during the post-war period, was the vulnerable status of the Welsh language in public life. Radical Welsh politicians, Aneurin Bevan among them, were motivated by the urgent need to improve health and welfare provision for working people. This was a much bigger priority than protecting aspects of Welsh culture, or giving Welsh problems more attention at Westminster.

Throughout the 1940s and 1950s, those fighting for equal rights for Welsh speakers found themselves openly ridiculed. The Revd Dr Leonard Hugh, minister of the Welsh chapel in Woolwich, had lived in the Rhondda in the 1940s. Appalled by the reluctance of Welsh speakers to use their native language, he had launched his own movement, *Yr Urdd Siarad Cymraeg* ('The League of Welsh Speakers'), to encourage its use. He loved to tell the story of his failed attempt to buy a rail ticket at Pontypridd station: the ticket office was manned by a Welsh-speaking chapel elder from Porth, who steadfastly refused to use Welsh at work (it wasn't 'proper'), and rejected Dr Hugh's attempts to buy a 'tocyn', but he happily spoke Welsh elsewhere.

The Welsh language was widely seen as an emblem of decay, and so were its main patrons, the Nonconformist chapels. They were a terminally unfashionable couple in the bright lights of the swinging 1960s. Social commentators noted that while society and youth had raced ahead, trashing old notions of respect and deference, most chapels had stayed still, clueless and obsolete.

These, then, were the reasons why membership numbers were decreasing, at King's Cross and elsewhere. Young Welsh people were still coming to London, and while some of them were making a dutiful beeline for the chapels, many more were giving them a wide berth. An ageing membership, no longer enlivened by a regular injection of younger company, found it very difficult to cope.

But cope they did, and this book was written partly in tribute to the hard-working, committed, loyal bands of members who have ensured that Londoners can still access Welsh-language religious services in the Nonconformist tradition.

Dr W. T. Owen and his wife, Janet, retired in 1981, celebrating their long and happy ministry at King's Cross, but refusing to hide from the big challenges facing the London Welsh chapels. In late 1979, Dr Owen had urged Borough and Radnor Walk chapels to form a joint pastorate with King's Cross, but his appeal had been unsuccessful. The result was that King's Cross decided to call its own minister to succeed Dr Owen: the Revd Ieuan Davies,

of Capel Mair, Cardigan, arrived in May 1984, much to everyone's delight. He was one of the most popular preachers in Wales, a gifted communicator and a friendly, hard-working pastor.

Ieuan Davies explained in his entertaining autobiography *Trwy Lygaid Tymblwr – A Gweinidog!* (2007) that the 'call' to King's Cross had been too tempting to resist. There were many links, some close to home: his mother had been in domestic

Interior of King's Cross chapel in the 1990s
© Rita Clark

service in London as a young woman, and had worshipped at the Tabernacle. The Davies family settled in quickly, enjoying the life of a busy church with 170 members on the books. The minister loved London life, taking full advantage of sporting fixtures and grand social events at The Savoy, where the London Welsh held their annual St David's Day dinner. He was supported by some exceptionally generous officers and members, including Hywel Thomas, Dr Eleri Rowlands (a daughter of Dr W. T. Owen), Sir Maldwyn Thomas, Marian Howell, Dewi and Mair Abel, and Jenkin ('Sianco') Davies. Eluned and Russell Jones were married by Dr Owen at King's Cross in 1960, and their daughters, Catherine and Susan, were christened by him. Eluned, originally from Maesteg, served the church loyally from her arrival in 1949. And there must be a special mention for another Maesteg woman, Catherine Davies, one of the original suffragettes who terrorised Lloyd George in the campaign to secure democratic rights for women. There were many others who added lustre to the King's Cross story.

But within two years, the minister and his wife informed the church that the family was moving to Cardiff, to secure Welsh-medium schooling for their daughters. There was understandable concern among the officers: keeping in touch with a London-wide congregation was already difficult, but doing so from Cardiff would be well-nigh impossible. The fears, it seems, were unfounded. The ministry continued to work smoothly until 1989 when Ieuan Davies accepted an invitation to become minister of Minny Street, Cardiff.

The 'what if?' conversation has been repeated hundreds of times in the context of the London Welsh chapels. 'What if' Borough and Radnor Walk had agreed to unite with King's Cross in the early 1980s? 'What if' the discussions and consultation papers on uniting several causes in the 1970s had led to concrete action? We shall never know. But we can say with certainty that if the Revd D. Gwylfa Evans had not agreed to take charge of King's Cross in 1998, the chapel would have closed long before 2006, when the final service took place.

When Gwylfa Evans and his wife, Buddug, came to Harrow in 1978, they could never have imagined the roller-coaster ride of the four decades to come. It is no exaggeration to say that Gwylfa has probably shouldered a bigger burden than most of the ministers mentioned in this book: his ministry

Annual dinner of the London Cardiganshire Society at the Savoy Hotel (1925)
© National Library of Wales

in Harrow spanned 34 years (1978–2012); he spent 23 years in charge of Radnor Walk (1983–2006); he looked after the Tabernacle, King's Cross, for eight years (1998–2006); and he was minister of the Borough for nine years (1998–2007). And all the while, he served the other London Welsh chapels when his diary allowed. He continues to do so in retirement. This is a prodigious record of service which deserves the highest recognition.

Despite healthy finances (there was steady rental income from various groups using the building), the decision was made to move from King's Cross, sell the building, and unite the cause with Radnor Walk and Eastcastle Street. The base for the new church would be the Welsh Baptist chapel near Oxford Circus. The final service at King's Cross took place on 22 October 2006, but the building wasn't sold until May 2009.

It is good to note that the chapel is still a centre of worship for the Ethiopian Christian Fellowship Church: to see the refurbished building today, with its pristine stonework, is to admire the sacrifice and endeavour of the Welsh in Victorian London.

To my great delight, I was able to visit the chapel a few months before the last service, as we filmed a BBC television series on the history of the Welsh in London. The building had clearly seen better days, but to stand in Elfed's pulpit, surveying the radiating expanse of pews, raising my eyes to the vast, hammerbeam roof, was a truly haunting experience.

It is good to report that the spirit and tradition of Capel Elfed are still very much alive in the Welsh Church of Central London.

CHAPTER 10

A DAIRY DISPUTE?

The opening scene of one of my favourite television dramas includes the briefest glimpse of the most eye-catching Welsh building in London. The camera pans across Cambridge Circus, capturing perfectly the grimy city of the late 1970s, as John le Carré's brilliant *Tinker, Tailor, Soldier, Spy* unfolds. Look carefully and there, in the background, is the dark, bewitching form of the Welsh chapel on Charing Cross Road. The building is hemmed in by banks and offices, but the octagonal dome rises triumphantly above the neighbouring rooftops.

A walk along Charing Cross Road today will reveal that in the three decades since the chapel closed, the exterior has changed very little. Its Grade II listing has no doubt helped. The interior, despite listed status, is a rather different story, reflecting the building's brutal transitions from a centre of worship, to a nightclub, to an all-day bar, and more recently to a centre for the performing arts. The arts charity, Stone Nest, backed by a Ukrainian philanthropist, is restoring the building to a high standard, ready for use as a location for 'experimental, unexpected and daring artistic practice across a diverse range of dance, theatre, music, video and performance art'.

Ken Kyffin, the chapel's former secretary, joined me on a visit in early 2014. We met the Stone Nest team and were impressed by their interest in the history of the building, and their sensitivity in devising the new spaces. If it works as planned, this could be one of the best examples of a chapel conversion anywhere in the United Kingdom. The original chapel design, by the English architect, James Cubitt, incorporated an airy, square, central place of worship, flanked by great arches: its cruciform layout, a grand design in what experts variously call 'late Norman' or 'English Romanesque' style, was light years away

Artist's impression of Charing Cross
Road chapel (1888)
© National Library of Wales

from the traditional styles of Victorian chapels. There was no other Welsh chapel like it – anywhere – and it is good that the building can still be seen and appreciated in its almost-original form.

Gwynne Pickering, a lifelong member of Charing Cross, was christened there and elected an elder many years later. He gave an informative talk at Jewin, in March 2003, on the man whose name was somehow overlooked in the official chapel history published in 1949. James Cubitt, the son of a Baptist minister, established a reputation as a leading designer of Nonconformist places of worship, including the Grade I-listed Union Chapel, Islington.

At Charing Cross, Cubitt designed something rather special, as Gwynne Pickering explained:

The worshipper steps in from a busy road, under a deep arch at the building's side, turns right and at once stands in another world of square Gothic drama, the central space massed under a great lantern. Two sides of the ground floor have no windows. At gallery level there are windows on two sides. Beneath the dome there are numerous windows casting a flood down into the middle of the chapel. Around the corner, at 136 Shaftesbury Avenue, the official chapel address, is a four-storey gabled imitation of a Bruges house, high and narrow, which houses the library and many other rooms.

Interior of Charing
Cross chapel in the
1960s
© Tudor Williams

Tom and Gwenllian Davies moved into the house as caretakers during the Second World War. It was a very brave decision to come to London when so many were fleeing the German attacks. Their daughter, Enid, was a schoolgirl at the time:

If there was one word to describe the chapel house, it was 'hectic'. Ministers, elders, members, visitors from Wales – everyone ringing the doorbell at all hours. It never stopped. The family needed its own signal, so we rang the bell three times, very quickly. That was my way in! It was very different to a chapel house in Wales. We were right opposite the Palace Theatre. Very busy! The house was huge, several floors including an attic and cellar. We lived in the caretaker's accommodation on the third floor. There was a minister's room, classrooms, meeting rooms and a library on other floors. The library was open all hours, it was used by people to write letters home to Wales, and the address was also used for receiving letters from home. We settled in very quickly, despite the 'doodlebug' flying bombs which destroyed neighbouring buildings. There was terrible damage across London.

As Enid explained, one of the first things that struck the visitor – and still does today – is the central location of the building, right in the heart of London's West End and its busy theatreland. It is less than a minute's walk from Leicester Square underground station, heading north towards Cambridge Circus. An important point to note is that 'Charing Cross' (as it was always misleadingly known) was nowhere near Charing Cross railway station. There are many stories of visitors wandering near the station looking in vain for a Welsh chapel. They needed to head instead for Charing Cross Road, the traffic-choked route which leads from Trafalgar Square to Tottenham Court Road.

During the first four decades of the twentieth century, until the eve of the Second World War, Charing Cross drew bigger congregations on Sunday evenings than any other London Welsh chapel. The London-wide attendance survey conducted by R. Mudie Smith in 1902–3, published in *The Religious Life of London* (1904), recorded a congregation of 623 on a Sunday evening in Charing Cross. King's Cross was next, with 570, and Eastcastle Street followed with 434. Jewin, with 307, drew less than half the congregation of Charing Cross. These are truly remarkable figures, and yet they account for just a fraction of the total number attending the 30 or so Welsh-speaking causes in London at that time.

Fairly or unfairly, Charing Cross was seen as the 'fashionable' chapel. Its minister, the Revd Peter Hughes Griffiths, was a national celebrity in Wales, and a prominent player on the London Welsh stage. The congregation included an unusually high percentage of parliamentarians, lawyers, doctors, civil servants, businessmen and teachers. The chapel was also hugely popular with young Welsh men and women who worked (and often lived) in central London. Charing Cross was a West End chapel in more ways than one: it was also a very effective Welsh marriage bureau – the Charing Cross tennis club in Finchley was said to be a matchmaking centre par excellence.

Despite the decades of razzle-dazzle, the overcrowded pews, the celebrity minister, the impressive list of societies and meetings, not to mention the inevitable parade of fur coats and new hats, the Charing Cross story ended more sadly than most. It became the first Welsh chapel in central London to close its doors, after a painful, protracted process. The last service was held in June 1982, and the chapel was eventually sold in March 1985 for £1 million (a record for a Welsh chapel at that time) to an American nightclub owner.

The man who locked the doors for the last time, handing over the chapel keys to the estate agent, was Ken Kyffin:

The feeling was not merely one of leaving a building and moving to a new address. It was more akin to abandoning a proud ship, sinking with the loss of countless irreplaceable treasures amassed during the course of a long and arduous voyage. A farewell to a way of life.

That, then, was the end of a century of Welsh worship in Charing Cross Road. James Cubitt's building had opened in 1888, but the history of Charing Cross started 40 years earlier, according to the official history published to mark the centenary, *Y Ganrif Gyntaf* (1951), written by the Revd E. Gwyn Evans. The origins might well have been earlier than 1847, as we shall see.

Most of the original members came from Jewin, where several disputes had rocked the cause during the early-nineteenth century. The controversies surrounding Edward Jones had alienated many; the dispute over Catholic emancipation in 1828–9 had caused great turbulence; and the appalling 'Deddf Elias' ('Elias's Law'), which discriminated against those who worked on Sundays, produced a decade of bitter division.

The main victims of Elias's Law were the dairy workers. Their numbers were growing in the mid-nineteenth century, a trend which made Elias's initiative even more perplexing. It has been suggested that the result of this move against the dairy workers was ten years of misery, a mini-exodus from Jewin, and the formation of a breakaway cause in central London. Even in the rigid theological context of the day, it was a very counterproductive move… for Jewin, that is. It could also be argued that in sowing the seeds of a new cause, Elias's hard line turned out to be abundantly beneficial.

Some accounts of the story of Charing Cross claim that this 'dairy dispute' was the main reason a group of people left Jewin in 1847, and started holding religious meetings in a rented room above a stable owned by the grocers, Nurdin & Peacock, in Wells Street, not far from Oxford Circus. The campaign to establish a new church in the West End was led by Dr Edward Richards, a Jewin elder since 1844, but he was opposed by many at Jewin who

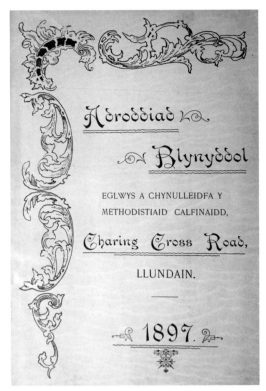

feared the consequences for their own cause. The breakaway group carried on regardless, and rented an old chapel in Grafton Street. The ensuing row was eventually settled by the denominational authorities, who found in favour of Dr Richards and a group of 67 members. Jewin was forced to admit defeat in August 1849, and within months would lose a similar case in north London. The 'mother' was notoriously reluctant to allow the 'children' their freedom.

The location of the chapel – Grafton Street – would turn out to be highly significant. This was not the plush, desirable Grafton Street which we find today near Berkeley Square. This was the old Grafton Street, which led through the area now called Chinatown, meeting West Street and Moor Street at the location of today's Cambridge Circus. In other words, old Grafton Street (which was demolished to make way for Shaftesbury Avenue and Charing Cross Road) passed right through the site where Charing Cross chapel would eventually be built.

So we can report that a new Welsh Methodist cause started in November 1849, in an old chapel in Grafton Street, and the origins of that cause lay in a 'dairy dispute'.

Can we really be that confident?

The waters are somewhat muddied by a few references to earlier religious meetings in the West End. J. W. Jones, who served for decades as secretary of the *cyfarfod misol* ('monthly meeting', or governing body of the Welsh Calvinistic Methodists in London), mentions services being held on Sunday afternoons in 1844 in Denmark Street, a narrow lane leading off the northern half of Charing Cross Road.

There is an even earlier reference: the Revd William Evans visited London for two months in 1831, preaching in 'Jewin, the Cambrian or Denmark

Street almost every week', according to his biography, *Cofiant y Parchg William Evans, Tonyrefail* (1892). This is a significant find, as Gwyn Evans underlined in his booklet. He added that a reference to the Revd John Jones, Talysarn, preaching in 1828 in 'the only' Welsh chapel in London (Jewin Crescent) suggested that worship in Denmark Street must have started between 1828 and 1831. The implication is clear: this would have been before the 'dairy dispute' erupted at Jewin, thus demolishing the accepted narrative about the origins of Charing Cross.

Indeed, it now seems increasingly clear that Dr Richards was motivated by the natural desire to expand, to provide a new place of worship for the increasing numbers of people living and working in central and west London. The dairy issue may well have played a part, but promoting growth was surely the main factor.

Denmark Street certainly qualifies as a West End location. Might it be possible to demonstrate continuity between Denmark Street and Wells Street, thus making a case for changing the primary dates (1849–1982) for Charing Cross? Yes, it might.

Richard Williams, writing in 1900, revealed how he had joined the cause at Denmark Street in July 1846. He described the meetings held in a 'small, run-down room, behind one of the houses, reached by a narrow passage', where he would attend 'a sermon on Sunday afternoon, a church meeting on Wednesday evening, and a prayer meeting on Friday evening'. It seems the room was not available on Sunday afternoons, which explains the decision to rent the room in Wells Street for Sunday school. It was not an ideal location (because of the stables) so they moved to a rented room in a coffee shop in Ryder's Court, at the north-east corner of Leicester Square.

So the evidence suggests that Denmark Street was being used from around 1831; it was still in use when Wells Street was rented in 1847; and it disappeared from the records after the move to Grafton Street. It seems entirely reasonable to assert, therefore, that the Charing Cross story started 'around 1831', though the new church was not formally established until 1849. After all, Jewin has always claimed 'around 1774' as its beginning, despite the fact that the church was not formed until at least 1785.

The chapel in Grafton Street had an interesting history: it belonged originally to a French Huguenot congregation (they called the chapel 'La

Grafton Street chapel, left of Grafton House (1880)
© London Metropolitan Archive

Charenton'); it was rebuilt around 1743 and used by a congregation of Particular and other Baptists; the Welsh Calvinistic Methodists had moved in by 1849; the records say it was acquired by the Metropolitan Board of Works for demolition between 1879 and 1883, long after the Welsh Methodists had left.

The chapel stood next to the old town house of the Dukes of Grafton, but forget any notions of grandeur. It backed on to a slaughterhouse and meat market, and to add to the hubbub, a street market was held outside on Sunday mornings. The location was said by one member to be 'less than favourable, but nonetheless good to have at the time'.

No wonder they wasted no time in finding a more suitable home. The new cause was growing, with 135 members by 1853, led by Morgan Jones (who founded a very successful building firm), and Richard Williams (whose son, Sir Howell J. Williams, would show exceptional generosity to the London Welsh community). They found a promising site within a few minutes' walk from Grafton Street.

They bought 9 Nassau Street, a town house with a stable and back yard, where they built a new chapel, accessed by a 'dark tunnel' (according to one report) on the right-hand side of the house. The property and building work cost £5,000. The chapel was opened in March 1856.

Nassau Street, like Grafton Street, had its practical issues. The tunnel was a favourite haunt of local youths who caused endless trouble during services. It became necessary to get a policeman to guard the doorway. The chapel was built on top of a wine cellar which belonged to the Horse and Dolphin (an ancient coaching inn nearby), and the fumes from the cellar became a very familiar feature of services at Nassau Street.

The name 'Nassau Street' disappeared in the late-nineteenth century when Shaftesbury Avenue was built, but the road still exists and is called Gerrard Place. The famous New World Chinese restaurant now occupies the site where Nassau Street chapel stood. The Horse and Dolphin yard is still there, behind the restaurant, and the only other reminder of the past is Nassau House, the block of flats around the corner on Shaftesbury Avenue.

A new chapel in Shirland Road, Paddington, in 1858, was formed entirely of Nassau Street members, but in 1863 there were still 277 members on the books in the West End. They included some influential people: William Davies ('Mynorydd') would serve as precentor for half a century; Thomas Richards, a prosperous builder, would be a mainstay; Hugh Edwards, a stockbroker, became a prominent figure in the London Welsh scene; and then the dairymen, William Edwards, Benjamin Davies, and Thomas Jones, who did so much to support the cause.

The first minister to devote all his time to Nassau Street was the Revd John Mills, a Llanidloes man who'd been appointed by the Welsh Calvinistic Methodists in 1846 to 'convert' London's Jews to his brand of Christianity. He was a fascinating, if controversial, character who made two visits to the Holy Land in the 1850s to deepen his knowledge. He was a member of several learned societies, and published the first musical handbook in the Welsh language, *Gramadeg Cerddoriaeth* (1838). John Mills became an assistant to Dr Owen Thomas and the Revd David Charles Davies in 1861, then took charge of Nassau Street in 1866, after Dr Thomas had moved to Liverpool, while David Charles Davies looked after Jewin. John Mills stayed at Nassau Street until his death in July 1873. He was succeeded by the Revd Griffith Davies, Aberystwyth, who was minister until his call to Cardigan in 1871.

Everything changed in 1884. The Metropolitan Board of Works

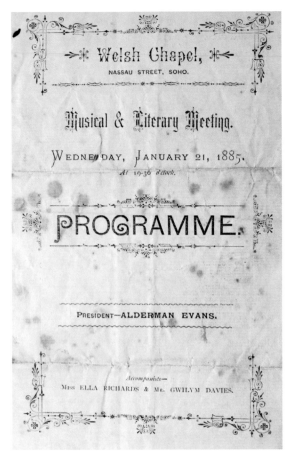

A rare copy of a Nassau Street programme (1885)
© Eglwys Jewin

announced its plans to redesign the area, constructing major new thoroughfares, later named Shaftesbury Avenue and Charing Cross Road, intersecting at a new point called Cambridge Circus. After protracted negotiations with the elders, the board lost patience and issued a compulsory purchase order. They bought the Nassau Street property for £11,000. The congregation remained there for two years, as the board's tenants, and then moved to Craven Chapel, in Foubert's Place, a narrow street leading off Regent Street and today's Carnaby Street.

There is a puzzling element to this tale: Nassau Street was never demolished, it was merely renamed some years later, and most of the building which housed the chapel is still there today. There is a case for suggesting that the compulsory purchase was never necessary, after all.

The elders worked hard to find a prime site on which to build a new chapel. Their ambition was astonishing: they found one of the best locations in central London, made possible by the very project which had forced their departure from Nassau Street. The point at which the new Shaftesbury Avenue met the new Charing Cross Road enclosed a large triangular piece of land. The elders were able to buy a substantial plot which extended from Charing Cross Road (where the main chapel entrance would be) to Shaftesbury Avenue (where the minister's house would be built).

The official financial appeal for the building fund was published in

December 1887. This set out the original £15,000 target cost of the new building (it would turn out to be £18,000), less the £11,000 received for Nassau Street:

> The new chapel which is to be erected in Charing Cross Road is to be the home of the Welsh Calvinistic Methodists formerly worshipping in Nassau Street, Soho. The chapel seats about 500. The building stands on almost the very spot where the few friends who some thirty-five years ago migrating from Jewin Crescent in the City (the parent of Welsh Presbyterianism in London) established a church in this district. It will be observed from the Estimate of Cost that the obligation of the Church amounts to about £4,000.

The opening services were held in November 1888, drawing huge crowds to hear some of the best preachers. This was, after all, one of the grandest Nonconformist buildings anywhere in the United Kingdom: it became a talking point in London and throughout Wales. Its design said a great deal about the people who just a few years earlier had been worshipping in a yard in Soho.

There were many press reports of the opening. The *Cardiff Times* on 24 November 1888 talked of the 'handsomest public building belonging to Welshmen in London', while *Y Celt* boasted that 'Charing Cross Road chapel will be the cathedral of the denomination in the capital of the world'.

There were 342 members when the new chapel opened its doors. The move had been supervised by the Revd R. E. Morris, whose arrival at 'Nassau' in 1885 was overshadowed by the talk of demolition and moving and fundraising. He certainly deserved praise for steering the church through such a challenging time: he resigned, possibly exhausted, in 1891, barely three years after the new chapel opened. He left behind a growing cause with 437 members.

His successor, the Revd Abraham Roberts, a native of Llanbrynmair, arrived in 1893 and established himself as an excellent preacher and pastor. He worked hard to draw young people to the church, and his death, at the age of 47, after a long illness, was a heavy blow. There were many tributes in the newspapers, including one by Mynorydd in the *London Kelt* on 31 March 1900 which praised his efforts to reach out to those Londoners whose Welsh was not fluent.

His readiness to include English in his services was attacked as 'affectation' by some, but Mynorydd considered that to be a 'bigoted and narrow view', and said Abraham Roberts showed 'sensitivity' towards those born and bred in London. There was some veiled criticism of his tendency to accept every invitation to preach in Wales, a tendency blamed (without evidence) for his final illness. There was a mixed message, too, in a tribute by his fellow minister, the Revd J. E. Davies, Jewin. Abraham Roberts's preaching was praised, but he was judged 'not the strongest thinker, not a natural organizer, not the most diligent student'. And with friends like that…

By the turn of the twentieth century, Charing Cross was a big church of 600 members, and had already earned a good reputation for looking after hundreds of young Welsh people who came to live and work in London. The women of Charing Cross were known for their care and generosity: so many young women from rural Wales, coming to work as domestic servants, were lonely and vulnerable, and needed guidance and protection. Charing Cross became a second home for many of them. Very often, their ministers in Wales would have written to their London contacts beforehand, asking for help.

One of those women in service needed rather less protection: Miss Anne Jones, a loyal Charing Cross member for decades, lived for many years at Buckingham Palace (and later at Clarence House) as the Queen Mother's housekeeper. It was said that the impressive flower displays at Charing Cross often came from the royal residences, with full approval!

The generosity of Charing Cross's women was especially evident during the First World War, when many young Welsh soldiers passed through London, attending what would turn out to be, tragically, their last service, at Charing Cross chapel. Those who did return, to recuperate in the city's hospitals, were often visited by the women of Charing Cross who provided practical support including food and clothing.

The notion of a 'golden age' will always be disputed: it is argued, rightly, that the spiritual life of a church is never dependent on numbers or finances. But it is surely right to draw attention to a period of great richness in the church's life, to the scale of its activity, and to the prominent part played in a much wider community. During the first four decades of the twentieth century, Charing Cross experienced what can reasonably called a 'golden age'.

Ken Kyffin highlighted the chapel's special appeal to so many young Welsh men and women who came to the capital:

> *Over the years, young people came in droves from Wales seeking a share in the new prosperity symbolised by the shops, restaurants and theatres of the new London in the West End with its focus at Piccadilly Circus. Situated as it was in the heart of the bright lights, Charing Cross chapel seemed to fit in with the rising aspirations of many of the youth of Wales; better living conditions without sacrificing the best of traditional culture.*

Those bright lights drew more and more people. Membership surged to new levels, rising from 691 in 1902, to 858 in 1917, to 1,114 in 1930, and to a record 1,222 in 1937. This peak was unbeaten by any other London Welsh chapel. But it also involved a range of activity rarely seen before or since, and a real sense that this was a congregation wanting to play its part in the wider world.

None of this would have been possible without exceptional leadership. The Revd Peter Hughes Griffiths, who served as minister from 1902 to 1937, was a uniquely gifted man who dominated the life of the church by the sheer force of his personality. That was the (rather guarded) verdict of one of the century's greatest preachers, the Revd Dr Martyn Lloyd-Jones, who attended Charing Cross as a boy, and whose recollections were published in *Y Ganrif Gyntaf*. He described his former minister as a 'complex character', a 'born aristocrat', a 'born rebel', and a 'rich personality'.

Tangnefedd etto a drigo yn ein **plith, a bendith anadl bywyd** ar ein gwaith.

Yr eiddoch **yn y gwasanaeth,**

13eg Ebrill, 1909.

Peter Hughes Griffiths signs the annual report (1909)
© Eglwys Jewin

Peter Hughes Griffiths, from Ferryside, Carmarthenshire, was ordained in 1900 and spent a few years at Crug Glas chapel, Swansea, before being called to Charing Cross. Let it be said right away that he wasn't the first choice: both the Revd John Morgan Jones, of Merthyr, and the Revd Thomas Charles Williams, of Porthaethwy (Menai Bridge), resisted the lure of London. But Peter Hughes Griffiths had no hesitation, and he spent the rest of his life at Charing Cross.

He was said to be an 'original' preacher: Martyn Lloyd-Jones said he 'scorned and disdained the orthodox type of sermon… and seemed to veto any attempt at detailed exposition or exegesis of a text… he was concerned about ideas… he thought in flashes and in phrases and always presented his ideas as word pictures… his art in handling his illustrations was consummate'. Very similar things were said about Elfed's preaching. Peter Hughes Griffiths was known for an economy of style (rare at that time), and his belief that the gospel was something to be 'felt and enjoyed', not 'understood or analysed'. His popularity probably exasperated those ministers whose approach to preaching was far more analytical, including Martyn Lloyd-Jones himself.

There is also more than a hint of the fussy dandy in his description of Peter Hughes Griffiths:

> *He was always well-groomed and well-dressed…*
> *and paid great attention to his hair. He generally*
> *wore a morning coat, and equally characteristic was*
> *his Gladstone collar and the flat black cravat type*
> *of tie with a gold pin in the centre. Out of doors he*
> *wore a silk hat. Everything about him suggested the*
> *aristocrat and he immediately attracted attention in*
> *every company.*

Peter Hughes Griffiths enjoyed an immensely successful pastorate at Charing Cross. The church newsletter he started in 1902, called *Y Gorlan*

An edition of *Y Gorlan* from May 1961
© Eglwys Jewin

Memorial card sent by Peter Hughes Griffiths after the death of his wife, Mary, in 1905. The verse reads: 'The one shall be taken, and the other left.'
© National Library of Wales

('The Fold'), was one of the best of its kind (its publication continued until 1982), and the literary society was known for attracting some of the biggest names.

But his decades in charge were also touched by serious illness and tragedy. His first wife, Mary, died in childbirth in 1905. His second wife, Annie Jane, an active member of Charing Cross, was the widow of the high-flying Liberal MP, T. E. Ellis, one of the leaders of *Cymru Fydd*, the campaign for Welsh home rule.

There were significant periods spent abroad for health reasons. Peter Hughes Griffiths travelled around Australia and the USA between 1909 and 1911, during which time Charing Cross refused his repeated attempts to resign. The same happened in 1919, when he left for South Africa and Southern Rhodesia (now Zimbabwe). He spent two years there, again offering to step down, but the congregation unanimously voted to await his return. There could be no greater tribute to his popularity and authority.

He died on New Year's Day, 1937, and was buried with his first wife and child at Salem, Pencoed, near Bridgend. His death, within two years of the outbreak of the Second World War, signalled the end of a phenomenal era for Charing Cross and the world of the London Welsh chapels.

Enid Morris (née Davies) left Port Talbot with her parents in the last year of the war, ready for the challenge of being chapel caretakers. They were welcomed by the minister, the Revd E. Gwyn Evans, who'd been appointed in January 1939. Enid was a schoolgirl at the time, and clearly a big fan:

> *He was my hero. Not a dry, formal preacher, unlike so many of the others. Gwyn Evans spoke naturally. He often ended his sermon abruptly. A simple sentence, and that was it. He was such a warm person, very sincere. He would often invite me into the minister's room after I returned from school and would discuss my homework with me. He was a farmer's son from Maesteg; he never forgot his roots. My mother always spoiled him! He would drive to the chapel from his home in Hendon and there was always tea and food ready for him. He was a very special man and I have such happy memories of that time. Going to London, even in the war, was the best thing that happened to me.*

Gwyn Evans – a veteran of the First World War who had suffered the effects of a poison gas attack – was preaching at Charing Cross on the morning of 3 September 1939 when the prime minister, Neville Chamberlain, broadcast to the world that Britain was at war with Germany. Later, the congregation heard the first air-raid siren of the war, and the footsteps of thousands of troops on the streets outside. Gwyn Evans contrasted this with the circumstances of his arrival:

> *Many times we heard people say we were foolish to come to London, but we came nonetheless. The outward signs were good, with the biggest membership of any church in our denomination, a significant Sunday morning congregation, a thriving Sunday school, and a Sunday evening crowd far too big to be accommodated. But there were clouds in the sky.*

The Revd E. Gwyn Evans (1898–1958)
© Eglwys Jewin

The post-war ministry saw much fundraising to repair the damage of 1939–45; a new organ was installed in 1949, a gift from Mr and Mrs T. B. Stephens in memory of their son, Tomos, who lost his life in the war; and more than £7,000 was spent modernising parts of the chapel and the adjoining house.

Gwyn Evans also found himself officiating at one of the biggest London funerals of the 1950s: Ivor Novello, the Welsh actor and composer, died in March 1951, and the service at Golders Green Crematorium was attended by more than 10,000 people. Novello, a Cardiff boy, was one of the most popular entertainers of the first half of the twentieth century.

Golders Green was also the location, seven years later, on 28 July 1958, of Gwyn Evans's own funeral service. His ministry at Charing Cross had lasted nineteen years, six of those in wartime, and he was widely respected for his work in sustaining the church in a period of gradual decline.

But it was soon clear that the decline was ceasing to be 'gradual'. It was accelerating, despite the superficial comfort of having more than 400 members listed in the early 1960s. Did anyone in 1965 seriously imagine that the doors would close within 20 years? A hasty plan to merge Charing Cross with Jewin in the late 1950s (as Jewin was about to embark on its new building project) came to nothing. The decline became a shocking collapse as the 1960s moved into the 1970s. The numbers tell their own story: 387 members in 1966, 352 in 1968, 319 in 1970, 265 in 1972, 220 in 1974, and on it went. This represented a fall of nearly 50 per cent in a decade. No church can survive a crash of this magnitude.

The extremely hard work of the last two ministers, the Revd Richard Jones (1960–9) and the Revd Owen John Evans (1971–80), a miner's son from Ammanford, certainly paid dividends: there were some memorable services, the literary society continued to draw prominent speakers, and the remaining members enjoyed a surprisingly wide range of activity given the church's relative weakness. Richard Jones had an interesting career: he was an industrial chemist before entering the ordained ministry. O. J. Evans was a very popular pastor who agreed to operate a joint ministry with Clapham Junction, a sensible solution at a time when ministers were increasingly reluctant to leave Wales for London.

The big debate during the 1970s focused on the iconic buildings,

Charing Cross is being redeveloped by the arts charity Stone Nest (2014)
© Richard Bryant

the cost of maintaining them, and the inevitable interest shown in them by developers and other business people. There was one scheme mooted in the late 1970s which would have created a kind of London Welsh social centre, to include a place of worship, but this was abandoned. How many times have the London Welsh chapels been urged to embrace such a project? It's worth remembering that Peter Hughes Griffiths, writing in *Llais o Lundain* (1912), had urged the chapels to fund a 'Welsh Home', a kind of hostel and social centre for the many vulnerable young Welsh men and women who came to London every year. He described London as a 'dungheap of sin' and warned the chapels that they needed to take action.

But the Welsh congregations in London have proved remarkably stubborn and resistant to plans which would have safeguarded both religious causes and buildings. The same debates are held today from time to time. One day, probably too late, common sense will prevail.

The decision to merge Charing Cross with Jewin (in partnership with Falmouth Road, which closed at the same time) was made after prolonged discussions. There were immediate offers for the purchase of the building, which should come as no surprise. The members were concerned about the suitability of some of the buyers. They eventually opted for the one with the deepest pockets: the chapel, sold for £1 million, would become the Limelight nightclub. Later on, it would be a Walkabout Bar, part of a big Australian chain. Only recently has it changed to a more suitable purpose. This prime freehold site, in the heart of one of the world's most expensive cities, is now worth in excess of £15 million.

On Friday evening, 9 July 1982, the last service was held at Charing Cross Road. There was a decent crowd (there would have been more had it not been for a rail strike) and Holy Communion was celebrated by the Revd O. J. Evans. The preacher was the Revd Elfed Williams, Jewin, and the Blessing was given by the Revd Geoffrey G. Davies, who had just arrived in London as minister of Clapham Junction, Walham Green and Sutton. Many years later, he would remark that attending the last service in Charing Cross, within days of his arrival, had made him doubt the wisdom of his decision to come to London. There was an unmistakable note of regret in his voice.

Gwynne Pickering, whose father's funeral in 1974 was the last occasion a coffin was carried into Charing Cross, eloquently expressed the feelings of so many:

> When you close a chapel, an emotional attachment is broken. It is like a personal bereavement. A flow of culture ceases. It is lost. We were happy and grateful to join our friends at Jewin, where I later became treasurer, but it wasn't the same thing. We had lost our spiritual home.

CHAPTER 11

BAPTIST BASTION

The date is 19 June 1917. The Great War is in its third year. David Lloyd George is prime minister, already emerging as a national hero, the man who is clearly winning the war. But on this day, he sets aside his onerous affairs of state and heads for the Welsh Baptist chapel in Eastcastle Street, near Oxford Circus.

With him in the car is his daughter, Olwen. It is her wedding day. They arrive outside the chapel to find a big crowd being held back by rows of policemen, and a military guard of honour waiting under the grand canopy erected for the occasion.

This is one of the biggest society weddings of the decade, and it is taking place not in a cathedral, not in a prominent church, not in even in a posh registry office, but in a Welsh chapel. London had never seen a wedding like this one… a prime minister's daughter getting married in shockingly modest surroundings.

But don't be fooled by appearances: the first telegram of congratulations arrived from the King and Queen at Buckingham Palace; gifts were received from the Lord Mayor of London and MPs and peers; the prominent parliamentarians attending included Sir Edward Carson, Dr Christopher Addison, along with Sir Ellis Griffith, Sir David Brynmor Jones, and most of the Welsh members of parliament.

The London press went into overdrive. The service, 'mainly in Welsh', was 'most impressive'. The groom, Captain T. G. Carey Evans of the Indian Medical Corps, was lauded as 'one of the most dignified and promising sons of Wales'. And there was high praise for the decision to reserve seats in the chapel for a group of injured servicemen.

David Lloyd George and his daughter, Olwen, arrive at Castle Street (1917)
© National Library of Wales

Castle Street on the day of Olwen Lloyd George's wedding (1917)
© National Library of Wales

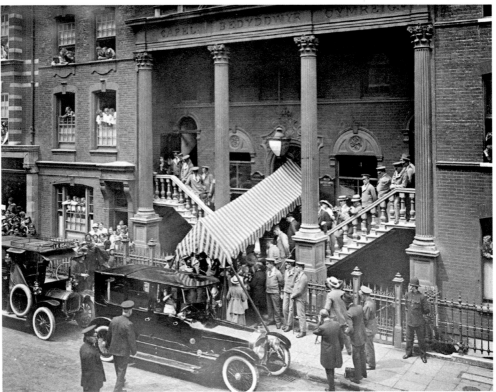

The Welsh press, it has to be said, worked itself into an even hotter state of frenzy and delirium. It was 'the brightest day in the long history of Welsh Nonconformity' – a statement of sublime madness – and all this taking place in 'a modest Welsh chapel amid the magnificence of London'. The crowd outside – and the congregation inside – were described as consisting of 'nobility and peasantry, rich and poor, high and low'. In short, there had never been such a Welsh wedding. Anywhere. Ever.

And here's the non-negotiable bottom line: the Welsh, after centuries of cringing, kowtowing, and flattering, were (thanks to Lloyd George) indisputably at the heart of government; they were (thanks to Lloyd George) the focus of London society; and they were (thanks to Lloyd George) being promoted and sponsored in all sorts of ways.

One Welsh journalist summed it up brilliantly:

Here was the prime minister of Great Britain, a world leader, a war leader, attending a Baptist chapel to give away his beautiful daughter to be married to one of Wales's best sons, and doing so in the Welsh language, without a shadow of shame about their culture, their language, their religion, their nation.

The last two lines hold great power and emotion for those of us (and we are many) who have spent a lifetime in London, juggling the demands of career and family with our desire to sustain Welsh life in the Englishman's capital. It is never an easy balance to strike. Those who have never tried (often because they have stayed in Wales, for perfectly valid reasons) tend to be the most critical and uncomprehending. But the effort required to maintain a Welsh life in London is not slight. The results are sometimes not ideal, but no one should doubt the commitment and sincerity of those who try.

And the struggle goes on. One of the latest initiatives to sustain the Welsh experience in London has been the creation of Eglwys Gymraeg Canol Llundain ('The Welsh Church of Central London') in 2006. The Welsh Baptists of Castle Street (the full name, Eastcastle Street, is rarely used) joined forces with the Independent churches of King's Cross and Radnor Walk to form a new cause under the leadership of the Revd Peter Dewi Richards. The three separate churches chose to use Castle Street as their new home. All three still exist in law but they worship as one congregation.

It is a Welsh church in the very heart of London, proud of its religious and cultural heritage, but its need to be an inclusive community in the world's most diverse city means that services are bilingual. Membership has increased since the new venture started, thanks in good measure to the leadership of Peter Dewi, who retired in 2013 but continues to serve all the London Welsh chapels.

No other Welsh cause in London has invested so much in its future: the Welsh Church of Central London has recently spent £1.3 million on a major renewal programme, refurbishing two flats above the chapel, creating new meeting spaces in the vestry, and returning the Victorian stained glass windows, plasterwork and paintwork in the chapel to their original glory. The result is truly spectacular, a great credit to all those involved. There is a confidence and buzz which impresses everyone who visits.

It is surely a fair bet that the early Welsh Baptists of London would be proud and delighted to see the progress at Castle Street, and, despite their rather tribal outlook, they might even be impressed by the decision to bring the three causes together.

It could also be argued that the Baptists of Castle Street – in the second half of the twentieth century – found themselves in a much stronger position than the other Welsh denominations. They could focus all their effort, energy and resources on a single church: by then, Castle Street was the only Welsh Baptist chapel left in London. This has been an unqualified advantage for them. While the Welsh Presbyterians juggled the demands of as many as sixteen chapels at one stage, and the Independents managed seven, the Baptists had just one to think about.

Theirs is a very different story, with more than a hint of the old Welsh Baptist reputation for standing apart, for emphasising doctrinal differences, and for warily guarding their independence. This is doubly ironic when we consider that Castle Street is now the home of an inter-denominational (or should that be non-denominational?) church.

The Revd Walter P. John and Gwilym T. Hughes, who jointly edited *Hanes Castle Street a'r Bedyddwyr Cymraeg yn Llundain* (1959), the centenary history of the chapel, acknowledged at the outset that the origins of Welsh Baptist worship in London were 'vague' and 'not easy to resolve'. They were clearly masters of understatement.

The original Baptists were in the vanguard of the campaign for full religious freedom. The origins of England's Baptist congregations were to be found in Amsterdam, in the early-seventeenth century, when an English pastor, John Smyth, declared his belief that baptism was only valid for professing believers, as opposed to (uncomprehending) infants. He also insisted that baptism be performed by complete immersion, rather than by the sprinkling of a few drops of water.

In London, sometime after 1611, Thomas Helwys established a Baptist meeting in Spitalfields, and by 1639 these 'General Baptists' had two churches, one in North Folgate, the other in Bell Alley. There was a separate grouping of 'Particular Baptists', with a stricter outlook, formed of two breakaway groups after 1638.

The first Baptist church in Wales was founded in 1649 at Ilston, near Swansea. One of its leaders was John Miles, who had been baptized in the famous Glass House church in London, and was sent by its officers to spread Baptist belief in Wales. There is no record of Miles preaching to Welsh congregations on his visits to London.

Rather more certain is our knowledge of Welsh Baptist activity in the London area in the period during the Napoleonic wars. We know that many Welsh came to work in the royal dockyards of Woolwich and Deptford and established religious causes there. The Revd David Saunders of Aberduar, Carmarthenshire, formed a Baptist mission at Deptford sometime in 1807, but he also preached in Woolwich and Borough. By 1810, when the Revd David Bowen, a leading Llanelli Baptist, visited London, the Welsh Baptists had invested in a meeting house in Deptford: there were several financial appeals made at the Baptist Associations in south Wales in 1808 and 1811 to support the London venture.

The first permanent ministerial appointment was made in December 1813 when the Revd John Philip Davies took charge. His experience was not a happy one, by all accounts, as he struggled to keep tabs on the small membership scattered across the city. Within two years, he left for Ferryside, Carmarthenshire. The timing was perhaps significant: by 1815, when the wars ended, employment opportunities had dried up and much of the dockyard workforce, including the Welsh workers, had dispersed. These two factors – the minister's departure, and the economic slowdown – prompted a real crisis for the Welsh Baptists in London. They lost the use of the building in

Deptford (possibly because of rent arrears) and there is no evidence that they were able to meet regularly.

It was a battle for survival, but thanks to the intervention of a rather special individual, everything changed in 1817.

The Revd Evan Evans visited London during that year to raise funds for Baptist churches in Wales, including his own at Cefn Mawr, Denbighshire. Evan Evans was a digger of trenches by trade, a man of immense physical strength and great independence of spirit. He was a self-taught preacher whose drive and energy got things done.

This was the man who put the Welsh Baptists in London on the right path. He moved to London in 1817, having married a wealthy dairyman's widow, and used his financial resources and status to help the London Welsh Baptists. His ability to gain the support of Jac Glan-y-gors, the satirist, and his friends at the Cymreigyddion Society, contrasted rather starkly with the priggish detachment of Edward Jones and the Methodists.

On 27 April 1817, at Evan Evans's instigation, the Welsh Baptists of London formed a new church. They met in a rented room in St Thomas Street, Borough, but baptismal services were held at Devonshire Square Baptist Church, Islington, where the Welshman, Timothy Thomas, was the minister. They moved from south London to Cheapside, in the City of London, sometime after 1819, and soon started looking for land to build a new chapel. They bought a plot in Eldon Street, Moorfields, and the new chapel opened in March 1823.

This is when the trouble started. Evan Evans, the hardest worker imaginable, was a country bumpkin in the eyes of some of the young dandies attending Eldon Street, and they started agitating. His hands-on involvement in the dairy business (he delivered milk on Sunday mornings, *quelle horreur*) offended their sensibilities. His friendship with Jac Glan-y-gors, and his evident liking of the Cymreigyddion company, also worked against him.

Evan Evans, true to form, was having none of it. He preached a robust sermon justifying his Sunday trading, handing his opponents the excuse they needed to break away and form a new grouping. The old Welsh amusement of strop and split was alive and well.

The rebels met, initially, in Hatton Garden, before moving south of the river to Chapel Court, in the familiar region of Borough. Their nagging efforts to secure the services of the Revd Daniel Davies, known as the 'Blind Man' (he'd lost his sight after suffering smallpox as a young boy), were eventually successful. This gifted young minister was a kind of 'Mr Memory', someone who could recite most of the Bible by heart, and developed into a very powerful speaker.

He certainly faced many challenges in the Borough: the Welsh Independents, under David Simon Davies, were less than thrilled to have some competitors in the neighbourhood, and they formed an alliance with Evan Evans to make life difficult for the Blind Man and his small congregation. Daniel Davies stayed in London for five years, preaching frequently in English in the city's Baptist churches, and left for Swansea in 1826. He was just 29 and already a preacher of fine repute.

His successor, the Revd J. T. Rowlands, who arrived in 1827, was the man who reunited the congregations of Chapel Court and Moorfields. Evan Evans had died in February 1827, at the age of 54, and was buried in Bunhill Fields, the pre-eminent dissenters' graveyard. He left behind a strong church, with growing membership, and was rightly praised for laying strong foundations for the Welsh Baptists in the capital. We should also note that he received no regular salary for his ministerial work: it is deeply ironic that the church had depended, in effect, on his controversial business income.

It should come as no surprise, therefore, to learn that Moorfields struggled to pay the new minister's salary. His income in 1828 was £52. Using a calculator based on purchasing power, this would correspond to an annual income of £3,800 today. No wonder the poor man struggled to make ends meet. His salary was increased to £60 in 1830, or £4,600 in today's purchasing terms. Relations between the minister and his members were tense, and he resigned in March 1832.

The chapel was rebuilt in 1834, complete with baptismal pool, during the ministry of the Revd Thomas Morris, and the membership increased again under the leadership of the Revd David Rees and his successor, the Revd David Rhys Jones.

Something rather curious happened in May 1841. A new Welsh Baptist cause was opened in Windmill Street, off Finsbury Square, advertised as a 'religious mission for Welsh seamen'. Why was it curious? It was no more than a ten-minute walk (at most) from Eldon Street. It was nowhere near the

Thames, where seamen's missions were usually based (the Cambrian Union Society was a good example). And its new minister was J. T. Rowlands, the man who'd abandoned Eldon Street because they couldn't afford his wages. He died the following year, at the age of 42, and it is likely that Windmill Street had closed its doors by 1848. On the face of it, this venture must rank among the craziest in the entire story of the London chapels.

Very soon the cause at Eldon Street was also in crisis. The Revd W. Lumley Evans, who'd arrived in 1843, left 'under a cloud' in October 1847: it was said that he'd spent a period in prison for drunken behaviour. He would nonetheless enjoy a remarkable rehabilitation, if we are to believe the references to his 'great popularity' in press tributes following his death in Caerphilly in 1899.

The volatile situation was stabilised by the Revd Thomas Rhys Davies, a renowned trouble-shooter, who spent a year in London from December 1847, but following his departure it was back to the unhappy old routine of supply preachers. Yet again, Eldon Street was in a rut. But yet again, there was a miracle-worker waiting in the wings. And this man would propel the Welsh Baptists into the heart of the West End.

The Revd Benjamin Williams arrived from Liverpool in August 1849. He saw the possibilities and devised a strategy to make them a reality. He knew, for example, that the Great Exhibition planned for 1851 would draw many thousands to London. He advertised his Eldon Street cause in the denominational press, reminding Welsh visitors to the capital to attend his services. It worked. They came in their hundreds.

There were some blips along the way. A dispute among the elders was probably responsible for the departure of up to 40 members in 1853. They began meeting in Store Street, off Tottenham Court Road, and later moved to nearby Chenies Street. It did not last long: Benjamin Williams was understandably hostile, despite the fact that he'd acknowledged the Welsh Baptists badly needed a presence in the West End. He organised what might be called a spoiling operation by holding Welsh services at Romney Street Baptist Church, Westminster. For a period, there was also provision south of the Thames, in Eleazar chapel, Borough, and in Palace Road, Lambeth.

Williams's project to find the Welsh Baptists a permanent home in

London's West End started in 1856. They rented a room in Chenies Place (not to be confused with Chenies Street), moving a few years later to Prospect Place, and then to Providence Chapel, Tottenham Court Road. In April 1859, the West End congregation made a formal appeal to be released from Eldon Street, seeking permission to establish a new, independent church. Despite his initial reservations, Benjamin Williams gave his approval.

This, then, was the start of the cause which eventually became one of the best-known Welsh chapels in the United Kingdom – Castle Street. It was formally established on 3 May 1859. The authors of *Hanes Castle Street* complain that few records remain from this period. We know that there were 59 members in 1863, by which time a 24-year-old minister, the Revd Llewelyn Jones, was in charge. He was said to be lonely in London and spent less than two years there. His successor, the Revd Hugh Cefni Parry, had no such preoccupations. He was said to be a 'big personality', a 'sharp debater', and 'restless by nature'.

He was installed in September 1864, a time of strong growth for the church, and soon there was talk of moving from the rather gloomy, cramped Providence Chapel (which they didn't own, in any case) and finding a better home.

In early 1865 they signed a rental agreement with the owner of the Franklin Hall, Castle Street East (today's Eastcastle Street), near Regent Circus (today's Oxford Circus). This was as central a location as it was possible to find. It brought the Welsh Baptists into the very heart of the West End, within easy reach of thousands of Welsh people living and working in central and west London. The hall, rented for £35 a year, was officially opened as a place of worship on 9 April 1865.

Hugh Cefni Parry, restless as ever, left in 1867 and seemed to spend the next three decades crossing the Atlantic: he went from Cardiff to Utica to Treffynnon to Dodgeville, and to other places in between, before returning to Llangefni, where he died in 1895.

It is astonishing to note that the church survived without a minister for the next fifteen years, a period of relentless growth and activity during which a stellar line-up of Welsh Baptists turned down invitations to come to London. By 1875, after so many rejections, they decided to lower their expectations and invited a student, Evan Jones, to take charge. His initial acceptance was soon withdrawn. His college tutor was unimpressed, but sent a revealing note to the elders:

> *The only plea I can put in for him is that several ministers in this and the adjoining counties have frightened him, by pointing out the isolation of a Welsh minister in London.*

They had a point, surely. More experienced ministers, such as William Harries, Aberdare, also gave London a wide berth: his son-in-law, D. H. Evans, had presided at the church meeting which voted to extend the invitation. Even the family connection failed to deliver! In those days, Dan Harries Evans, a leading member of Castle Street, was running a small drapery business at 320 Oxford Street. By 1894, he had created one of the biggest stores in the capital, employing 400 workers. The DH Evans department store would be a familiar London landmark until 2001.

The official report for 1881 recorded 150 members, many of them newly-arrived workers, a creditable performance for a church without a minister. There was strong representation from small communities in Wales, including Llanrhystud, Penrhyncoch, and Talybont in Cardiganshire.

It is worth noting, however, that this long period without a pastor had a lasting (and very healthy) effect on the leadership culture of Castle Street: its elders and officers became used to providing direction and vision; they readily handled church meetings and made decisions on practical matters; the result was that Castle Street became known for the quality and calibre of its lay leadership.

One of the best decisions they made, in 1880, was to buy the remaining lease on The Franklin Hall for £860. They spent £500 on refurbishing the building, and they worshipped on Sunday evenings at Moorfields until the work was finished in October 1881. An article in *Seren Cymru* described the new-look building as 'a very convenient, exceptionally pretty, little chapel'. By March 1882, after a grand fundraising 'soirée' (their posh word for a chapel tea party) the debt had been cut to £500, and would (remarkably) be repaid in full by April 1883.

At last, the Welsh Baptists had their own home in the West End. They established a hugely successful Mutual Improvement Society, which would meet on Saturday nights for decades to come, organising concerts and lectures and debates featuring prominent names. And very soon they would have their first minister since the distant days of 1867. The Revd William Jones, a highly-respected preacher from Fishguard, was installed in early 1883. It was a time of great optimism and energetic activity. The 'pretty little chapel' was regarded by many as a temporary home, simply because it was already far too small for the congregation. Plans were already being made for much bigger things, and a building fund was launched.

William Jones never settled in London, much to his regret, and returned to Wales after a few years. His friends suggested that he, too, had suffered a lonely life in the busy city, and much preferred the tranquillity of west Wales. There is an even sadder story to be told about his young successor, the Revd Robert Roberts, who arrived from the Rhondda in 1886. He was very popular, building up the membership to 227 and the Sunday school membership to 130. But his health was not robust, and he died at the age of 29 in October 1888.

It was a huge blow to the young church, which was already committed to a big fundraising project for a new chapel building. It is a sure tribute to the quality of the officers that they remained seemingly undaunted throughout. They faced a rapidly-approaching deadline for the end of the lease (in 1894) and were under great pressure to submit plans for the building work to the landowner, the Duke of Portland.

The architect, Owen Lewis, was a Castle Street elder. His clever plan to maximise the use of a narrow plot was accepted. A financial appeal brought a significant £200 contribution from D. H. Evans, and several gifts of £100. They made immediate progress on the work of reducing the £4,800 cost of the new building.

The work began in April 1889, and by July the Welsh newspaper, *Baner ac Amserau Cymru*, was reporting on the laying of the memorial stones:

> *Thirty years ago, Castle Street began with around a dozen members. Today, there are 250. For 22 years, they were meeting in rented rooms in challenging circumstances. The members have collected nearly £3,000 in recent years, and they can now approach the Baptist Building Fund for an interest-free loan. The architect is Owen Lewis, and the plans give us confidence that the chapel will be both handsome and convenient.*

The new chapel, opened on 17 November 1889, was described in *The Baptist* as 'an edifice exclusively chaste in design and worthy of a West End reputation... the architect deserves unstinted admiration... the chapel is admirably adapted for nineteenth-century conditions, having its own lecture hall, library, committee rooms and housekeeping facilities... this is a church of most aggressive character, doing a grand work amongst young people.'

And that last sentence is a perfect summary of the Castle Street story in the century that followed. It has been 'aggressive' in the best sense, confident and determined, a church led by some of the best preachers Wales has produced.

The Revd R. Ellis Williams, installed in January 1890, summed up his vision for Castle Street soon after his arrival:

> *To provide a spiritual home for newcomers from Wales, surrounding them with goodly influences, helping resist the pleasures and excesses of our big city; protecting our members from the noxious air; and nurturing them in all good things.*

Protecting young people from the vices of London was a big selling-point for the chapels: they knew that concerned parents in rural Wales would value this aspect of London life, and encourage their sons and daughters to make a beeline for the nearest Welsh place of worship.

Castle Street could also claim to be in the vanguard of gender equality and democratic reform, long before such issues became fashionable. Elders were elected on a three-year basis (re-election was possible); and the trust deed deleted any mention of 'men members', a decision which meant that Castle Street, unlike many Welsh chapels, never held a *cwrdd brodyr* ('brothers' meeting'). It is important to note that Ellen Williams, a lay preacher, was one of the most influential members. She served as minister of a Baptist church in Pennsylvania for a period.

There were 475 members on the books in 1904. Castle Street, with its attractive building in such a convenient location, drew scores of young people to its services and meetings. Many of those who worked in some of the big stores and businesses of the West End lived 'above the shop'. They formed a living Welsh community in the heart of London, a strange concept today, but a familiar feature of that time.

Even more prominent were the successful businessmen (they were usually men) who operated in central London, of whom D. H. Evans was a prime example. It is not surprising that The Drapers' Chamber of Trade was formed in Castle Street in 1899, nor should we be surprised, given the strong Welsh connection, that its first official solicitor was a rising politician called David Lloyd George.

The story of Lloyd George's link with the Welsh Baptists of Castle Street deserves its own volume. It is a story full of contradictions: should that really surprise us? Lloyd George had been elected to parliament in April 1890, after which he spent most of his time in London. And yet it took him sixteen years to become a member of Castle Street. Some have claimed that his own Baptist church in Criccieth, a hardline faction, refused to release him. So he managed an exception to the rules in 1906 when he joined Castle Street, thus becoming a member of two Baptist churches, a highly unusual situation.

That wasn't the only unusual thing about Lloyd George and Castle Street. How on earth did he manage to make an annual service on the last Sunday in June a national event? The so-called 'flower services' had been instigated in the early years of the twentieth century by the women of Castle Street, including Ellen Williams. The day included a women's breakfast, a meeting of the Baptist Missionary Society, and a special afternoon service for Sunday school members to which Lloyd George was invited for many years.

His president's address – delivered from the pulpit – became one of the highest points of the London Welsh calendar. The pronouncements he made there during the Great War – as prime minister – were of global significance. Among the many parliamentarians who accompanied him over the years was Winston Churchill. What on earth he made of the crazed welcome for Lloyd George's pulpit performance is anyone's guess: the act of worship must have seemed dangerously misdirected.

These were years of unqualified growth in most of the London Welsh chapels: but as Castle Street gained new members every month, the old cause in Moorfields was struggling. There were fewer than a hundred members, the church had been without a minister since the Revd William Rees's departure in 1892, and to make matters worse, the lease on the building expired in 1902. They soldiered on, moving several times before settling in Leonard Street, off City Road, near the site of the famous Wesley's Chapel. It was a slow decline: the old Moorfields cause would finally be wound up in 1917.

The Revd Herbert Morgan, who'd enjoyed a brilliant academic career at Oxford, became minister in October 1906. He inherited a typical London church with its rapid turnover of members (his predecessor had accepted 1,200 new members and released 600) and made a notable impact on the work of the chapel's literary society and its Welsh language classes for young Londoners.

It was during his time that Castle Street invested in a new organ (a small pipe organ had been installed after the chapel was built) as part of a major refurbishment costing £1,000 in 1909. The organ was built by Alfred Hunter, a well-known south London firm which built some fine organs including the magnificent example in Holy Trinity, Clapham Common. The Castle Street organ, a powerful three-manual instrument, seems almost too big for the building as the pipes barely fit under the ceiling. Refurbished by Noterman of Shepherds Bush in the 1960s, the organ makes a wonderful sound and has greatly enhanced the congregational singing at Castle Street for the past century.

Herbert Morgan left Castle Street for Bristol in 1912, after six very successful years, but faced a difficult time at the city's famous Tyndale Baptist Church during the Great War because of his uncompromising pacifism. He was a staunch Labour supporter (this must have caused some tension between

Castle Street chapel before the renovations of 1909
© National Library of Wales

Interior of Castle Street before the removal of the elders' seat
© London Metropolitan Archive

The Revd James Nicholas (1877–1963)
© Eglwys Gymraeg Canol Llundain

The Revd Walter P. John (1910–67)
© Eglwys Gymraeg Canol Llundain

him and Lloyd George) and later spent twenty years as director of extra-mural university studies at Aberystwyth. He was elected to the presidency of the Baptist Union of Wales in 1945, a year before his death.

At the outbreak of the First World War, in August 1914, the Castle Street elders did their best to maintain 'business as usual', but no one could have foreseen the extent of the devastation ahead. The scale of the carnage was unprecedented: more than one million British and Commonwealth troops died in the war; more than 2.2 million were wounded; the total number of deaths around the world included seven million civilians in addition to ten million military personnel.

One of those serving in France in 1915 was a young minister called James Nicholas. He had been temporarily released from his pastorate in Tonypandy to serve with the YMCA, helping troops on the front line. On visits to London he had preached at Castle Street, where members decided he was the right man to become their next minister. He accepted the invitation and started his ministry in October 1916.

Lloyd George, then Secretary of State for War, rushed from his office on the evening of Thursday, 26 October, to preside at the installation service. That tells us a great deal about the importance attached to such an event. By Sunday, 10 December 1916, Lloyd George was back at Castle Street being congratulated on his appointment as prime minister. It was said to be the first time that Lloyd George had spoken in public since his elevation: again, this just underlines the central importance of the chapel in the life of a Welshman whose public duties were burdensome, to put it mildly.

The memorial tablet unveiled after the war – naming all those members who'd lost their lives – was paid for by Mr and Mrs John Hinds, whose son Willie was among the fallen. The Hinds family showed exceptional loyalty to the cause over many decades.

After the war, in 1920, Castle Street secured a 999-year lease on the building and land, a major step forward which allowed a grand refurbishment in 1924. The accumulated debt was cleared by 1929.

The Revd James Nicholas worked hard on his pastoral duties: he was known for his generosity and his care for the many young people who came to London. During the economic hard times of the 1920s and 1930s, more than a quarter of a million people left south Wales for London. The London Welsh chapels experienced an unprecedented membership surge: Castle Street passed the 1,000-mark in 1931 and maintained this level until the outbreak of the Second World War. Sunday evening services were the most popular, and Castle Street installed a sound system so that an overflow congregation could follow the service in the vestry.

James Nicholas resigned in September 1934 (his health was failing) but was persuaded to stay on. He resigned

The Castle Street annual report for 1929
© Eglwys Gymraeg Canol Llundain

again a year later, but agreed to return in 1937 after many appeals. By the summer of 1938 it was clear that he could not carry on, and he retired with the title of 'Honorary Minister' of Castle Street. He remained in London, becoming president of the Baptist Union of Wales in 1952, and died at his home in Fulham in July 1963.

James Nicholas had accepted the challenge of leading a central London church in wartime: his successor would find himself facing a similar set of circumstances. The Revd Walter Phillips John, Pontarddulais, accepted the call in October 1938, just eleven months before the outbreak of the Second World War.

The minister, writing in *Hanes Castle Street* in 1959, was far too modest to describe his own gifts. He was widely acknowledged to be in the first rank of preachers – not just of the Welsh Baptist variety – and served the church faithfully until his death at the age of 57 in March 1967. He became a successful broadcaster, and his belief in cooperation between Christian denominations made him many friends. He was the very opposite of a tribal Nonconformist.

He certainly left his mark on Castle Street: the church abandoned the strict rules on membership (it was no longer limited to immersed Baptists); this openness was symbolised by the removal of the rail enclosing the deacons' 'big seat'. Walter P. John wanted no 'barrier' between the congregation and the Communion table, so the rail was removed. A new table was designed by Frederick Gibberd, the leading English architect and designer, who sometimes accompanied his wife to Castle Street. The table rests on two extended arms which reach out to the congregation, a gesture much appreciated by the minister.

The Revd D. Hugh Matthews was welcomed as the new minister in 1968, a challenging time for the London Welsh chapels at a time of great social change. He explained that the church still held on to some of the old ways:

In keeping with times, the church was quite formal in its ways. The minister was always addressed as 'Mr', the members were Mr, Mrs or Miss, and only children and young people were addressed by their first names. Dress on Sundays and to the Thursday prayer meetings was also very formal. I can still remember being shocked when someone came to a service for the first time in jeans – and to make it even worse, the culprit was a female student! No one would dream of bringing a child to the chapel dressed in a football shirt. When I went to London in 1968 we were fifteen ministers serving the Welsh chapels around the city. We met in Castle Street monthly for a fraternal. Slowly the chapels became redundant and the ministers retired and/or returned to Wales.

He explained the wide catchment area of the church and the part it played in London Welsh life in the 1970s:

Members attended regularly (though not necessarily every Sunday) from as far away as High Wycombe in the west, Letchworth in the north, Horsham in the south and Kent in the east. Living as we did as a family in Kingsbury, my wife Verina and I were among the members living nearest the chapel. The morning service normally numbered 15–20 and the evening service 100–120, sometimes more in winter months. In the summer there was a mass exodus, usually back to Wales. The small Welsh dairies dotted around London had all but disappeared by 1968, but London, with its teaching posts, universities, teaching hospitals, etc., was still a magnet for young people from Wales. We were able to attract many of these for a Sunday afternoon young people's fellowship, held in a large committee room upstairs. The attraction was the variety of well-known speakers who accepted our invitation. These included such people as Vic Feather, the union leader, Donald Sinden, the actor, Bishop Trevor Huddlestone, and Quintin Hogg, the Lord Chancellor.

The minister also had some interesting points to make about the chapel's central location, seen by many as an unqualified advantage:

Castle Street's site in the West End was both a strength and a weakness. Many of the younger people who came to London were able to find 'digs' in the centre of London and by attending Castle Street met up with other young people from Wales. The church was jokingly referred to as a Welsh marriage agency as a number of the young people met their spouses there. These then felt that they owed some sort of allegiance to the church and became active members of the church, feeding its numbers. Because the church practised 'open membership' since the days of Walter P. John, many of these were from other denominations but remained faithful to Castle Street while they lived in London. However, many Welsh Baptist families coming up from Wales, unacquainted with the centre of London, chose to attend chapels nearer their homes.

Castle Street after the major renovations of 2014

After Hugh Matthews's day, the burden was shouldered by the Revd Byron Evans, another popular preacher who believed strongly that the Welsh chapels of London should make a determined effort to come together. He was convinced that a single ministry could serve the needs of the Welsh in London, but his appeal fell on deaf ears. It is a familiar story. Byron Evans did manage to start a joint pastorate with the Welsh chapel in Ealing, a promising venture, but this came to an end because of the minister's serious health problems.

Had he lived, Byron Evans would have been the first to celebrate the historic coming together of King's Cross, Radnor Walk, and Castle Street in 2006. The Revd Peter Dewi Richards, a Llanelli man, had come to London in 2003. His decade at Castle Street, most of which was as minister of the Welsh Church of Central London, was a great success. He managed a complex process of change with great skill and sensitivity.

The new-look Castle Street, unveiled in October 2014, is a church with a future.

Lloyd George would be rather pleased.

CHAPTER 12

ALONG THE DISTRICT LINE

It's time to take a useful journey westwards along the District Line, starting from Victoria, one of the capital's busiest transport hubs. It's an area of London where many thousands of Welsh people have settled over the past century, owning small bed-and-breakfast hotels, corner shops, and the ever-familiar dairies.

The green Tube line will take us to Sloane Square and the expensive shopping area of the King's Road, Chelsea, once the undisputed manor of the stars of the swinging 1960s. One of the routes leading off the King's Road is Radnor Walk, a narrow street lined with multi-million-pound properties. One of those buildings, right next to a pub called the Chelsea Potter (the old Commercial Inn), has been bought and refurbished by London's most exclusive preparatory school, Hill House International. This is the former home of the Welsh (Annibynwyr) Independents' chapel, Radnor Walk.

In January 2013, a group of people from London's Welsh chapel community gathered at the newly-converted building at the invitation of the headmaster. We had come to see the results of the conversion, and it is fair to say we were very impressed. The main school hall (they call it the Founders' Hall) was formerly the main body of the chapel. The other rooms have been converted into teaching spaces. The overall effect is airy and light, with good use also being made of the extensive basement area.

It had always been a bizarre building for a chapel. The clue was in its location, right next to a public house. It is likely that the original building, in the garden of the pub, was a kind of music or concert hall. There would have

Radnor Walk chapel
in 2005
© Radnor Walk Trust

been plenty of earthy entertainment and plenty of good London beer to go with it. The 'commercial hall' (as one record described it) clearly didn't fit the bill, so it was sold in 1855 to the London Congregational Chapel Building Society, and registered as a chapel in 1856.

How did the Welsh Nonconformists come to settle in this area? We need to go back to 1846, when a group of members from Borough Independent chapel decided to start their own cause in Aldersgate Street, in the City of London. This was the congregation which later moved to Barrett's Grove, Stoke Newington, and worshipped there until the Second World War.

Among the Aldersgate congregation were people who lived in west London: their journey to the City every Sunday, with no trains or buses at their disposal, was time-consuming and tiresome. Understandably, they were keen to worship closer to home. They took advice from the Revd John Roberts of Aldersgate Street and went on to rent a room in the Belgrave Hall, Pimlico, where a new religious cause was founded. It was known by some as 'the women's chapel' because of the number of prominent women involved from the outset.

The first meeting, held in January 1859, drew no more than 20 people, but with strong support from Aldersgate Street, Borough, and Fetter Lane, the numbers started to grow. Within a year the congregation had moved to Ebenezer, a small chapel in New Road (today's Pavilion Road, running parallel with Sloane Street) where they would stay for a decade. Miss Mary Rees and David Griffiths, two of the founders, both died in their 40s, and the church struggled to find stable leadership. There were many other problems to overcome in those early years. The chapel was badly damaged by fire in 1869, and by December 1871 they had moved to Union Chapel in the same street. There were 140 members on the books, and the congregation was boosted by regular visitors on Sundays.

The next obstacle came in the person of Earl Cadogan, Lord of the Manor of Chelsea, whose large estates covered a huge area. He showed exceptional generosity to some local causes, including Holy Trinity Church, but he clearly had no sympathy for Welsh Nonconformists. When Union Chapel was bought by the local authority, to allow a new road scheme to go ahead, there was plenty of money available to build a new chapel, a luxury rarely experienced by Welsh congregations.

The Revd J. Machreth Rees (1855–1911)
© Radnor Walk Trust

But Earl Cadogan simply refused to give the Welsh Independents permission to build on his land. They were homeless, holding religious services in a room at the YMCA in Sloane Square, where they stayed for a year before moving to Cadogan Terrace in April 1877.

A very exciting prospect presented itself in the winter of 1878: an old chapel in Radnor Street, owned by the Primitive Methodists, was offered for sale. The owner, Dr Walker, eventually struck a deal with Isaac Williams, acting for the Welsh Independents, to sell the chapel for £1,950. Earl Cadogan did everything in his power to stop the sale, offering much higher sums, to no avail. Dr Walker kept his word and sold the chapel to the Welsh.

The new home was opened on 1 February 1880, and before the end of the year, the first minister had been appointed. The Revd Joseph Rowlands, Beaumaris, laid strong foundations during his eleven years in charge, and was succeeded in 1895 by the Revd J. Machreth Rees, a former Anglican, who'd worked as a collier, quarryman and railwayman before his ordination as a Nonconformist minister. Machreth Rees was a gifted man – a champion poet, author of a first-rate biography of the great Dr John Thomas, Liverpool, one of the most eminent of late-nineteenth-century British Independents – and proved to be a very popular and successful pastor at Radnor Street, serving for sixteen years until his death in 1911. The Revd J. Edryd Jones was installed at the end of the Great War, and stayed until 1922, followed by the Revd Ifor O. Huws, Ferndale, who arrived in 1929.

Ifor Huws, writing in the Annual Meetings Handbook of the Union of Welsh Independents in 1937, provided a wonderful description of the old chapel before the major renovations which took place in 1924:

I remember visiting the place in 1916, and it left a strange impression on me. The odd-looking stage looked out of place in a chapel, and it was used to prepare food for the congregation who stayed after Sunday school for the evening service. There were no facilities in the basement in those days. But the public house had access to some very dark cellars, and we would often hear the loud rolling and rumbling of beer barrels during the services.

The work done in 1924, devised by the architect T. Jay Evans, an elder at Radnor Street, changed the layout to great effect. The basement became a hall and kitchen, making it possible for members to enjoy tea and sandwiches between services. The distances involved in travelling across the city for services meant that provision of food was always an important feature of life in most of the London Welsh chapels.

Membership rose from 187 in 1907 to 260 in 1931: Radnor Walk (the street was renamed in 1938) was certainly part of the London 'surge' in the 1930s, though membership rose to even higher levels in the 1950s. The church community also shared the common experiences of the Second World War, including damaged buildings, and a widely-scattered membership. Finances were badly dented, which meant that the Revd Ifor Huws had to be released in 1941. The church would have to wait until 1947 to find a replacement.

But what a replacement they found. The Revd Cyril G. Williams came from Tabernacl, Pontycymer, an Independent chapel in the Garw Valley. He spent just four years in Radnor Walk, leaving for the stronghold of Priordy, Carmarthen, in 1951. The officers and members were bitterly disappointed by his decision to leave London, but they might have reflected instead on their good fortune in securing his services for even a brief period. He was one of the brightest scholars of his generation, and spent much of his career in senior academic posts.

His successor, the Revd Dewi Eirug Davies, was a leader in the same mould, a talented preacher and academic, who spent seven years at Radnor Walk from 1952. He would serve as minister of Tabernacl, Morriston, the so-called 'cathedral of Welsh Nonconformity', after which he devoted his time to academic work, producing substantial volumes of theological studies, and becoming chairman of the Union of Welsh Independents in 1990. Under his leadership, Radnor Walk's membership reached 280.

The chapel was served by four ministers after Dewi Eirug's departure,

The Revd Dewi Eirug Davies and elders of Radnor Walk in the 1950s
© Radnor Walk Trust

the longest serving of whom, indeed the longest in the history of the chapel, was the Revd D. Gwylfa Evans, who added Radnor Walk to his ministry in 1983 and stayed in charge until the momentous decision to unite with King's Cross and Castle Street in 2006. He had succeeded the Revd Jonathan Thomas (1960–5), the Revd Elwyn Jones (1966–73), and the Revd John Baker (1977–9).

The final service took place on 1 October 2006, when Gwylfa Evans was joined by one of his predecessors, Elwyn Jones, to lead the worship and celebrate Holy Communion. Gwylfa recalled his early years at Radnor Walk ('a hive of activity… a good congregation including around fifteen young people') and warmly thanked those who'd served with great loyalty over the years, including Megan Jones, the secretary; Simon Davies, the treasurer; and Michael Phillips, the organist. Among those taking part on that Sunday were Dr Hefin Jones, Dennis Evans, Dr David Thomas and Megan Jones, who sang a solo during the service. In true London Welsh style, the members held a special dinner the following night in the plush surroundings of the East India Club, St James's Square, where Gwylfa and his wife, Buddug, were presented with gifts to mark their exceptional contribution.

For 147 years, the Welsh Independents maintained centres of worship in

The former Radnor Walk chapel is now Hill House School (2013)

this (now very affluent) part of south–west London. It is good to see the old chapel building in immaculate condition, and full credit is due to Hill House School for restoring the small pipe organ, a rare example of an unaltered instrument built in 1860 by Henry Jones of Fulham.

Back to the District Line we go, travelling westwards a few stops to Fulham Broadway (which until 1952 was called Walham Green) station. Best to avoid a Saturday afternoon because this is the main stop used by thousands of Chelsea football fans making their way to nearby Stamford Bridge. Turn right out of the station, take the first left on to Harwood Road, and then an immediate right on to Effie Road. A short distance away, on the left-hand side of the street, is The Haven, a breast cancer support centre.

The building is clearly a former place of worship, though its form is not typical of a Victorian Welsh chapel, with its high porch dominating the impressive frontage. The building has been sympathetically restored and is easily recognisable as the former Welsh Calvinistic Methodist chapel, Walham Green.

The Walham Green story started in 1891 when the Welsh chapel in Hammersmith decided to open a Sunday school in a 'rented room at a doctor's surgery in the Broadway'. From there the congregation moved to 'a comfortable room above Lockhart's Cocoa Rooms' near Walham Green station. There is something curiously appropriate about both locations. By 1892 they had added a weekly prayer meeting, and two years later they started a regular Sunday morning service. They moved to a bigger room in Effie Road in 1897 and submitted an application to the London governing body, the 'monthly meeting', to break away from Hammersmith and start a separate new cause in Walham Green, an area defined as being 'on the border of Fulham and Chelsea'.

One of the prime movers (and the main financial sponsor) was Timothy Davies, a Llanpumsaint man whose name pops up time and again in the story of the London Welsh around the turn of the century. He was a hugely successful businessman (his large department store, 'Timothy Davies of Fulham', was known throughout London) and an active Liberal politician closely associated with David Lloyd George. He served as mayor of Fulham, represented Fulham in the House of Commons (1906–10), and later, the constituency of Louth, Lincolnshire (1910–18). He maintained strong links with Wales until his death at the age of 94 in 1951, and remained a notably generous sponsor and supporter of the London Welsh chapels.

The date chosen by the 'monthly meeting' of the Calvinistic Methodists to start the new cause was 21 March 1897. There were 38

Photo]   [Elliott & Fry.
      MR. T. DAVIES.

Timothy Davies, Walham Green (1857–1951)

founder members at the outset, worshipping in Effie Road until December 1900 when they moved to the vestry of the new chapel being built nearby. The memorial stones had been laid by Lloyd George and others, according to *Y Werin* on 21 June 1900:

> *Mr Lloyd George remarked that the spiritual initiative of the Welsh in recent times – years of ample Saxon pride – had led to the creation of thirty places of worship in London. In the past five years alone there had been five chapels opened where services are held in the Welsh language in different parts of London, mostly by one denomination, the Calvinistic Methodists. Mr Lloyd George stressed the debt of Wales to the London Welsh chapels, which act as shelters for the young Welsh men and women who come here every year. Mrs Timothy Davies, wife of the founder and leader of the Walham Green church, who contributed £1,000 to the new building, laid one of the stones. The new chapel, in a very convenient part of Fulham, is estimated to cost £8,000.*

The new chapel opened in February 1901 with 150 members. Note the relaxed attitude of the London Welsh chapels (when it suited them) to denominational divisions: the usual cast of celebrity preachers included Elfed, then at Harecourt Congregational Church, whose presence was always guaranteed to draw a big crowd.

But there was nothing relaxed about the fundraising effort. Newspaper adverts, including one in the *London Kelt* on 28 December 1901, offered six per cent interest on a loan of £300 to the chapel building fund. Numerous concerts (one chaired by the businessman Peter Jones, whose name still graces the famous department store on Sloane Square) and bazaars were held to reduce the hefty debt.

A press report six years later noted that the total building debts of the London Welsh chapels stood at an eye-watering £42,780. In today's terms (using a simple purchasing power comparator) that would be £3.5 million. A broader economic cost comparator would suggest a sum in excess of £20 million. The latter is probably more realistic: just imagine the cost of building a dozen new chapels in London today.

Timothy Davies ensured that 'his' new chapel got all the local publicity he could muster. *The North Wales Times* of 23 November 1901 gave a sense of the man's style and purpose early on in his political career:

Mr Timothy Davies, of Walham Green, a well-known London Welshman, was on the 9th [November] elected mayor of the borough of Fulham. Mr Davies, who is a Nonconformist and chairman of the London Welsh Presbytery, invited the aldermen, councillors, and officers of the borough to Divine service on Sunday morning at the Welsh Calvinistic Chapel, of which he is a deacon.

What Fulham's Anglican bigwigs made of their simple Welsh surroundings is anyone's guess, but Timothy Davies was used to getting his way. His loyalty to the chapels was beyond reproach: he went on to chair a special committee ('The Committee of New Causes') tasked with creating several new London Welsh chapels in the late 1890s.

Walham Green had already appointed its first minister before the new chapel opened in Effie Road: the Revd J. Tudno Williams was inducted in October 1898 and laid solid foundations during his seven years as pastor. The *London Kelt* reported in January 1899 that his preaching was drawing a capacity crowd on Sunday evenings, prompting demands for a new chapel – demands that would be met within two years. Tudno Williams's name should ring a bell with anyone familiar with the story of the London Welsh chapels. His son, Arthur Tudno, would serve as minister of Lewisham Welsh chapel, and his grandson, Professor John Tudno Williams, would become one of the most distinguished ministers and leaders of the Presbyterian Church of Wales.

Tudno Williams was a cultured man who no doubt influenced the chapel's policy on promoting the use of the Welsh language. Catering for London-born Welsh men and women – whose grasp of Welsh was often shaky – was a challenge in all of the chapels. Walham Green moved to deal with the problem in July 1908, according to an article in the *Weekly Mail*:

Eglwys y Trefnyddion Calfinaidd,

WALHAM GREEN,

LLUNDAIN.

TRYDYDD

ADRODDIAD BLYNYDDOL,

1899.

An early annual report for Walham Green chapel (1899)
© National Library of Wales

An important movement has been inaugurated by the Walham Green Welsh Calvinistic Methodist Sunday School. Last Sunday the teachers almost unanimously passed the following resolution: 'That this meeting of the teachers of the Walham Green Welsh Sunday School (C.M. Chapel), in order to be consistent with the object of the establishing of Welsh causes in London, hereby pledge themselves henceforth (i) to limit the prizes awarded to children to books printed in Welsh; (ii) to use every influence to create a totally Welsh atmosphere in their church and homes; and to forward a copy of this resolution to (a) all the Welsh Sunday schools in London, (b) the monthly meeting, (c) the two-monthly meeting, (ch) the foreign-mission committee of the connexion.'

It is amusing to imagine the impact of the '(ch)' on English readers. The original resolution (clearly written in Welsh with its alphabet points 'a, b, c, ch, d, dd…') had been translated letter for letter. The unwitting printer was probably blamed…

Tudno Williams was succeeded in February 1909 by the Revd David Davies, a native of Tregaron, who moved to Conwy in 1913. He was a preacher whose popularity was growing, but he was taken ill in April 1917 and died at the young age of 39.

The Revd D. J. Williams of Treorchy arrived during the Great War, in November 1917, and proved to be a very able leader who settled in to London life with ease. He was expected to stay for many years but could not resist a call from the historic church of Heol Dŵr, Carmarthen, in 1933. There were more than 300 members at that time. There is a magnificent photo of D. J. Williams with his ministerial colleagues taken at Walham Green at the time of his departure.

Many Walham Green members returned to Wales during the war, and those who stayed often sent their children to stay with relatives. The young Anthony Williams was one of them: he spent the war years with his maternal grandmother in Rhostryfan, near Caernarfon. Anthony's mother, Elen, was a faithful member at Walham Green. He returned to London after the war, and as a young man was greatly influenced by the ministry of the Revd Denzil Harries. Anthony went on to become a civil servant, but responded to a lifelong calling in 1989 when he entered the ordained ministry. He has served all the London Welsh chapels with unstinting loyalty and care for decades. Without his support and leadership, there is no doubt

The Welsh Presbyterian ministers of London in 1933: (back, left to right) Emlyn Jones (Holloway), D. Jeffrey Davies (Ealing), Eliseus Howells (Lewisham), W. J. Jones (Clapham), T. H. Williams (Wilton Square), D. W. Stephens (Shirland Road), Dr Francis Knoyle (Hammersmith); (seated) D. S. Owen (Jewin), Peter Hughes Griffiths (Charing Cross), W. R. Williams (Mile End), John Thickens (Willesden), D. J. Williams (Walham Green), Maurice Griffiths, M. H. Edwards (Falmouth Road)
© Eglwys Jewin

that the challenges facing the capital's chapels would have been even more daunting.

Anthony shared his memories of Walham Green and the experiences which influenced him:

> *Virtually every minister who preached in Walham Green remarked on the 'heavenly' hymn-singing: hardly a hymn was sung without the final part being repeated, often more than once. I was overwhelmed as a teenager by the older members who had experienced the Revival of 1904–5, which continued to burn within them. I feel so privileged to have become a member in 1953, an elder in 1967, and, from 1989, the chapel's last minister. Through God's good grace I have been granted over 50 years of unparalleled joy.*

There are many other happy shared memories of life in Walham Green in the years before and after the war. Glenys Pashley (née Ball) was married in the chapel in 1954. Her mother was nineteen when she came from Llanarth to London in 1909 to work in a milliner's shop near Selfridges:

Don and Glenys Pashley's wedding at Walham Green, with minister the Revd H. Denzil Harries (July 1954)
© Glenys Pashley

At that time she spoke very little English. She had left Llanarth school at fourteen and had learnt her sewing skills in her aunt's dressmaking workshop in Llanarth. She stayed with a family called Lloyd, also from Llanarth, who had a dairy in Moore Park Road, Fulham. I think she went to Walham Green chapel with them. I was born in 1929 when Mam was 39. We lived in Wandsworth, apart from the war years in Llanarth, until I got married. It was just a short Number 28 bus ride to Fulham. Mam remained a member at Walham Green until she and Dad moved to Saffron Walden to live near us just three years before she died in 1966.

Glenys also recalled the lively social life of the chapel, and its deserved reputation as a 'marriage bureau' whose reach was not limited to chapel members:

After the war, I attended Sunday school at Walham Green. My class of teenagers and young adults was taken by Denzil Harries and there was a lively discussion group. I became known as 'the heretic' because I questioned the accepted beliefs! Music played such a big part of chapel life. Lyn Harry, from Llanelli, was our organist in the 1950s. During the early 1960s he was director and conductor of the London Welsh Male Voice Choir, and after he moved back to Wales he conducted the Morriston Orpheus Choir. I have a memory of staying behind after the evening service to listen to Lyn improvising with popular music on the piano in the vestry. I also have good reason to remember the table tennis competitions: I persuaded Don (my future husband) to join the team. It was quite brave of him, as an English boy.

It is never easy for those who've enjoyed a lifetime of worship in one chapel, with close family associations, to see that building close its doors for the last time. That was the Revd Anthony Williams's experience in June 1998 when Walham Green decided to join forces with Clapham Junction under the ministry of the Revd Geoffrey G. Davies. A centenary service had been held in 1997 to mark the contribution of Walham Green chapel, and to give thanks for the dedication and vision of Timothy Davies and his remarkable generation.

A happy coincidence leads us from Fulham to Hammersmith, our next stop on the westbound District Line. In the early 1990s, I was looking through a pile of old records (the term 'LP' seems so incredibly old-fashioned now) in a street market on the North End Road, which leads from Fulham Broadway, when I came across an 'official souvenir' LP from 1969 by the Hammersmith Welsh Male Voice Choir called (inevitably) *We'll keep a welcome*, released following the investiture of Prince Charles at Caernarfon in 1969.

I was intrigued: a Welsh male voice choir in… Hammersmith?

Had I realised the chapel connection, the mystery would have been easily solved. A ten-minute walk from Hammersmith Broadway and its manic one-way traffic system leads us to Southerton Road. The Tawheed Islamic Centre is based in what most of us would immediately recognise as an early-twentieth-century Welsh chapel. This, until 1972, was the Welsh cause of Seion, Hammersmith. And this is where, for many years, the Hammersmith Welsh Male Voice, a well-known and successful choir, was based. The well-known composer John Peleg Williams served for a period as the Hammersmith chapel organist.

The intricate interlinking between chapels and choirs was often difficult to unpick. Ieuan Morgan and his brothers, all natives of Maerdy, were stalwarts of the Hammersmith choir. But their London roots were in Walham Green, and after it closed Ieuan joined the congregation in Clapham. There were more connections: Gareth Davies (who became caretaker of Ealing Green) was raised in Hammersmith, where his father John Davies was an elder. His mother, Olwen, was elected an elder at Ealing. Dan Morgan Jones, who conducted the Hammersmith choir, was the brother-in-law of Idris Roberts, the secretary of Ealing.

In other words, Hammersmith and Ealing were closely linked long before they would become formally united.

The first Hammersmith chapel, built in 1885
© National Library of Wales

The story began in 1883 when a Sunday school was started in Bridge Street, Hammersmith, under the auspices of the Welsh Calvinistic Methodist chapel in Shirland Road, Paddington. The initiative, led by J. D. Jones and Robert Parry, proved to be a good move, because there was enough support by January 1885 to start a new cause in the area.

One of the earliest press references to Hammersmith is in the *Weekly Mail* of 20 June 1885. It is well worth quoting because it underlines the immense work done by the Welsh Sunday schools at that time, and the importance attached to their activity. The report centred on a centenary convention held at the Exeter Hall in central London:

> *All the rank and file of Welsh nationality in the Metropolis were there. The children assembled in their thousands to commemorate the old Ysgol Sul, in whose classes all of them had received their first instructions in Cymraeg and Scriptural knowledge. Late on Wednesday afternoon I happened to be in one of the streets leading into the Strand, when my ears suddenly caught Welsh words spoken by someone behind me, and on looking back, which I did as if I had suddenly heard a strain of music, I saw marching up the street a long string of children. They were little ones on their*

The new Hammersmith chapel, built in 1907, now the Tawheed Islamic Centre (2014)

way to the meeting in Exeter-hall, with their Sunday School superintendent at their head. On arriving at the hall I soon found representatives of the following London Welsh Sunday Schools arriving in rapid succession: New Jewin, Nassau, Wilton-square, Holloway, Shirland, Crosby-row, Stepney, Camden Town, Pimlico, Hammersmith, and Peckham. These Welsh Sunday Schools, be it remembered, did not consist merely of children, but of adults also of both sexes. Each school was also a musical choir, which could render most harmoniously the hymns of religious Wales. The great hall was quickly nearly full, while the platform was crowded.

The Hammersmith Sunday school was, therefore, part of this powerful network, and without doubt, drove the growth of the congregation in this part of west London. The new chapel was built in late 1885 in Southerton Road. The Revd John Thickens, writing in 1939, admitted that details of the origins were rather sketchy, but he found accounts suggesting total building costs of £1,454 for the chapel and the adjoining house. Shirland Road had stepped in at a late stage to provide some financial guarantees. This is hardly surprising: a church with only 101 members could not afford to take too many risks.

The church grew and called its first minister in 1901. Dr Francis Knoyle, a Llangennech man, had trained in medicine before entering the ministry. He became one of the longest-serving ministers in the history of the London Welsh chapels, a hugely respected and popular figure. Membership had increased to 229 by 1912, and continued to grow. He stayed at Hammersmith until 1943, having completed nearly a half-century as pastor. Early in his ministry, the chapel was completely rebuilt and a good pipe organ installed. Dr Knoyle's name is still to be seen on one of the memorial stones laid on 16 June 1906. The new chapel opened on 13 January 1907, as the *London Kelt* recorded:

> *Last Sunday the church met in its new home for the first time, drawing big congregations throughout the day. The building project has weighed heavily on the minister's mind, but he and the officers and members are confident of success. The buildings are spacious, including a chapel and house, a school hall and two classrooms, all arranged in the best way. The architect, L. Wynne Williams, Birkenhead, and the builders are evidently experienced. There has been a huge rise in the population of Hammersmith, Shepherd's Bush, Chiswick, and Acton, and this will no doubt benefit the Welsh cause in Hammersmith.*

That rise continued for many years. Among the newcomers in the 1930s (boosting membership numbers to 260) were the Morris family, who moved into chapel house as caretakers in 1931. Their son, John, explained that his parents had been living in a room above the Rees Price dairy shop in Hammersmith Grove, and enjoyed their busy new surroundings:

> *Hammersmith chapel was large, with a half gallery, seating around 600 people. There was a full-size hall in the basement with a kitchen and smaller rooms. A large number of dairymen and factory workers and shop workers with young families made up the large and buoyant congregation. It was a 'working-class chapel' drawn from a wide area. During the war the basement was used as a centre where homeless families could sleep. The area was badly bombed, houses were multi-occupancy, and we would go scavenging for stuff on bomb sites. The local people had a great respect for the chapel and would pop in to hear the singing on a Sunday evening. It was non-stop meetings all week, with the male voice choir practising on Fridays, too.*

Nest Beynon's father, the Revd W. T. Phillips, Llansteffan, came to Hammersmith in 1946, as the chapels were trying to rebuild in the immediate post-war period:

My memories as a child and teenager in Hammersmith are of three Sunday services, Sunday school in the afternoon (there were six classes) and a well-attended evening service. We had a table tennis club competing against other chapels, and of course the annual eisteddfod in May. In those days they had to have 'prelims', so not everyone competed on stage. There was a strong drama group, and I remember the Hammersmith Welsh Male Voice Choir whose conductor was Dan Morgan Jones, one of our deacons. During the 1950s, Dad also became minister of Wembley chapel, which was in a side street off Wembley High Road. It was a hall, not a chapel, and is no longer there. As a child I remember my father going to Paddington station many times, and taking a funeral service on the platform to send a coffin back to Wales.

The process of rationalisation had begun as early as the 1950s, despite the continued flow of young Welsh people to London:

Sometime in the late 1950s, Dad added Ealing Green to his pastorate. My father died in 1963, and the Revd Gwilym Rees became our minister for a number of years, until Ealing and Hammersmith shared Walham Green's minister, the Revd Denzil Harries. The chapel closed in June 1972, and as the building had not been sold, I was married there in September. When Hammersmith closed most of the members went to Ealing Green, which is why we now have Seion, Ealing Green. All memorial plates from Hammersmith are in Ealing.

The reorganisation Nest referred to took place in 1968. It was felt that Ealing, the western terminus of the

The Revd W. T. Phillips (1906–63)
preaching in Hammersmith chapel
© Nest Beynon

Margaret Lloyd George lays the foundation stone at Ealing Green, October 1908. On her right: Sir Howell J. Williams and John Thickens. On her left: Timothy Davies, T. Jay Evans (architect), Peter Hughes Griffiths, J. E. Davies ('Rhuddwawr').
© Eglwys Ealing

District Line, was a more convenient location for most of the members, so it was the natural choice as the home of the newly-united church. The merger has been an unqualified success, boosting Ealing's strength and making it one of the liveliest Welsh chapels in London. It certainly has the biggest Sunday school, by a long way.

The early work in Ealing was done by D. Clifford Evans, an elder at Shirland Road, and J. R Jones of Hammersmith. The first meetings were held at the YMCA on Uxbridge Road in October 1903. They moved later to rented space in Swift's Assembly Rooms, holding evening services and a Sunday school.

The new church was formally established on 17 February 1907 and plans were soon made to build a chapel. The land, off Ealing Green, was bought in 1908, the foundation stone was laid by Margaret Lloyd George, and the new building was opened on the first Sunday of 1909. There were 78 members at that time.

The big puzzle is why it took the new church two decades to find its first minister. The 50th anniversary booklet, *Hanner Can Mlwyddiant yr Achos yn Ealing Green* (1957), suggests that some members were 'uncomfortable' with the situation. It is hardly surprising. A young, growing church needs

The Revd J. Herbert Roberts and elders of Ealing Green (1955)
© Eglwys Ealing

a pastor's guidance. The process started in 1926 and even then it took three years to get a result.

The first minister, the Revd David Jeffrey Davies, Ferndale, was inducted on 23 April 1929. He stayed at Ealing Green for twelve years and presided over a significant rise in membership, which reached a peak of 241 in 1933. After the war, the Revd J. Herbert Roberts, Wrexham, accepted a call, ending an eight-year period without a minister. The chapel community had recovered quickly after the war and members had returned with plenty of energy and goodwill. They built a new hall in 1952 for concerts, meetings and nurseries.

Graham Griffiths, the chapel secretary since 1999, made the point that a lack of funds restricted much activity until the late 1950s when the debts were finally cleared. He succeeded J. Idris Lloyd Roberts, whose notable 43-year term had started in Hammersmith. With people like his predecessor in mind, Graham provided an admirable summary of the work of so many unsung heroes and heroines:

> *As in many other chapels, the journey has not been easy, with mini-crises along the way. But, somehow, answers have been found. No summary of a chapel's history will reveal the contribution of so many individuals over the years, or the duties they're still performing, but our debt to them is immeasurable. We owe thanks, too, to ministers, preachers, elders, organists, members and friends who keep the candle burning, with such dedication, from year to year.*

The Revd Anthony Williams and elders of Ealing chapel (2007)
© Eglwys Ealing

That eloquent tribute can apply to thousands of chapels and churches across the United Kingdom today.

Ealing experienced two big ministerial changes in its history: the first was the decision to unite with Hammersmith in 1972; the second was the inter-denominational pastorate established with the Baptists of Castle Street, under the Revd Byron Evans, in 1994. They both worked extremely well. The tragedy was that Byron Evans's health did not allow the arrangement to run for more than three years.

Since then, Ealing Green has been led by the Revd Anthony Williams (1998–2009), including a joint pastorate with the Revd Dafydd H. Owen (2000–3), and the Revd Richard Brunt since 2010.

Ealing Green is the envy of most other London Welsh chapels because of its thriving Sunday school. There are strong links with Ysgol Gymraeg Llundain (the Welsh School, based in Stonebridge Park, north-west London) and families are within easy reach of Ealing at weekends. There is a strong sense

Interior of Ealing Green chapel in 2014

of community and an infectious optimism about the future. The newsletter, *Newyddion Seion*, is produced on a monthly basis. One of the best articles in 2014 informed members of the hundredth birthday of Mrs Dinah Cyster, originally from Bala, who has spent most of her life in London, and came to Ealing from Hammersmith in 1972. She embodies the spirit of loyalty and devotion which characterises so many of her generation.

Ealing Green is the only Welsh chapel left in west London, and has already outlasted the mother church, Shirland Road, by nearly three decades. It is a great success story. Graham Griffiths and his fellow officers and members are to be warmly congratulated on their achievement.

The mention of Shirland Road, a brisk 20-minute walk heading northwest from Paddington station, brings us back to earth with a crash. It is a sadly familiar tale of spectacular growth followed by long, painful decline.

It starts with the touching story of William and Jane Hughes and their disabled daughter, Ellen. They were an Anglesey couple who'd come to London in 1856. William was a carpenter who worked for the Great Western Railway at Paddington station. Ellen needed special shoes and was taken to see an English cobbler called Hudson, a religious man. William Hughes happened to mention that they walked three miles to Nassau Street every Sunday for chapel services. Hudson encouraged him to think about starting a

Welsh cause near Paddington and even offered to arrange a meeting room for him, free of charge.

The offer was discussed by the officers of Nassau Street, and they responded with enthusiasm. One of the Welsh missionaries in London, Hugh Lloyd, held a service on 13 September 1857, with seven people present. They started regular meetings in Chichester Mews, Harrow Road, with eighteen members including Hudson the cobbler.

The new cause was formally started on 25 January 1858. No Sunday school was possible at the time because the room was only free in the evenings, but by September 1858 a meeting place became available in Union Street, Notting Hill. Hugh Edwards, one of the Nassau Street elders, became one of the mainstays of the Paddington cause.

There was a good deal of moving around before a plot of land was bought, not without difficulty, in Shirland Road. The landowner was a Roman Catholic with no sympathy for Nonconformist worship. But he relented after receiving a parliamentary petition, and a new chapel was opened on 4 June 1871, at a cost of £2,358. The members were mainly working-class people employed in local industries, especially the railway. But in the later years of the nineteenth century, the flood of Welsh migrants included shop workers (the department stores of Whiteleys and Selfridges were not too far away) and young women in domestic service. They included my mother's great aunt, Elizabeth Pugh, a housekeeper in Formosa Street, Paddington, working for an Aberystwyth family.

The best fundraisers, according to Meurig Owen, in his valuable book *Ymofyn am yr Hen Lwybrau* (2001), were the young women. They collected contributions for the building fund and would often bring money back from Wales after their holidays. The Revd John Davies paid a tribute to them in 1898 for their loyalty and dedication. Any intelligence on local Welsh people was eagerly sought and shared: everyone was a potential chapel member.

Shirland Road was rightly respected for the strength of its Sunday school: the branches in Hammersmith, Portobello Road, Seymour Place and St Mary's Institute were all active. The branch at Regency Hall, High Road, Willesden Green, which opened in 1896, was the start of Willesden Green chapel, where the Revd John Thickens spent a remarkable four decades from 1907. There were other branches in Kensal Rise and Harlesden. It was a thriving network.

The former Shirland Road chapel, now the Amadeus Centre (2014)

The chapel's first minister, a former Welseyan Methodist called Michael Roberts, had been a controversial choice. He was invited to take up the post in 1865 and was ordained in 1867. He was liked by the people of Shirland Road, but not by others, apparently, so he concentrated all his efforts on Paddington. He left within two years and joined the Anglicans. He left behind a church with 121 members.

Among his successors were the Revd John Davies, Llandeilo, who came in 1898, at a time when membership had swollen to 325. It would rise again to 400 by 1912. He was a great organiser and a strong preacher – the perfect mix for a London pastor. It was no surprise that he left for the USA in 1902, where he stayed until his death in 1926.

It is important to mention the contribution of Hugh Edwards, who died in 1906. He'd come to London in 1851 and established himself in the ship-broking business. He became a member at Nassau Street, where he was elected an elder in 1858, and joined Paddington in 1871, a week after Shirland Road opened. He was, quite simply, a tireless worker, a very bright man who spared nothing for the cause. His many articles on aspects of chapel life in London are priceless, as are his biographies of Owen Thomas, David Charles Davies and John Mills. He fell on hard times later in life, but he was helped out by his fellow members at Shirland Road.

The decade of the 1930s brought great things to Shirland Road: an engaging new minister, ever-rising membership, a week packed with lively meetings, and an extremely talented organist in Mansel Thomas, one of the most influential musicians of his generation.

The Revd D. W. Stephens took charge in 1931 when there were

431 members, with 64 children attending Sunday school. The chapel was redecorated in 1937 at a cost of £900. All the money was collected in a matter of weeks. There was a real sense that anything was possible.

And then came the Second World War.

Shirland Road was fortunate in one sense: unlike many of the other chapels, they held on to their minister throughout the war and beyond. D. W. Stephens retired in September 1949, moving to Llansamlet, where he died in 1962. He was widely admired for his quiet determination and gentle pastoral skills.

There are still plenty of people in London who brighten up and enthuse about the minister who arrived in 1951. The Revd Geraint Thomas, Aberystwyth, was a superb preacher and a strong, engaging personality. He was very popular with congregations throughout Wales, and soon became a big hit with the Londoners. He added Willesden and Ealing to his pastorate in 1978 and retired in 1985 after a hugely successful 34-year ministry.

His farewell service on 24 July 1985 drew a crowd from every chapel in London. It was a powerful statement about the man, his contribution, and the

The interior of Shirland Road chapel in the 1980s
© Rita Clark

respect in which he was held. Geraint Thomas and his wife retired to Llanelli where he sadly died the following year.

He was the last minister of Shirland Road. The numbers had declined, and following his departure, the vulnerability of the cause was more apparent. In January 1988 a decision was taken to close the doors after 130 years of Christian witness in the Welsh language in this part of London.

The final service of thanksgiving took place on 15 December 1988. Among the ministers taking part were Elfed G. Williams, Jewin; Huw Llewelyn Jones, Holloway; Dr W. T. Owen, King's Cross; and Geoffrey G. Davies, Clapham Junction.

Most of the remaining members joined Willesden Green or Ealing chapels.

It was entirely fitting that a memorial tablet for Geraint Thomas, one of the best Welsh preachers of his generation, was unveiled at Seion, Ealing Green, in November 1991.

It was Geraint Thomas who foresaw, back in 1962, the speed and force of the reversal which would affect the chapels, and the sharpened responsibility which resulted:

> *This situation forces us to take our religion and our chapels more seriously. If we are to make an impression on the faithless Welsh, we have to show that worshipping God is all-important to us. Christianity has to be utterly central to our lives or it is nothing. Every member must demonstrate that his or her religion is wholly relevant, a privilege, and a necessity.*

His words are as fully relevant now as they were more than half a century ago.

CHAPTER 13

BEYOND THE JUNCTION

I have a personal interest to declare before this story begins: the Welsh chapel in Beauchamp Road, Clapham Junction, is my spiritual home in London. I first attended in 1996, during the outstanding ministry of the Revd Geoffrey G. Davies, and it is where all my children were christened.

I would be unable to give it a bad press, even if it deserved it… which it doesn't.

I had lived in London since 1984 but had not felt the desire or need to attend a place of worship for a long time. The situation changed in 1996 when I greatly appreciated the warmth and fellowship of my friends in Clapham. They have even put up with my amateurish attempts at playing the organ. I am greatly in their debt for all of these reasons.

We should also clarify the nomenclature. Just as Charing Cross (chapel) is nowhere near Charing Cross, Clapham (chapel) is nowhere near Clapham. Its official name is the Welsh Presbyterian Church, Clapham Junction. The famous railway station is indeed just a few minutes away. But the accepted shorthand in the chapel community is 'Clapham'. Visitors have been known to take the underground to Clapham Common or Clapham South only to find that they have a bracing walk to get to Beauchamp Road.

The Clapham story goes back to the late-nineteenth century, when south-west London was booming. Row upon row of terraced homes – for thousands of workers and their families – were appearing across Wandsworth, Battersea and Clapham, all of which are comprehensively gentrified areas today where a modest terraced house can sell for £1.5 million. It was very different in the 1880s and 1890s, as thousands of Welsh workers joined the throng and soon started demanding religious provision in their native language.

By 1893, the people of Falmouth Road chapel approved the creation of a Sunday school in a rented room behind the 'Time Coffee Shop', near the site of today's Springfield Methodist Church. Within two years they had moved to the Felix Educational Institute on Lavender Hill (the site of an old manor called Highbury House), and then to New Hall, Battersea Rise. The venture was certainly a success and encouraged the governing body of the Welsh Calvinistic Methodists in London to establish a new chapel in the area.

In the best Welsh tradition, a committee was formed, but that tradition was shattered by a startlingly rapid decision-making process. The committee first met in December 1885 and within a month, on 18 January 1896, the new cause was formalised. By October of that year, the first minister, the Revd Llewelyn Edwards, had arrived. His pedigree was rather impressive: he was the son of Dr Lewis Edwards of Bala, the prominent educator and minister, and the brother of Thomas Charles Edwards, the first principal of the University College of Wales, Aberystwyth.

The problem was that Llewelyn Edwards and his new flock did not have a permanent home.

The ever-useful Timothy Davies, Fulham, stepped in with his 'new causes' committee and started looking for a suitable location. They found an intriguing property, an eighteenth-century villa owned by the Battersea miller, Thomas Dives, until his death in 1880. His rather grand house had then been used by the builder Alfred Heaver while he was developing the new streets of (today's) Ilminster Gardens and Beauchamp Road. It was Heaver who sold the plot to Timothy Davies and his committee for £600.

John Erskine Clarke, vicar of St Mary's Church, Battersea, claimed that Dives's house was never demolished. He argued that when the new chapel was built in 1896–7, the builder merely encased the old villa in

Eglwys y Methodistiaid Calfinaidd
BEAUCHAMP ROAD,
CLAPHAM JUNCTION.

Gweinidog - - Parch. D. TYLER DAVIES.

Dadorchuddiad
Ffenestr Liwiedig

Er Coffadwriaeth am = =

MISS MAIR LLOYD GEORGE

Prydnawn Dydd Sul, Mehefin 27ain, 1909,
AM 3.30 OR GLOCH.

The programme of service for the unveiling in 1909
© Eglwys Unedig De Llundain

The Mair Lloyd George memorial window, installed in 1909
© Eglwys Unedig De Llundain

red brick. He said the 'unusual thickness' of the chapel's walls would support his claim. Griffith Davies, the architect, also built three 'matching' houses around the chapel (numbers 28, 30 and 32). This configuration would change when the chapel was extended in 1924.

The new premises were completed in 1897 at a total cost of £5,800. When Llewelyn Edwards took charge as minister, there were 91 adult members and 87 Sunday school members. Within five years the numbers had grown to 204 adults members and 145 Sunday school names. This was impressive but by no means exceptional at that time.

There is a strong Lloyd George link to the Welsh chapel in Clapham, a far more intensely personal link than the 'flower services' mentioned in the context of Castle Street. One of the little-known treasures of the London Welsh chapels is the wonderful stained glass window installed in Clapham in 1909. It was commissioned in memory of Mair Eluned Lloyd George, the eldest daughter of David and Margaret Lloyd George who died of peritonitis in 1907 at the age of seventeen. The window was designed by Thomas Figgis Curtis and produced by Ward & Hughes of Soho.

There appeared several press reports of the unveiling, including this one in *Y Clorianydd* on 1 July 1909:

> *In Clapham Junction (MC) Chapel, Sunday, a coloured window was unveiled in memory of Miss Mair Eluned Lloyd George, daughter of the Chancellor of the Exchequer, who died in November 1907, aged 17 years. The young girl used to attend this place of worship. The drape was drawn from the window by the Revd John Williams, Brynsiencyn, while Mr and Mrs Lloyd George and their four children were present.*

The chapel was full to overflowing, and all cheeks were 'wet with tears of longing'. The presence of John Williams, several years before the outbreak of the Great War, is revealing. Williams was a preacher of stunning power, a close friend of the Lloyd George family, who would take an active part in backing the formation of a dedicated Welsh division during the First World War. He became its honorary chaplain and outraged many by appearing in uniform in the pulpit. His words at the dedication of the window were transcribed:

Young people, young women especially, permit this window to speak to you for a brief moment, it will tell you about the brevity of existence and the uncertainty of life. I am unveiling this window today to the glory of God, and in everlasting loving memory of Mair Lloyd George.

There were other changes to the built fabric of the chapel in 1909: a carved wooden screen, commissioned by Mr and Mrs T. H. Jones, who owned a dairy on Battersea Rise, was placed behind the pulpit. Electric lights were installed during 1913. A major renovation in 1925 changed the layout dramatically to accommodate a growing congregation. Mrs Margaret Felix, a lifelong member who died at the age of 101 in 2011, summed up the thinking of that time:

Maybe it doesn't make sense now, the way things are, but we just didn't have enough room. There just weren't enough seats for the Sunday evening service. And no one could have imagined that things would change like they have. Mind you, it was a big improvement. It was small and dark before, it's much better now. We had a pew in the front row on the side, it was quite a squash for a family of seven.

The Jones dairy, 23 Battersea Rise, one of several Welsh businesses around Clapham Junction

We had Welsh lessons and our New Testaments were bilingual. The young people got together regularly to play tennis, we'd go all over London playing the various chapels. I met my future husband, Glynne, at a chapel drama club. We were married in 1938 at Clapham Junction chapel and Glynne always said the best thing he did in his life was to marry me.

Margaret Cynwydwen Williams (she was named after her father's village of Cynwyd) was born at Glynde Dairy, 105 East Hill, Wandsworth. She vividly recalled the long hours and relentless work of the dairyman:

There were three deliveries daily. Dad did the round before breakfast, wheeling the empty barrow to Clapham Junction station at 4 a.m. to collect a churn. He would have a nap in the afternoon. The dairy was open every day til 11 p.m. except Sunday, and even then there might be a knock on the door from someone wanting something. The dairy was my home for 25 years. We sold milk (in a big china container), butter (on a cold shelf), eggs, bread, tea, tinned fruit and biscuits. When I was born, there were buses pulled by horses up East Hill.

Margaret's recollection of the Great War brought home the impact on almost every family in Britain:

I remember a troop of soldiers in khaki on East Hill breaking step and falling out, sitting to rest on the kerbs and doorsteps. The women, including Mum, came out with tea and food for them. The Welsh boys from Cynwyd would come to the house when passing through London on leave. Every Sunday we would hear that another boy in the local gang had died, they were such sad times. My Uncle Huw was lost just before the end of the war in August 1918.

In times of grief and in times of joy, their lives revolved around the chapel.

The original Clapham building, based on the old villa, was square, but the renovation extended the structure to incorporate the caretaker's house at 32 Beauchamp Road. The pulpit was moved from the east (today's main entrance) to the opposite end; new offices were added at the back; and a new chamber was built ready for the new pipe organ installed in 1926. David Lloyd George presided at the first recital concert.

As many as 62 young men and women from Clapham had served in the

Clapham Junction chapel before it was rebuilt in 1925
© National Library of Wales

Great War, including Gwilym Lloyd George, the second son. Of these, eight young men died on active service. Their names, and those of men lost in the Second World War, are recorded on memorial tablets in the chapel. Between 1939 and 1945, the vestry beneath the chapel served as a bomb-shelter for the local population.

Membership peaked in the 1930s, as it did in most of the other London chapels. In Clapham, the record high was 478 members in 1938, caused by economic hardship in south Wales and the flow of jobless heading for London.

One of the prime features of Clapham life has been the quality of its ministry. Llewelyn Edwards was succeeded by D. Tyler Davies (1907–17), whose ministry was tragically cut short by his death at the age of 50, and then by W. J. Jones, who served for an astonishing period of 36 years (1919–55). His really was a 'golden age', a time of high attendance, especially by young Welsh men and women, a time of activity and generosity, and a time when the Welsh chapel really was an indispensable part of London Welsh life.

W. J. Jones was nonetheless considered by some to have a rather narrow outlook. He was followed by (the far more easy-going) R. G. Alun Richards (1955–61), and then in 1962 by the popular O. J. Evans, whose ministry also took in Croydon and Sutton in 1969, and then Charing Cross from 1971 until he retired in 1981. Membership had fallen steadily, but 'OJ's' ministry was seen as universally beneficial.

Over the years, Clapham has been proud of its association with some prominent public figures, including Sir David Hughes Parry (vice-chancellor of the University of London), Lord Morris of Aberavon KG PC QC, the former attorney-general, and the Lloyd George family.

There have been some exceptional contributions by officers and members. Mrs Eluned Idris Jones, who lived to a very grand age, served as organist for five decades. She missed the old Rushworth & Dreaper pipe organ and shared my aversion to the electronic replacement. Her daughter, Eleanor, is equally loyal and organises services which are greatly enjoyed by members; Eleanor's husband, Dr Hywel Thomas, has served as secretary over four decades. The late Ellis Jones gave his all to lead the congregational singing and is greatly missed. There are too many good people to mention. They know who they are.

In July 1982, the Revd Geoffrey G. Davies, his wife, Wendy, and daughter, Lowri, arrived to take charge of Clapham, Sutton and Walham Green. Geoffrey regaled me many times with the story of his decision to come to London and the response among family and friends. 'You're nuts', said one. 'But you hate London!' said another. 'Stay in Oswestry, it suits you', was another piece of advice.

Geoffrey admitted that all these comments were valid, in their own way. He often wondered why he'd decided to make the move from rural Oswestry,

The Revd Geoffrey G. Davies (1932–2008)
© Lowri Williams

where he'd served happily for more than two decades. But London is a magnet, and Geoffrey fancied a challenge. By his own admission, he had not bargained for the speed of the decline (an elderly congregation, a high frequency of returns to Wales) but he did his very best to contain the losses.

He suffered his share of health problems, focused his attention on Clapham and Sutton, and served loyally until the late spring of 1999 when his wife, Wendy, died. Geoffrey retired and moved to Cwmgwrach, Neath, to live with his daughter, Lowri. Geoffrey was an erudite, cultured man who won our affection with his wry sense of humour and his occasional outbursts of frustration. Nothing irked him more than the slowness of the London Welsh congregations to join forces to build a stronger future.

In fairness, his successor, Dafydd Owen, took important practical steps to shore up the position of some of the London causes. He formed a joint ministry with his colleague, Anthony Williams, looking after all the London Welsh Presbyterian chapels. Dafydd, using his expertise as a former general secretary of the Presbyterian Church of Wales, restructured some of the chapels (creating a united cause in north London, Eglwys-y-Drindod, and a parallel structure in the south, Eglwys Unedig De Llundain) designed to safeguard some of the assets if or when chapels are sold – to sustain the work and witness of those remaining.

We are, however, having to grapple with the centralised structure of the Presbyterian Church of Wales which means that the central bodies have the final say on pretty much everything, including money. The situation has been made much worse by the booming London property market: selling some of the chapel properties would yield millions of pounds for central funds. Tight denominational control minimises the freedom of congregations to use the money that they and their forebears have raised and contributed. It can be argued that this money – by any reasonable, rational, moral consideration – is theirs. Chapels begging to access their own money to pay essential bills are struggling to understand the motives for these rules.

I strongly believe that we need far-reaching improvements in understanding, cooperation, and mutual support between the London chapels and the denomination centrally to give the churches a real opportunity to flourish once more.

The man left to pick up the pieces – in Clapham and right across

London – is the current minister, the Revd Richard Brunt. He is handling matters with tact, wisdom and sensitivity. At the time of writing, Clapham is planning a major refurbishment, including the installation of a lift from the basement: health and safety regulations can be another drain on chapel finances.

There is a very positive note on which to leave Beauchamp Road. The Welsh playgroup, Dreigiau Bach ('Little Dragons'), which uses the vestry during the week, has given the cause a huge boost. They attend special services, bringing joy and sparkle to events in the chapel, allowing Clapham to give Ealing a run for its money!

It is one more reason to believe that Clapham Junction chapel, for 118 years a spiritual and cultural home for Welsh people in London, can continue to serve its community well.

Let's follow the footsteps of countless worshippers over the years, and leave the chapel by making our way along Beauchamp Road to Lavender Hill. We are now in the heart of 'the Junction', as Battersea locals call it, and within minutes we are in sight of the famous railway station, one of the busiest in Europe.

Beyond the Junction lies Wandsworth, the borough in which Battersea is

Revd and Mrs W. T. Owen (King's Cross), the Revd and Mrs Elfed G. Williams (Jewin), and the Revd Huw Llewelyn Jones (Holloway) at the Clapham Junction centenary services in 1996

Welsh chapel, Beauchamp Road, Clapham Junction (2014)

The Revd Anthony Williams at Clapham Junction chapel (2014)

located. Running parallel to Lavender Hill is Battersea Rise, a steep hill which leads to Wandsworth Common, the extensive playing fields of Emanuel School (founded 1594), and Spencer Park, an eye-wateringly expensive enclave for City bankers, footballers and celebrities.

Battersea Rise is rather grey in comparison, with its run-down ambulance station, its rows of rather tired-looking shops, and its pounding traffic. Opposite the ambulance station, on the corner of Auckland Road, is a new block of flats, built a few years ago on the site of an old used-car forecourt.

There is nothing, apart from a few sections of ridged Victorian stonework, to suggest what used to be here. This was the location of Battersea Rise Independent Welsh chapel, a relatively short-lived cause established on 28 June 1903 at a meeting in Battersea Town Hall. The Union of Welsh Independents had established its own evangelising 'forward movement' in 1898, with the aim of raising £20,000 to build new chapels. Battersea Rise was one of the fruits of that investment, though there are suggestions that some disgruntled members of Clapham Junction were also involved.

The Revd J. Machreth Rees, Radnor Walk, was there to bless the new venture, as his church was the main sponsor, releasing around 35 members to help establish it. The Revd D. C. Jones, Borough, also took part.

The origins of the church went back to the early 1890s, when a Sunday school was held in Battersea. A meeting held on St David's Day, in 1903, at the Felix Educational Institute, Lavender Hill (where the Clapham people had also met in the early days) decided to hold regular services. The move to Battersea Town Hall came three months later.

The plot of land on the corner of Auckland Road was bought for £1,300 and the small chapel was ready by October 1906. The Revd J. T. Davies of the London City Mission was among those taking part. There was a new minister standing by to take over, a Methodist called E. T. Owen from Richmond College, a Wesleyan theological training centre… yet further proof of the flexibility of the time. He moved to Llangeler in 1909, the first and last full-time minister of Battersea Rise.

The Revd Ben Davies, formerly of Pant-teg, spent many years in London in retirement and took great care of the new Battersea chapel for eight years between 1929 and 1937. His ministerial colleague J. T. Davies of

A rare image of the interior of Battersea Rise chapel, built in 1906
© National Library of Wales

the City Mission showed even more generosity to the cause, and celebrated Holy Communion countless times over the years.

The membership total stayed stubbornly around the 40 mark, even in the thriving 1930s, and was still at 40 in 1951, shortly before the chapel closed.

Glyn Morgan, a lifelong member at Clapham Junction, remembered attending the occasional service at Battersea Rise as a young boy. He said it was opened while the effects of the religious revival of 1904–5 were still being felt in Welsh chapels across London. But he explained that the cause, being so close to Clapham Junction, never really grew from its modest beginnings. It was sustained by some devoted officers and visiting preachers, but its long-term prospects had clearly been misread.

This is in no way to decry the work done by the Union's 'forward movement' in the early years of the twentieth century. The significant sums invested in East Ham, Woolwich and Battersea would be a burden for many years to come, but in the case of Woolwich, in particular, the investment paid very impressive dividends.

A short walk from Battersea Rise to Clapham Junction station will allow us to catch a fast commuter train to Sutton, a large suburban area of southwest London, where we can find one of the best examples of a wise chapel investment.

Sutton Welsh chapel was established – in response to growing local interest – on 23 April 1933, under the leadership of the Revd D. S. Owen, Jewin, in his capacity as president of the London Presbytery. There were 80 members registered by 1938, with promising numbers attending Sunday school and weekly meetings.

But how did those first meetings take shape? Whose initiative was it? Here we have a Lloyd George link again. Dame Margaret was presenting prizes at a concert in Clapham in the early 1930s. The crowd included Mrs Catherine Roberts, a widow, originally from Porthmadog, who lived with her daughter in Sutton. She was a member at Clapham Junction. Also in the crowd was David Edwards, another Porthmadog native, who made contact with Catherine when he realised the connection between them.

With Dame Margaret's encouragement, they discussed the possibility of starting religious services in the Sutton area. David Edwards put his home at their disposal, and this is where the first meetings took place. Soon they needed more room, so they moved to the Salvation Army hall. Next stop was Sutton Adult School (two rooms, one for services, one for the all-important catering), and contemporary reports were full of enthusiasm and optimism about the future of the cause.

They presented their case – to join the London Presbytery as a new cause – to a committee chaired by Professor David Hughes Parry. There were detailed questions about the financial projections, but formal permission came in 1933.

The Second World War presented immense challenges, but Sutton nonetheless emerged (with just 39 members) and survived after 1945. How the church would have lasted without the courageous leadership of that wonderful man, the Revd Eliseus Howells, Lewisham, has to be a matter of grave doubt. Membership had recovered to 60 by 1960, with seventeen children on the books.

Sutton was again fortunate in its next minister, the Revd Denzil Harries, Walham Green, who led the church with dedication and unfailing diligence

Anniversary services at Sutton in the 1960s, with the Revd Denzil Harries and the Revd Glanville Davies
© Catrin Unwin

from 1947 to 1969. This was a very exciting period for the Sutton members. Their meetings were moved from the Adult School to the Red Cross Hall, where they stayed until the mid-1960s. A rumour that the English Methodists were vacating a chapel in Lind Road turned out to be true, and Denzil Harries mounted a lively campaign to buy the property, making several successful financial appeals along the way. The congregation moved in at the start of 1965.

The ministerial musical chairs of 1969 meant that Sutton lost the valued services of Denzil Harries but gained the equally impressive gifts of the Revd O. J. Evans, Clapham, until July 1972. He was replaced by the Revd Glanville Davies, Falmouth Road, who stayed until his retirement in 1980. Another reorganisation in 1982 meant that the new minister, Geoffrey G. Davies, looked after Sutton, Clapham and Walham Green.

Geoffrey and Wendy's daughter, Lowri, chose to be married in Sutton chapel because she loved its similarity – in size, warmth and atmosphere – 'to a chapel back home in Wales'. That's probably the best compliment of all.

Bryn Lloyd, the secretary for the past 35 years, has made a superhuman

Sutton Welsh chapel (2014)
© Eglwys Unedig De Llundain

Sutton's officers in 2015: Bryn Lloyd, Gwyndaf
Evans, Bethan Clarke, Gwen Wildman
© David Lloyd

effort to keep Sutton on the map, helped by a small group of active elders and members including the organist, Gwyneth Thomas, who has served for decades. Gwyneth's father, W. R. Williams, a prominent Labour MP, was also a loyal member and elder. Sutton is now part of Eglwys Unedig De Llundain, and collaborates closely with Clapham Junction. It is sad that Lewisham, the third member of the group, is no longer with us.

But Sutton is alive and well, in its southernmost suburb beyond The Junction, where the Welsh presence is sustained by a small group of devoted officers and members.

Hir y parhaed. Long may it continue.

CHAPTER 14

NORTHERN PANORAMA

It took a Welshman, Sir Hugh Myddelton, the seventeenth-century entrepreneur and engineer, to provide Londoners with a permanent supply of clean water. Supported by King James I, Sir Hugh masterminded the creation of the New River, one of the most ambitious engineering projects of the seventeenth century, completed in 1613.

Sir Hugh's inestimable contribution was recognised by the erection of two statues, one on the Royal Exchange, in the City of London, the other on Islington Green, where the New River ended its 38-mile journey from Hertfordshire. The latter, by the sculptor John Thomas, was unveiled in 1862 by William Gladstone.

The statue of Sir Hugh, at the southern end of the green, is easily the most prominent Welsh presence in one of London's trendiest and most prosperous areas. Islington – once a run-down inner city zone – is now hugely popular, thanks to its elegant terraces, its proximity to the City, and its enviable range of shops, restaurants, bars, and arts venues.

There are other Welsh connections to explore in the area, as we embark on a sweeping tour of north London, working our way northwards and westwards from Islington until we reach Willesden, Wembley and Harrow.

Islington breaks the pattern of our story so far: it was the location of what was, to the best of our knowledge, the only English-speaking Welsh chapel in London. Meurig Owen, in *Ymofyn am yr Hen Lwybrau* (2001), explained that there may have been others elsewhere in London, but no records have survived.

Sometime in 1864, the 'monthly meeting' of the Calvinistic Methodists in London concluded that English-language provision was needed for those who could not follow services in Welsh. The idea was put to the officers of Crosby Row, but they were unimpressed. We should not be surprised: the debate about English-language provision would prove to be rather toxic in the decades to come, as the 'traditionalists' (whose Nonconformity found expression exclusively in the Welsh language) battled with the 'expansionists' (whose dream was to extend their brand of Nonconformity to English-speaking Welsh congregations).

It took another five years for a new English-speaking cause to be established at Myddelton Hall, Islington, opposite the modern site of the famous Almeida Theatre. It is also referred to as Wellington Hall in some records. The most active members of the new church had come from Wilton Square and Jewin. The banker and Jewin elder, Hugh Lloyd Hughes, and his wife, Megan Watts Hughes, a well-known singer and composer, were prominent supporters.

Megan Watts Hughes, who'd been educated at the Royal Academy of Music, and had performed with Joseph Parry, was a very popular concert performer. Her hymn tune, 'Wilton Square', is still regularly sung in chapels today. But her greatest achievement, without question, was the founding of a home, in Barnsbury Square, Islington, for destitute boys, which opened in 1881. She died in 1907 and was buried in Abney Park Cemetery. There were 30 former residents of her home at the funeral.

The first minister, the Revd C. Leon Stephens, stayed until 1877 when he and his wife started preparations to leave London to become missionaries in India. They would spend 30 years in the Khasi Hills in the north-eastern state of Meghalaya (then part of Assam). It was during his ministry that the congregation leased a plot of land in Highbury Station Road and built an 'iron church with cupola' in 1874. There are few details available about the life of the church, but we know that the Revd John Jones took over in 1879, and stayed for at least five years.

He would be the last minister: the building was sold to the influential Union Chapel, Islington, in around 1886, and was used as a 'mission church', known as 'Union Hall', until its demolition in around 1904.

Hugh Lloyd Hughes and Megan Watts Hughes did not return to Jewin or Wilton Square: they became valued members of Union Chapel, though Hugh Lloyd Hughes continued to support mission work among the Welsh in London, as well as the Welsh Charitable Aid Society.

Artist's impression of Wilton
Square chapel
© Eglwys Jewin

The Islington venture had been a rather dismal failure. The original aim was to establish a Calvinistic Methodist chapel in the Welsh tradition – for an English-speaking congregation – drawing people from a wide area. The chapel register suggests that most of the members (around 30 of them) all lived near Highbury station. It had not proved to be the magnet that some had confidently predicted.

The failure would not deter others from exploring English-language provision in the decades to come, but the Islington project would be brandished by those who believed that the whole point of having Welsh chapels in London was to offer services in… Welsh. They liked to point out that there was no lack of choice for those who preferred their sermons in English. Their argument was difficult to rebut, and still is.

Those who'd stayed at Wilton Square chapel, barely a mile away from Highbury Station Road, did not have to contemplate failure in any form. They belonged to one of the thriving London Welsh chapels of north London, established in 1853 in a part of London known as Hoxton. (Some insist Dalston would be more accurate, but the difference is minimal.) The cause had started, like so many others, as a local Sunday school vestry, though it has to be said that the officers of Jewin, the sponsoring church, had been less than enthusiastic in the early days.

Lemuel Pierce, a tailor from Rhyl, and Simon Griffiths, a bank messenger from Rhuddlan, were two of the Wilton Square pioneers. They started by renting a room in Cropley Street, New North Road, in May 1848, before moving to Wenlock Hall a year later, and then in 1851 they leased some land in Wilton Square, New North Road, from the Clothworkers' Company.

The architect, Henry Hodge, designed the chapel, which was built by two Jewin members, David Hopkins and Robert Roberts, Islington. They would both become elders at Wilton Square. Edward Rowlands of Coleman Street, a Jewin elder, was chosen to lead the new church when it opened in May 1853.

Meurig Owen described Wilton Square as an 'active and influential church' served by a succession of able ministers, including Joshua Davies, John Mills, Robert Roberts, John Elias Hughes, Gwilym H. Havard, Morgan W. Griffith and T. H. Williams. The high calibre of the officers certainly contributed to the success of the cause. It was a Wilton Square man, David Williams, who was chosen to become one of the first London City missionaries to work among the impoverished Welsh in London.

Lemuel Pierce is another who deserves a special mention: he served as the first secretary (in effect) of the 'monthly meeting', recording the important denominational debates and decisions over many years. He is known to have produced an official record of the origins of the Welsh Calvinistic Methodists in London, 'Llyfr Coffadwriaeth yr Amseroedd' ('The Book of Time and Memory') in 1889, a work of supreme importance on the history of the Welsh in London. This irreplaceable book disappeared during the Second World War.

We are fortunate, however, to have a first-hand account of life at Wilton Square in the first decades of the twentieth century. Alun Jones came to London from Brynsiencyn, Anglesey, in 1912 and was a member of Wilton Square until his marriage in 1929. Pennant Jones kindly provided a copy of his father's memoirs which included his experience at Wilton Square:

> I was a 17-year-old youth when I came to London, in October 1912, to work
> for a company in the City of London. It was a business dealing with the rubber
> industry. I found a room with a widow called Mrs Morgan who lived in Highbury.
> She was a member of the Tabernacl, King's Cross, and the famous organist, David
> Richards, had been one of her tenants. I travelled by Tube from Highbury to my
> office at Moorgate. The nearest Welsh chapel to my digs was Wilton Square, so I
> became a member there. It was two miles away, and I made the journey on that first
> Sunday by horse-drawn tram. The fare was a penny. That was my way of getting

to the chapel for years until the electric trams came. The preacher that morning was the Revd David Oliver, Mile End, and in the evening, the Revd M. P. Morgan, Blaenannerch.

It was clearly a good Sunday to be visiting Wilton Square. The opportunity to listen to M. P. Morgan, a preacher of the highest grade, would have been too good to miss. Long after Alun Jones had left Wilton Square, serving for many years as an elder at Willesden Green, he retained a deep fondness for the cause in Hoxton:

I was a member there for 17 years, and I consider that period among the most blessed of my life. Wilton Square was an exceptionally welcoming church, its people were kind and accommodating, its services well attended, morning and evening. Most of the members lived nearby in Dalston, Canonbury and Highbury. There were some brilliant individuals there, such as Sir Wynn Wheldon, and they made a significant contribution to the Sunday school and the literary meeting. The minister, the Revd Morgan Griffith, was one of the greatest influences on my life. He was a true friend and a natural leader, and he wasn't afraid to confront those whose standards were deficient.

Wilton Square chapel converted into a hostel (1973)
© London Metropolitan Archive

Alun Jones's lively description of Morgan Griffith could fill an entire chapter. He was a keen runner (unusual in those days), often to be seen in his shorts, jogging on a Saturday evening, defying anyone to make a comment as he passed. He could also provide unusual guidance for a Christian minister: he told one member that turning the other cheek was fine, but any aggressor who then struck again should be 'half killed'.

It should come as no surprise that the Revd Morgan Griffith lived to a grand old age.

At the outbreak of the war, in September 1939, there were 174 members registered at Wilton Square, with just nineteen children attending Sunday school. It was a much weaker cause than Jewin, the 'mother' church, and far less robust as it faced the turmoil of wartime. The chapel was bombed in the early stages of the Blitz in 1940, and again in November of that year. The minister, the Revd T. H. Williams, moved to Chester, promising to return once a month to hold services at the church of St Phillip, Linton Street. The chapel was hit again by German bombers in May 1941, and the minister tendered his resignation the following month, after eighteen years in London.

Alun Jones recalled the scene after that first German strike in 1940:

My saddest memory of Wilton is of the morning I beheld the devastation of one of the biggest attacks of the war. That dear, sacred place, its walls torn down, the fine pulpit and organ covered in rubble. I could barely hold back the tears, and saddest of all was the failure to revive the church after that deadly blow. I shall never forget the glory of Wilton Square.

It was a traumatic time for all who lived through those years in London, and no one could be blamed for seeking peace and safety elsewhere. Some of the members and officers returned to Wales, but there were still 133 members and fifteen children registered in 1944. Services were still being held after the war in a local schoolroom, but by 1947 the arrangement ended. A committee chaired by Sir David Hughes Parry oversaw the process of examining the deeds, letting the caretaker's house (45 Wilton Square), and exploring the option of rebuilding the chapel. It was clear by 1953 that rebuilding was not an option: there was already talk of building a new chapel in north-east London. The new chapel at Leytonstone would open in 1958.

Capel Coffa y Gohebydd, Barrett's Grove, opened in 1885
© National Library of Wales

Wilton Square was formally decommissioned at a special service held in Charing Cross on 27 June 1956.

The German bombers claimed another Welsh chapel in this part of London. A ten-minute bus ride along the busy A10, heading from Wilton Square, brings us to Barrett's Grove, Stoke Newington, not far from the non-denominational Abney Park Cemetery, where so many London Welsh are buried.

The chapel in Barrett's Grove started in May 1846 as a branch of Borough, the oldest Welsh Independent (Annibynwyr) cause in London. There were just 65 members at the first home in Aldersgate Street, in the City of London, where they stayed until the expiry of the lease in 1870. The congregation – 32 by that time – then decided to move out of the City to north-east London, to the Cymry Hall, Hackney Road. They stayed there for five years. There was another move to Ware Street, Kingsland Road, where ambitious plans were made for a final move to a purpose-built chapel in Stoke Newington.

This was the chapel in Barrett's Grove, opened on 11 January 1885, known as 'Capel Coffadwriaethol y Gohebydd' ('The Correspondent's Memorial Chapel'), after John Griffith, the well-connected newspaper correspondent, education campaigner, and fervent eisteddfod supporter, who had served as the chapel secretary for many years. Building and paying for this new chapel was an exceptional venture for a congregation of just 70 members. The entire debt of £5,155 was repaid by 1905, which was a remarkable fundraising achievement.

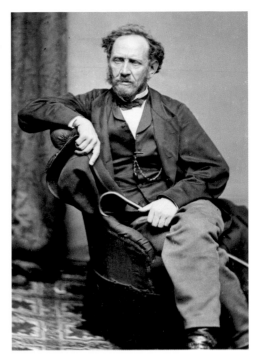

John Griffith ('Y Gohebydd') (1821–77)
© National Library of Wales

Barrett's Grove enjoyed a notably active period in the 1930s under the leadership of the Revd D. J. James, when membership increased from 60 to 166, and then under the Revd T. Glyn Thomas, whose ordination took place in the chapel on November 1936. There was growing optimism for the future of Barrett's Grove, but the building was badly damaged during the Second World War. Services were suspended and the 95 remaining members moved to King's Cross.

Morfudd Jenkins reported that Barrett's Grove was sold after the war and the proceeds used to support the three new chapels in Harrow, Slough and Luton. She and some fellow Annibynwyr visited the building in April 1986 to take part in special services held by The Church of God World Fellowship, a Pentecostal group which had bought and refurbished the building. Among those who spoke was Emrys Edwards, a King's Cross member, and a former mayor of Stoke Newington who had attended Barrett's Grove as a child.

With her customary faith, Morfudd expressed quiet satisfaction that Barrett's Grove was once again a place of Christian worship. It still is today, 130 years after the chapel was built.

Happily, the same can be said of the former Welsh Presbyterian chapel in Sussex Way, Holloway, some three miles north of Barrett's Grove. Holloway is now the home of the Greek Orthodox Community of Saint Anthony The Great and Saint John The Baptist. The Welsh congregation vacated the building in 2004 when Eglwys-y-Drindod was established in Cockfosters.

In its heyday, Holloway was one of the most active, enterprising Welsh chapels in London, known for its good-natured community, its lively Sunday school, and the density of its links with Cardiganshire. People who left London decades ago still recall their experiences in 'Capel Holloway' with notable warmth and affection.

The origins of the cause in Sussex Way go back to 1865, when members of Wilton Square met initially at the Holloway Institute, and then in a rented loft room called, rather grandly, Tollington Hall. It was a grim location, above a shop selling wild birds and animals, according to the Revd Edward Matthews, Ewenni:

> *It was a poor, run-down place, and it was as if Hell itself was opening its jaws wide open beneath us, with bulls and wild birds making unearthly noises.*

There are more details of Tollington Hall in the biography of Richard Owen, the noted revivalist who became Holloway's first minister:

> *Tollington Hall was a most inappropriate place for worship, a loft room, with second-hand seating organised as conveniently as was possible, a rickety floor, bare walls, and to make matters much worse, the floor below had been leased by a man who sold fish, four-legged creatures, birds, and the like.*

These were the bizarre, exotic circumstances in which Holloway started. Richard Owen, Llangristiolus, came to London in 1871 and soon took charge of the congregation at Tollington Hall. He was not a leader in the traditional mould, as the Revd Richard Thomas explained in the *Dictionary of Welsh Biography Down to 1940* (1992):

> *He had neither eloquence nor liveliness of gesture, and yet when he stood face to face with his congregation, and the inspiration of the moment was upon him, the lucidity of his thoughts and the vividness of his descriptions had an overwhelming effect.*

Despite his lack of showmanship, Richard Owen proved an able leader of the campaign to build a 'fitting chapel' in Holloway. He was supported by some generous colleagues, including Stephen Evans, one of his committee members. This was the building which opened, in Sussex Way, as described by the *Cambrian News* on 25 July 1873:

Holloway chapel opened in 1873
(1990)
© English Heritage

Interior of Holloway chapel (1990)
© English Heritage

The new Methodist chapel at Holloway [...] was opened for public worship on the 12th, 13th, and the evenings of the 14th and 15th July. On Saturday evening the Rev O. Thomas preached; Sunday morning the Rev. Edward Mathews; Sunday afternoon, in English, the Rev. Henry Simon (Cong.); and in the evening the Rev. Thomas Charles Edwards, M.A., Oxon., principal of the University College of Wales [...] The meetings were very well attended. About three or four years ago this little church formed an acquaintance with our patriotic countryman, Mr Stephen Evans, to whom she is greatly indebted for bringing her to her present condition. It is very probable that the church would be still worshipping in Tollington Hall if she had not met with a friend such as Mr Evans. Instead of a poor place like Tollington Hall she has now a building considered by men capable of judging, in all respects, equal to, if not better, than any other place of worship belonging to the Welsh in London. The new chapel cost £1,600, and the congregation have already subscribed and collected the sum of £800. This is worth notice, considering that they are comparatively poor people. We wish the little church every success in her new home.

Richard Owen was ordained in 1873 and acted as minister until his return to Anglesey the following year. Few men could claim to have made such an impact during a relatively brief stay in the capital. The foundations he laid were solid ones: Holloway chapel blossomed in the decade that followed, despite a thirteen-year period without a minister. The Revd W. Ryle Davies, a former quarryman from Waunfawr, who arrived in 1887, was welcomed in a special service which featured effusive addresses by 'Mabon' (the trade union leader and politician, William Abraham), and T. E. Ellis, the senior Liberal parliamentarian. Ryle Davies – rather unusually for a Welsh minister of that time – warned the packed congregation that he was no fan of 'soft soap'. His four years at Holloway were widely considered to be productive ones.

Membership had risen above 330, with 115 children registered at Sunday school. Ryle Davies was noted for his work among the chapel's young people, who excelled for many years at the inter-chapel eisteddfod and gymanfa. He established a Holloway tradition which lasted until the 1960s.

But Ryle Davies's story ended in tragedy. He lost his wife in January 1901, and he died three month later, at the age of 57, leaving three children without a mother or father. There were several appeals in the press for contributions to a special fund for the children.

He was followed in 1904 by the Revd R. O. Williams, who enjoyed consistently good relations with the church during his twelve years, and then by the Revd Griffith Rees, who came to Holloway as a student from Oxford. In 1928, after six years in London, he accepted a call to Princes Road, Liverpool, one of the biggest Welsh chapels ever built.

Holloway's membership reached its peak in 1936, with 455 adults and 120 attending the Sunday school, under the ministry of the Revd Emlyn Jones. It was, in the words of the Revd D. Elwyn Edwards, who'd attended Holloway as a child, a golden age:

Emlyn Jones was the minister, and no church has ever had a more conscientious and committed pastor. The Sunday morning service was well attended, better indeed than any other London Welsh chapel, and the Sunday evening service was very busy, boosted by students and domestic servants. The floor was full and a good number in the gallery. Emlyn Jones was at his best in the Communion service, and these were always intense occasions. His other great skill was teaching children, and the Sunday school was a huge success. He would take us to see Arsenal playing football, to see cricket at Lord's, and tennis at Wimbledon. He left in 1937 and it's fair to say that things were never the same after that.

In fairness to the successor, the Revd D. R. Jones, any new minister arriving three months before the outbreak of the Second World War would have faced a major challenge. To his eternal credit, he stayed in London throughout the war despite 'several opportunities to leave', according to Elwyn Edwards, who added that 'not every minister from Wales had honoured his commitments in London' during that time. Elwyn Edwards remarked that D. R. Jones 'did not see the church at its best', because of the mass evacuation of Welsh people from London in 1939. But he did, surely, experience the spirit and bravery of those who remained in Holloway's close-knit community, and that must be why he stayed until 1948.

By the time the Revd W. Lloyd Price arrived in 1949, membership had fallen to 290 (with 72 at Sunday school) but Holloway was still known as a very busy chapel community. It turned out to be a period of expansion, energetically supported by the minister, thanks to a bequest of £3,000 from Louise Jane Evans. Holloway's members had often talked of adding a new hall to the chapel, but resources or circumstances had made it impossible. But in February 1957 the dream was finally realised, when the new hall, kitchen and adjoining meetings rooms were opened. The total cost was £8,000. Within five years, the debt had been reduced to £600.

Holloway's membership in 1960 stood at 260. The minister agreed that it made sense to unite the cause with Wood Green, where membership had fallen to 60, to set things on firm foundations for the decade to come. W. Lloyd Price left for Porthmadog in 1962, after such a beneficial period in London, but the congregation was deeply saddened by news of his death in January 1964. His widow kindly provided some of the information used in this chapter.

The last minister of Holloway was its record-holder, the Revd Huw Llewelyn Jones, who came from Ystalyfera in March 1963 and stayed until his retirement in 1992. He enjoyed great respect and popularity across the entire London Welsh community, and played a leading part in managing the strategy of the Welsh Presbyterian chapels in London over a long and difficult period. Leytonstone was added to his ministry in 1970. Huw Llewelyn Jones came to London when the chapels were still relatively strong, and witnessed,

London Welsh ministers visit Coventry Cathedral in 1963: (left to right) A. Tudno Williams (Lewisham), Glanville Davies (Falmouth Road), Michael Parry (Leytonstone), Denzil Harries (Walham Green), Richard Jones (Charing Cross), Elfed Williams (Jewin), D. Hughes Jones (Willesden), H. Llewelyn Jones (Holloway), O. J. Evans (Clapham Junction)

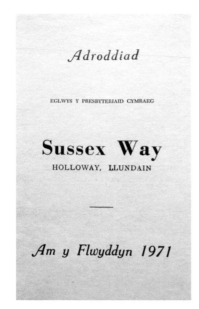

Adroddiad

EGLWYS Y PRESBYTERIAID CYMRAEG

Sussex Way

HOLLOWAY, LLUNDAIN

Am y Flwyddyn 1971

Annual report for Holloway chapel (1971)
© Eglwys Jewin

despite his sincere efforts, the collapse of the network. Despite what must have been his deep disappointment, he never lost his sense of duty or mission. He retired to Blaenpennal, Ceredigion, where he died in March 2011.

In July 2002, the decision was taken to create a new cause, Eglwys-y-Drindod ('Church of the Trinity'), uniting Holloway, Wood Green and Leytonstone in a newly-acquired building, the former United Reformed Church in Freston Gardens, Cockfosters. The last service at Holloway, conducted by the Revd Anthony Williams, was on 8 February 2004. The first service at Cockfosters took place on 7 March 2004, led by the Revd Dafydd H. Owen, the former minister, who saw his strategy come to fruition.

Wood Green, in north-west London, was one of the smaller chapels established by the Welsh in the capital. It started in Enfield, in 1899, with members from Wilton Square and Holloway meeting to worship at the Waldron Hall, near Enfield Town railway station. From there they moved to a hall in Lordship Lane, near the modern site of Wood Green underground station. A new church, comprising 23 members, was established on 23 October 1904.

The church grew slowly but steadily (there would be 76 members by 1909) so they built a 'corrugated iron' chapel on Bounds Green Road, on the corner of Northcott Avenue, where the Wood Green Community Seventh-Day Adventist Church stands today. It was known affectionately as the 'Capel Tin' (the 'Tin Chapel') and it was a Welsh base for nine years. They moved to a former Baptist chapel in Palace Road, Bounds Green, in February 1915. This would be their home until the formation of Eglwys-y-Drindod in 2004.

The chapel had a stage, but no pulpit or 'big seat' for the elders. Thanks to the generosity (yet again) of Sir Howell J. Williams, a major development

Wood Green chapel was built by the Baptists in 1915
© Haringey Archives

plan was devised, adding a hall (it was called the 'Tudor Hall' because of its beamed ceiling) and giving the chapel a more traditional look. The work was completed in time for special services in January 1923. Wood Green was said to have some of the best facilities of any London Welsh chapel at that time.

The 1920s and 1930s were good years for Wood Green, despite the absence of a full-time minister, and the community played its full part in the wider world of the capital's religious and social life. It all changed, predictably enough, in the Second World War. Wood Green chapel was badly damaged in the Blitz, its roof partially blown off, its windows shattered. But services continued in the elders' room, and new seating was brought from Stratford chapel, which had closed its doors in 1940 after a similar attack.

The church had always wanted to call its own minister, but the finances had not made this possible. They had enjoyed the leadership of the Revd D. R. Jones, Holloway, from 1941, but his departure in 1948 prompted new action. They invited the Revd E. Alun Thomas, Burry Port, to become minister of Wood Green. He accepted and was installed on 21 September 1950. It was an inspiring moment for the members, celebrating the appointment of their first-ever minister.

The Revd E. Alun Thomas and elders of Wood Green (1950)
© Eglwys-y-Drindod

Meurig Owen noted that Alun Thomas's arrival brought 'a sense of revival and purpose' in all areas of Wood Green's life. The minister's daughter, Delyth MacDonald, now living in Llanrhystud, said the family spent a happy, busy decade in London before returning to Wales in 1960:

My parents moved to London while my mother was expecting me, and I was born less than a month after my father's installation service – quite a start! I have a child's memory of that time, our easy walk to chapel while others had long journeys, and a big tea after Sunday school as many people could not be expected to get home and back again in time for the evening service. The 1950s were a good time for the London chapels, new faces appearing regularly, many young teachers among them, including Hafina Clwyd. There were lots of dairy families, and the Morgan family were farmers. Evan and Rosemary Morgan were pillars of the cause at Wood Green. Their son is the Revd Evan Morgan of Salem, Canton, Cardiff.

Delyth also recalled the practical challenges faced by her father at that time:

He had no car while he was there, and relied on the underground for most of his preaching engagements. He would sometimes fall asleep on the way home at night, and wake up at Cockfosters, the end of the line. Our home in London was a magnet for family and friends from Wales, and there would be people staying with us quite often. My father's salary was small, but he and my mother would always try to show visitors around the West End. London life was seen as 'glamorous' at that time, with St David's Day dinners at the Savoy, and my mother's emerald green 'evening dress' made quite an impact on a young girl.

There were several notable contributions by individuals to Wood Green over the years. The Morgan family of Home Farm, Queenswood, were certainly key members, as was the former missionary to India, Gwen Evans, who joined Wood Green in the 1960s.

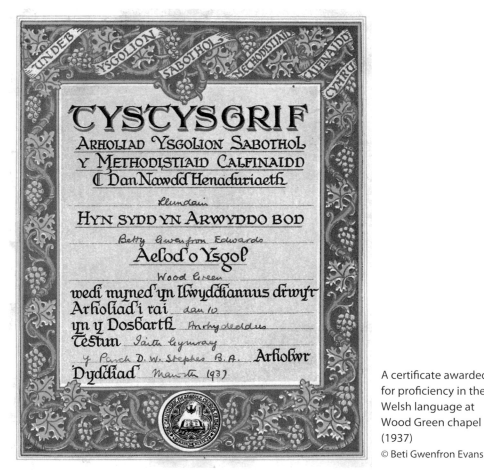

A certificate awarded for proficiency in the Welsh language at Wood Green chapel (1937)
© Beti Gwenfron Evans

Gwen Evans was a remarkable woman. She spent many years in northeast India as a teacher, establishing the Presbyterian High School in Shillong. She was proud of her work in India, but modest about her achievements. She told me what happened after her return to Britain:

> I returned in 1969 and lived with my sister in Enfield. Wood Green chapel was nearby, so I joined there. We were looked after by the Revd Huw Llewelyn Jones, Holloway, a good preacher and pastor. Wood Green was a lovely, warm community, very homely. I started preaching in 1970, and in 1975, to my surprise, I was elected an elder at Wood Green. At that time, in the 1970s, there was still a bit of life in the Welsh chapels in London. A decent crowd at Charing Cross on a Sunday morning, and again at Jewin in the evening. A strong chapel in Willesden, and really good at Ealing Green. Clapham was thriving. I didn't like the journey to Falmouth Road. Walham Green was friendly enough, but maybe not quite as welcoming as the others.

Gwen Evans served all the London Welsh chapels for four decades after her retirement from missionary work. The tributes paid at her memorial service in Cockfosters in 2014 underlined her good influence on the lives of so many people, including thousands of schoolchildren.

One of those who took part in Gwen's service was Bowen Williams, a member at Wood Green since the 1930s. He was born in Stockwell, in south London, in 1921, where his parents, originally from the Llan-non area, were among the last dairymen to keep a herd of cows in a city dairy. In 1932, they moved to Hornsey, in north London, where Bowen was involved in the family dairy business for 53 years until his retirement in 1985. The family were all members at Wood Green, as he explained:

> It was a small chapel on Palace Road, not easy to find. They had to put up a sign saying 'Welsh Chapel' on the corner of Palace Road and Bounds Green Road. It was an old Baptist chapel, with a baptism pool under the floor. There was a very good Sunday school there, six classes in the years before the war, plenty of room in the Tudor Hall and the rooms behind the chapel. We had trips to Broxbourne in the summer, great fun. I also played football for the London Welsh and played some matches with the Falmouth Road boys.

Go for a stroll along Palace Road today, and you will find no evidence

Artist's impression of Willesden Green chapel, opened in 1900
© National Library of Wales

of the old chapel. The sign at the corner has gone, and the building has made way for a block of flats.

Services ended at Wood Green in 2002, and the remaining members joined their friends from Holloway and Leytonstone two years later.

By that time, Eglwys-y-Drindod was the only Welsh Presbyterian cause left in north London, as Willesden Green chapel had closed in June 1999, just eleven months after marking its centenary in July 1998.

On the eve of the Second World War, Willesden had 351 adult members and 54 children, forming a strong church under the leadership of the Revd John Thickens, one of the biggest names in the story of the London Welsh chapels.

John Thickens, born in Cwmystwyth in 1865, spent thirteen years as minister of Tabernacl, Aberaeron, during which time he was influenced by the preaching of his uncle, Joseph Jenkins, New Quay. They organised meetings

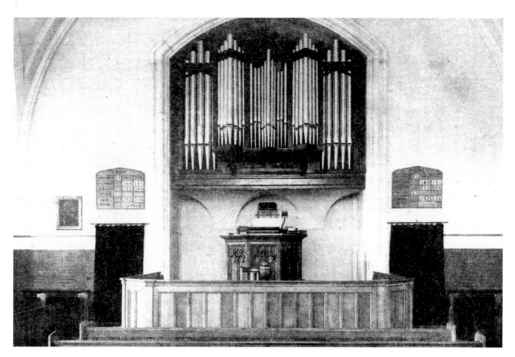

Interior of Willesden Green chapel after the organ installation (1928)

which would contribute to the religious revival of 1904–5, spearheaded by Evan Roberts.

He accepted a call from Willesden Green, a relatively young London Welsh church, in 1907, and stayed there until his retirement at the end of the Second World War. He died in 1952 in Leamington Spa, but his ashes were buried at Hen Fynyw churchyard, Aberaeron.

Gomer Roberts described him as 'a notable preacher at the height of his power… a mystic by nature, and despite his great interest in theology, his favourite study was the history of hymnody of the mystics'. When his widow, Cecilia, died in 1953, the tributes praised her ability to keep her 'otherworldly' husband 'in touch with this world, from time to time'. He was a prominent Welsh Presbyterian, serving as moderator of the South Wales Association in 1938, and moderator of the General Assembly in 1945.

John Thickens 'steeped himself in the history and ethos of the Presbyterian Church of Wales', and, despite 'his pedantic and over-grammatical style', wrote authoritatively on the origins of the London Welsh chapels. He devoted years of effort to the search for original historical sources. His Davies Lecture, later

The Revd John Thickens and elders of Willesden Green in the 1930s

published as *Howel Harris yn Llundain* (1938), was a detailed study of a year in the life of the great Methodist pioneer.

He was a thoughtful, serious man who despised cynicism and sarcasm. There are several accounts of his tendency to reprimand ministerial colleagues – for cracking the tamest of jokes – and to remind congregations of their obligations to the church.

Verdicts on his preaching tended to vary: many judged him 'dry' and 'dull', while others insisted he could be 'fiery' and 'spirited'. It clearly depended on the mood of the day. What could not be denied was his quality as a pastor. He was unfailingly concerned for people's welfare, and his work during the Second World War, rushing to members' homes after German bombing raids to check on his people, was never forgotten.

The centenary services in 1998 provided an opportunity for members and former members to share their memories of life at Willesden Green. Among those who contributed was Iola Bilson, one of the third generation of the big Morgan family which played an essential part in the story of the chapel.

Iola's father, Trefor, was one of eight children of Dafydd and Lisa

The Revd Richard Williams and elders of Willesden Green in the 1950s

Morgan, who ran a dairy business in Willesden High Road. Her mother, Audrey, born in 1915 in Bangor, came to London in 1936 to find work, and settled in the Willesden area. She met Trefor at the Welsh chapel, where they were married by the Revd John Thickens, who also baptised four of their five children.

I visited Audrey Morgan at her home in Aberaeron in January 2012. She was then 96, her mind as sharp as ever, and keen to share her memories of four decades at Willesden Green:

> *When I came to London in 1936, Mrs Cecilia Thickens would invite me for tea on Sunday afternoons. She was from Dowlais, and although she could speak Welsh, she preferred to speak English. Her husband always spoke Welsh. They were a very kind couple. Mr Thickens could appear distracted, lost in his thoughts. I remember one occasion when he walked past the window, and his wife said to me: 'Please can you pop out and tell my husband that this is where he lives?' He was an excellent pastor, always walking in all weathers, or using the Tube to cross*

London. He showed great courage during the Second World War. After every night of bombing, he'd check on the chapel and then visit members' homes. We had a dreadful experience one night when a rocket hit our home. Had I not taken little Iola from her cot, and taken refuge in the shelter, things would have been very different. The people next door were killed.

Audrey's brother-in-law, Tom Morgan, who was born at the family dairy in Willesden in 1922, attended the chapel for nearly 60 years before retiring to Wales in 1981. He held John Thickens in the highest regard, and loved chapel life:

The minister was a great man, Mr Thickens, a good and loyal friend to our family. When I was young, he secured me a place at Haberdashers' School, an excellent school. He went to see the headmaster on my father's behalf. He was very warm and interested in our welfare as children. I can still see Mr Thickens walking along the street in his black homburg hat, he always wore it. We attended chapel three times every Sunday, always sitting in the family pew in Row 38.

Tom played an important part in the musical life of the chapel, and paid tribute to Kenneth Thomas, the conductor who set the highest standards:

The singing in the chapel was always good. Kenneth Thomas was an excellent musician and led the singing. We had a good choir at the chapel, the Willesden Choral Society, set up by Kenneth and me. We took the choir to Eisteddfod Pontrhydfendigaid several times and performed with Anne Evans and Gwyneth Jones. After the performance we'd go back to the Feathers in Aberaeron where the singing was often better than it had been at the eisteddfod! This was also the beginning of the London Welsh Festival Choir, and our first concert was at the Royal Festival Hall with Owain Arwel Hughes conducting, and Anne Evans as soloist. I was a very active member of the London Welsh Male Voice Choir, and after a very unfortunate disagreement among the choristers, I helped to form the Gwalia Male Voice Choir in the 1960s. We did very well at the Llangollen International Eisteddfod, coming second in our first appearance there.

Audrey Morgan shared her brother-in-law's love of competitive activity:

It was busy, very lively. I won several prizes in the chapel eisteddfod for poetry and essay-writing. I won two chairs for poetry at the inter-chapel eisteddfod, open to all the London Welsh community. I was also asked to adjudicate, and remember an eisteddfod at Clapham Junction, where the vestry was full of young children rehearsing. It was a wonderful sight.

A range of old Willesden friends recognised those experiences. Russ Jones, a founder member of the London Welsh Male Voice Choir, later joining the Gwalia Male Choir, stressed the quality of the music at Willesden. Kenneth Thomas was always in demand as a conductor of oratorios and the gymanfa ganu, and he also directed the St David's Singers and the London Welsh Youth Choir. He was a great asset, as was the organist Cyril Anthony FRCO, who later moved to King's Cross. His brother, Trevor Anthony, had a very good voice and was a popular soloist. Among the big names who performed in concerts over the years were Ryan Davies, the multi-talented Welsh entertainer, and the soprano, Isobel Baillie, one of the leading oratorio singers of the twentieth century.

Rita Clark remembered 'après-chapel jaunts into London on the bus to sing Welsh hymns at Hyde Park Corner, and a visit to Lyons' Corner House for a meal'. Rita also underlined the impact of marriage on the identity of the London Welsh community, noting that surnames changed from Roberts, Evans, Morgan, Daniels, and Jones, to Butlin, Bilson, Miles, Buckner, Clark and so on. The effect, as Rita said, was 'to throw a smokescreen over our very Welsh identity'.

Thelma Butlin recalled many annual coach trips to Chorleywood, Hertfordshire, which 'for town children was a lovely outing to the wilds of the country'. Beryl Miles remembered 'a full vestry for the St David's Day and harvest suppers', and the competitive world of table tennis, drama, and singing competitions. Tegwen Hughes said they played 'with the dedication of minor professionals', and matches in the chapels' league were taken very seriously.

Iola and Bob Bilson were just one of so many couples married at Willesden Green, and Iola underlined the emotional attachment to a building where so many important family events had taken place.

The Willesden story began in 1895 when a group of people started meeting at the home of John Davies, a pharmacist and member of Jewin.

They grew in number and hired a room at the Regency Hall, Willesden High Road, where two Sunday school classes were formed in January 1896. Soon there were five classes, and religious services were held on a non-denominational basis. By 1897 a majority felt drawn to the Calvinistic Methodists, and by April 1898 they had built a new schoolroom on a plot of land at 265 Willesden Lane. This is where the church was established and it would remain there for a century.

Some notable individuals contributed to the Willesden story. They included the man known as 'Yr Anseisnigadwy' ('The Unenglishable') – an unforgettable nickname. John Williams, one of the great cultural benefactors of the London Welsh in the first half of the twentieth century, fully deserved the compliment.

'JW' was a Gwynedd man, a roofer who came to London in 1900 and established a very successful business. His autobiography, *Hynt Gwerinwr* ('A Worker's Tale'), published in 1944, is one of the best accounts of a young Welshman's experience in London at the turn of the century. He was a keen poet and eisteddfod competitor, and a stickler for accuracy in the Welsh language. John Williams joined Willesden chapel and remained a member until his return to Wales before the Second World War. His grandson, Pennant Jones, underlined his achievements:

> His autobiography recounts his childhood in Rhostryfan, his first work in the slate quarries, then jobs in Liverpool and London. It contains an impression of London Welsh life in the 1930s, including comment on the central role of the chapels in the capital. He also wrote a regular column for Y Cymro headed 'O'r Brifddinas' ('From the Capital') under the byline of 'JW Llundain', for which he became famous. He wrote similar columns for Y Brython entitled 'Ymhlith Cymry Llundain'. With his great friend, D. R. Hughes, he was the co-editor of the London Welsh monthly journal Y Ddolen which was published from 1923 to 1941. It is a goldmine of information about every aspect of London Welsh life in that period.

Pennant's family story thus connects two of the strongest Welsh chapels in north London before the Second World War. His father, Alun Jones, had moved from Wilton Square in 1929 and became a long-serving elder at Willesden Green.

The Revd John Thickens was by far the longest-serving minister. His predecessor, the chapel's first minister, Dr Richard Roberts, arrived in 1900 and stayed for just three years. John Thickens was succeeded, in 1949, by the Revd Richard Williams, a charismatic preacher who revived the church after the Second World War and was especially popular with the younger members. The Revd D. Hughes Jones, a Llanelli man, was minister during the 1960s, and he was followed by the Revd Geraint Thomas, who'd added Willesden to his pastorate at Shirland Road. The Revd Anthony Williams was the last minister, serving for a decade from 1989.

Willesden Green chapel was also widely known for another reason: for many years it was the home of Ysgol Gymraeg Llundain (the Welsh School in London) and there are hundreds of former pupils who recall the building with warmth and affection. It is no exaggeration to say that Willesden Green, in that sense, made an impact unlike any other chapel in London.

The story of Willesden overlapped for a significant period with that of the small Welsh chapel in Wembley, some five miles away to the west. This was a relatively short-lived cause which opened in 1939 and closed in 1972, but packed a significant amount into those 33 years. Its origins were in the Welsh Society formed in the Wembley area in September 1927, and a non-denominational Sunday school established the following year. The opening of the Gwalia Hall, London Road, in October 1929, was described as good news 'for Welsh exiles in London', and weekly religious services were organised there. It is important to underline, again, that the cause belonged to no one denomination at that time. But the opening of Harrow Independent chapel in 1937 drew people away, so the remaining Wembley congregation applied to become part of the Presbyterian Church of Wales. The new cause was formed on 12 March 1939. The Revd John Thickens and the Revd Eliseus Howells were among those who preached.

The first report, listing 34 founding members, stated bleakly:

We expected great things, but within six months war was declared, and the horrors of the blackout were with us. Many of our services were cancelled. We are a small flock but we are determined to keep faith.

Mrs Tudor Edwards opens the Gwalia Hall, Wembley, watched by the Revd Peter Hughes Griffiths (right) (1929)

Tom and Myra Davies, both natives of Brynaman, were members at Wembley from 1952 until it closed. Myra had come to London as a teacher in 1947. Tom was an aircraft engineer with the de Havilland company. They heard of the chapel in a conversation with neighbours, and decided to join. Their daughter, Janet, was christened there by the Revd D. W. Stephens in 1955.

Tom explained, in a conversation we had in 2012, that he and Myra were the only remaining former members of Wembley, and he went on to qualify the use of the world 'chapel':

> *It wasn't a traditional chapel building. It was a small, simple hall. A big room with a wooden roof. It was called the Gwalia Hall, built on a plot which had been 'spotted' by Jordan Jones, who owned a tailor's shop in Wembley. The members included a local consultant, Dr Tudor Edwards, whose wife had opened the Gwalia Hall, and Kenneth Thomas, the musician, who'd transferred his membership from Willesden. Dr Edwards was more or less in charge.*

Myra recalled her earliest memories of settling in Wembley, and the advantage of being able to meet other Welsh mothers in the area:

> *It was 1948, and Wembley was very busy with the Olympic Games. I remember taking Janet in the pram on Tuesday afternoons to the chapel in London Road. There were lots of young mothers and babies there. It was a great community, and at Christmas we would clear all the seating and organise a big dinner in the hall. We didn't have our own minister, we shared with Willesden and Shirland Road, and that seemed to work very well.*

Wembley closed in 1972 following the imposition of a compulsory purchase order by the Post Office, which wanted to expand the telephone exchange next door. It is interesting to note that there were still 70 members on the books in 1972, a perfectly respectable number in today's terms. Wembley had never been a strong cause, but as the Revd Geraint Thomas noted in the final report, the decision had been taken 'deliberately and purposefully to unite with Willesden Green'.

Myra and Tom were members at Willesden until it closed in 1999, and then transferred their membership to Harrow, which was more convenient for them than Ealing Green. They received a warm welcome from the 'Annibynwyr' of Harrow, a church known for its spirit of friendship and inclusivity.

As Morfudd Jenkins explained in her excellent booklet on the history of Harrow Welsh Church, *Hanes Eglwys Gymraeg Harrow 1937–87* (1987), the period between the two world wars was the most flourishing and prosperous in the story of the London Welsh chapels. Better transport facilities and better housing tempted many people to move out of London and settle in the new suburbs. Many Welsh people were drawn to Harrow, and they established their own place of worship there.

The Harrow Welsh Society was formed in November 1929, and religious services in the Welsh language were started the following year in the English Congregational Church, Hindes Road. It is interesting to note that the preacher was a Baptist, the Revd James Nicholas of Castle Street. There were 120 present, a response which led to other services being organised in 1931. Enthusiasm waned over the years to 1935, and services ended. Everything changed the following year when Morfudd Jenkins's father, J. R. Thomas

Elfed, 'JR', and the Revd Idris Jenkins at the opening of Harrow chapel (1949)

of King's Cross, urged the Independent churches to extend their influence. A working party was formed, and Harrow was identified as an ideal target. Special services were arranged in April–May 1937, including sermons by Elfed, which took place at the YMCA building in Station Road.

A public meeting in Harrow on 11 October 1937 concluded that there was sufficient demand in Harrow to establish a new Welsh cause, under the auspices of the 'Annibynwyr', and within a few years, similar decisions were made in Luton and Slough. The Welsh cause in Slough, 'Capel-y-Lôn', was founded in 1938 and was based for many years in a chapel in Stoke Poges Lane, but has since moved to St John the Baptist Church. It was started by Welsh people driven from the valleys of south Wales by the economic depression. Similar factors created the Welsh chapel in Luton, called 'Noddfa', also formed in 1938. It was an active church for many years, especially in the 1950s, and survived until 1991.

Harrow Welsh Church was formally established on 7 November 1937 at the Labour Hall, Wealdstone, featuring Elfed and other guest preachers. There were 94 founding members, 141 by the end of the year, 211 by the end of 1938, and plans were being made to build a chapel in the area. A plot of land was bought in Marlborough Hill, not far from Harrow and Wealdstone station, an architect was appointed, plans were drawn up, but the events of September 1939 put everything on hold.

The first minister, the Revd J. Idris Jenkins, was called in 1946. He married Morfudd, J. R. Thomas's daughter, and they gave their all to the new church. 'JR' was prevailed upon to share his time between King's Cross and Harrow, such was the demand for his advice and wisdom.

The need to find a permanent home was the first priority. A disused chapel in Lower Road, Harrow, built by the English Wesleyan Methodists in 1856, became available. It had been used as an unemployment centre, an engineering workshop, and a furniture warehouse. Repair work on the building began in 1947, and furniture was obtained from Barrett's Grove chapel, which had closed in 1940. The pulpit was a perfect fit, and so was the pipe organ.

The renovated chapel was opened on 16 July 1949. The special services drew huge crowds from London and Wales, and a BBC broadcast was produced. The opening ceremony was performed by J. R. Thomas, who linked arms with Elfed as the historic deed was done. 'JR' was there, too, in his capacity as chairman of the Union of Welsh Independents. It was a great occasion.

Harrow has been exceptionally fortunate in its ministers: Idris Jenkins, who was also a great friend to the congregation in Slough, served until 1965; Alwyn Charles, who would become professor of Christian doctrine at Bala-Bangor Theological College, stayed for just a year; W. Eifion Powell, another distinguished scholar, served from 1967 to 1972; E. Stanley John, who would succeed Alwyn Charles at Bala-Bangor, arrived in 1973; the record-holder, D. Gwylfa Evans, came from Pwll, Llanelli, in 1978, and

he still cares for Harrow today. At one stage, he was minister of all the Independent chapels in London. His service has been exemplary. Gwylfa celebrated his half-century in the ordained ministry in 2012 with a special service at Harrow attended by hundreds of friends and admirers. His

The Revd D. Gwylfa Evans celebrated 50 years in the ministry in 2012

The interior of Eglwys-y-Drindod, Cockfosters (2014)

wife, Buddug, was rightly praised for her unstinting support throughout that time.

The extensive sphere of Welsh worship in northern London – from Islington to Harrow – has included some of the strongest examples of Christian witness in the story of the London Welsh.

The tradition is still alive in Cockfosters and Harrow.

We pay homage to the workers in the vineyard.

CHAPTER 15

WESLEY'S WAYS

A visit to the historic City Road, home to the prominent dissenters' burial ground, Bunhill Fields, brings us to one of London's most famous Nonconformist churches.

Wesley's Chapel is often called the 'mother church' of Methodism. And just in case there's any lingering doubt about the identity of its founder, a statue of John Wesley dominates the forecourt. This was the church, a sublime example of Georgian architecture, built by him in 1778.

The superintendent minister, the Revd Dr Lord (Leslie) Griffiths, a Burry Port man, has enjoyed a phenomenally successful ministry here for the past two decades. His is a flourishing church, packed with a richly diverse congregation every Sunday, proud of its heritage, confident of its identity. This is a brand of Methodism that clearly works.

The 'brand' is relevant to our story: Wesleyan Methodism was (and is) theologically different to the Calvinistic Methodism which dominated Wales for so long. And though the differences might seem less than drastic today, the fact is that these two branches of Methodism developed in radically different ways.

Leslie Griffiths kindly accepted my challenge to provide clarification on this most perplexing of issues:

> *'Calvinistic Methodism' is a straightforward contradiction in terms. Almost the only theological battle which John Wesley fought was against Calvinism. His contemporary and one-time friend and collaborator, George Whitefield, did, however, insist on keeping Calvin's doctrine of predestination and limited grace within his own understanding of Methodism. The two friends fell out on this, and Whitefield's*

Wesley's Chapel was built in 1778 (2013)

formula was picked up by the Countess of Huntingdon's Connexion in England and, via Howell Harris, in Calvinistic Methodism in Wales. In order to maintain this distinction, it became necessary to qualify the use of the simple term 'Methodist' when applied to the followers of John Wesley. They became known throughout Wales as 'Wesleyan Methodists'.

In Wales, the vast majority of Welsh-speaking Methodist congregations were in the Calvinistic fold; the Wesleyans, while strong in a few areas, were slower to penetrate Wales and always struggled to get a country-wide foothold.

The relative weakness of the Welsh-speaking Wesleyans was vividly demonstrated by their experience in London, where, despite a relatively early start, they failed to achieve the kind of progress made by other denominations. Indeed, their story is often one of missed opportunities, endless financial difficulties, and sheer bad luck.

There are some high points to counter the gloom. The Welsh Wesleyans managed to build one of the grandest chapels in London, a fitting home for some of the best preachers Wales had to offer. The City Road chapel, which opened in 1883, was located just a few yards away from Wesley's Chapel.

Madness? Maybe. Here were the Welsh building a Wesleyan Methodist chapel almost next door to the church built by the great John Wesley himself. They were part of the same 'brand'. The crucial difference was the language of worship, but it still seems shockingly brazen to set up shop so close to head office.

Having said that, the Welsh Wesleyans had certainly been active in the area for several decades. The Revd Hugh Carter had come to London in 1809, and it was under his leadership that the first Welsh Wesleyan chapel was built in St Mary Axe, opening in March 1812. St Mary Axe, a street in the heart of the City of London, is best known today as the location of 'the Gherkin', the famous skyscraper designed by Norman Foster.

There were daunting financial challenges from the outset. Workers with little money to spare were asked to make significant contributions. A £40 gift from the Cymreigyddion Society boosted things, but there were too few members to share the burden comfortably. There were just 62 members in 1823, barely rising to 75 in 1826.

No wonder that things fell apart in 1830. The chapel at St Mary Axe was transferred to the English Wesleyans, while the Welsh rented a chapel in Aldersgate for £80 a year. This move may have attracted more backers – there were 109 members in 1830 – but soon they were back in trouble because of the extra City taxes levied on the cellar space under the chapel. By 1839 they were back in St Mary Axe, and that is where they stayed until 1848. After that they moved again to Friar's Street chapel, Doctors' Commons, near St Paul's.

This is where the first Welsh Wesleyan cause in London came to an end. The records mention countless visiting ministers (many of them sharing the same name, hence David Jones II, Edward Jones III, William Davies I etc.) in line with the Wesleyan 'circuit' system which encouraged the regular switching of preachers. The system had clear advantages, but stability, in a London context, would probably have been a much more powerful means of keeping congregations together.

Thanks to a new wave of migration from Wales in the mid-nineteenth century, the Welsh Wesleyans were able to regroup. Services were held in

Jewin Street (an important English Methodist church not far from the Welsh Calvinistic chapel in nearby Jewin Crescent) from 1852, always on Sunday afternoons, and by 1856 they were given use of the vestry at Wilson Street chapel, no more than five minutes' walk from Wesley's Chapel.

This arrangement worked well, encouraged by the Revd Humphrey Jones II whose missionary work among the London Welsh had been financed by North Wales Home Mission Committee. The result was that they rented Wilson Street chapel (all of it) and by 1863 had bought and renovated the building for £1,322.

During the building work they worshipped jointly with the Welsh Independents in Aldersgate. It seems entirely fair to ask why, if joint worship was so readily acceptable, was there any desire to spend money building a separate new cause? Fair, but probably not sensible. The question could apply to congregations in any number of villages, towns and cities. The answer lay in a potent mix of denominational tribalism, theological differences (manufactured or otherwise), personal preference, and simple vanity.

Dr Owen Thomas of Jewin preached at the opening services (no sign of denominational schism there) in June 1863. Some frenetic fundraising (especially in Wales) helped to eliminate the entire debt by the following year. It was a stunning result, especially for the Welsh Wesleyans with their record of financial horrors. But membership was still disappointingly low (85 in 1865) and there was no sign of any dramatic improvement. Not yet, at any rate.

It all changed in late 1878 with the arrival of the Revd John Evans, Eglwysbach, one of the most brilliant preachers ever to emerge from Wales, a spellbinding speaker who had the power to sway and influence thousands. His arrival transformed the life of the Welsh Wesleyans in London, but people still argue about the decisions he took and the priorities he identified.

The press reports of his welcoming ceremony are full of breathless, swooning speeches delivered by the Welsh 'grandees' of London. He was a 'prince' who deserved a 'royal welcome', a 'giant' who had 'deigned to bless a handful of London Welsh people'.

They were right about the 'handful': there were just 63 members at Wilson Street in 1878 (a significant fall since 1865) and 45 at Poland Street (a relatively new Welsh Wesleyan cause in Soho, in London's West End).

The Revd John Evans, Eglwysbach
(1840–97)
© National Library of Wales

It is remarkable to think that 'Eglwysbach' (as John Evans was affectionately known) left Wales, where chapels were invariably crammed for his sermons, to take charge of a flock of 108 members in London. No wonder some people questioned his sanity in accepting the posting. But John Evans had ambition, vision, and iron determination, as we shall see.

He gave the strongest hint of what was to come when he addressed Hwfa Môn's leaving service in May 1881:

> *The London chapels are small and plain, the congregations thin. In Wales, the chapel is the most prominent building. This is much to the preacher's advantage, because a big chapel attracts people. No matter how good or bad the sermon, an imposing chapel draws a crowd. But in London we have no attractive Welsh chapels. The biggest holds 700 people, and what is that in London?*

The '700' swipe would have been aimed at New Jewin, which had opened in 1879 and was, by all accounts, a very handsome building. Even worse was his line about 'imposing' chapels, given that Wales would be saddled with far too many 'imposing' chapels with too few decent preachers to fill them.

But John Evans was not a man to be deflected. There were plans to extend Wilson Street (despite having just 130 members) but the pub landlord next door demanded £1,500 for two yards of his land. This might well have been the excuse John Evans needed to press for grander plans. The Wilson Street site was sold to the trustees of Wesley's Chapel for £2,000 while the Welsh Wesleyans started searching for land on which to build a new chapel.

They came across a plot for sale 'a few yards from the cathedral of Methodism', according to one report, on the corner of City Road and a narrow street called Oliver's Yard. The total cost, including the purchase of adjoining warehouses and the freehold rights, was in excess of £13,000 – a crippling sum for such a small congregation. John Evans was the driving force behind the plans, fired up no doubt by dreams of preaching to big crowds in a grand chapel near Wesley's final resting place. He displayed all the strengths and weaknesses of a conviction leader: there was remarkable energy and drive, accompanied by stubborn refusal to heed advice.

To be fair to Eglwysbach, he advanced other reasons for aiming high. He reckoned there were more than 3,000 Welsh-speaking Wesleyans in London (it must have been based on the roughest guesswork) and yet no more than 250 could be accommodated in Wilson Street. He stressed the need for a 'centrally-located chapel, in a prominent place, with room for 500 people, and a suite of comfortable rooms and facilities for Welsh people coming to London'.

He was also highly critical of the London situation compared with the thriving Welsh Wesleyan set-ups in Liverpool and Manchester. The Londoners, it was said, may have been marginally stronger than the weakest circuit of all, in Utica, New York State, but it was a close-run thing. It had to change, and John Evans was convinced that his big ideas for City Road would transform the London scene.

The foundation stones were laid in the winter of 1882; the memorial stones were added in December, and in the two years it took to build the new chapel, they worshipped at the YMCA in Aldersgate Street, St Mark's Hall in Old Street, and at Wesley's Chapel.

The impressive City Road Welsh Wesleyan Church – one of the grandest

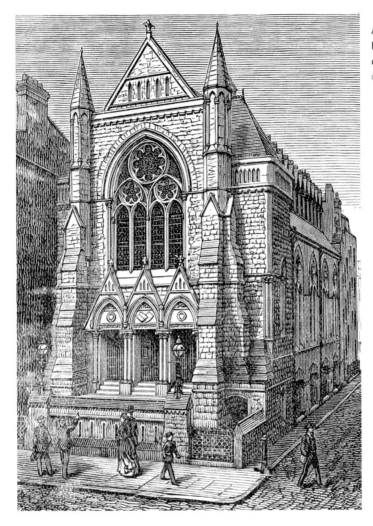

Artist's impression of City
Road Welsh Wesleyan
chapel (1883)
© National Library of Wales

Welsh chapels ever built – opened with a series of services, featuring no fewer than ten celebrity preachers, in September 1883. The first sermon in the new building was preached, not unreasonably, by Eglwysbach himself, taking as his theme: 'My house will be called a house of prayer for all nations.' (We have no way of knowing if he strayed into the next line: 'But you have made it a den of robbers.') Press reports of the opening were predictably frothy.

It is clear that the stress and strain of driving such an ambitious project, not to mention establishing new branches in Blackheath and Kentish Town, had damaged John Evans's health. Despite the elation of seeing the chapel open and attracting new members, there were thousands of pounds still to repay, and no easy ways of finding the money. By March 1884, he was forced to spend time in Caernarfon, resting and reflecting on the work ahead. There were hints that he was on the verge of a breakdown, with talk of 'nerves giving way' and being 'haunted' by the City Road venture. He was frequently let down by people who pledged money but never handed over the cash. Costs had spiralled to £15,000 ('unreasonably expensive', in his own words) but he pledged to pay off the balance by the end of 1885.

John Evans did not achieve that goal, to his deep and lasting regret, because he was obliged to move from London by 1886. He had dreamed of leaving behind a thriving, debt-free church. It was certainly thriving (there were 293 members at the time of his departure) but the financial challenges were still shocking. The debt stood at a mighty £3,000.

It is easy to imagine Eglwysbach's successors cursing his ambitions and grandiose plans as they fumbled for shillings in bazaars and concerts to raise much-needed funds. It is no exaggeration to say that the life of City Road, until the debt was finally cleared in 1910, revolved around money. It must have been a rather depressing experience.

The Revd Ishmael Evans, whose ministry in London ended in 1901, offered these reflections on the City Road experience:

> Let me say right away that the chapel is a handsome, pleasant building, seating 500 people, with a big hall in the basement, and other useful rooms attached. John Evans did all he could to repay the money, and he certainly had rich and powerful friends, but he had to leave London in 1886 with much of the debt outstanding. Promised help did not materialise. He was a deeply disappointed man.

He went on to shed light on the thoughts of Eglwysbach's successors in London:

> It is not for me to go into detail about the anxiety and the overwhelming burden imposed on those who followed Mr Evans. Interest payments on £3,000 and ground rent of £240 annually! Yes, the ministers and loyal members of City Road worked hard to overcome these challenges. I have, however, come to the view that Mr Evans was right to pursue his dream. Welsh Wesleyan Methodism has never been as influential in London as it is today. The size and beauty of our chapel has contributed to this.

More (unintentionally) damning, though, was Ishmael Evans's concluding thought:

> There are 170 members, and on Sunday evenings we often welcome more than 200 people there. And we could recoup our money at any time, if there was a desire to sell and move to a quieter place, which is unlikely. People have said very hard things about City Road, but those who know best are those who know its workers and their achievements.

The membership, therefore, had fallen since John Evans's departure, and even on a good Sunday evening, more than half the chapel seats were empty. It is very difficult to accept Ishmael Evans's spinning of the facts. This was one of London's grandest Welsh chapels, established by one of Wales's best preachers, losing members at a time when other Welsh chapels were booming.

The eternal struggle at City Road became painfully evident in the annual reports of the 1930s, when the other denominational fortresses – Jewin, Charing Cross, King's Cross and Castle Street – were all having to manage membership lists of more than 1,000 people. City Road, given its status, size, and prominent location, deserved to be in the same category. It is rather shocking to read the officers' frank foreword to the 1936 annual report:

> The financial burden facing our circuit is carried by a small number of people. Some of our churches face exceptionally heavy pressures, with very few members to share the burden. Levels of enthusiasm and zeal vary a good deal. It would be good to be able to convince ourselves that poor attendance on Sunday mornings is the result of entirely lawful activity.

YR EGLWYS FETHODISTAIDD

CYLCHDAITH

City Road, Llundain

Adroddiad Blynyddol

AM Y FLWYDDYN 1936

Gweinidogion y Gylchdaith :
Parch. R. CONWAY PRITCHARD,
20, Baalbec Road, Highbury, N.5.
Parch. J. IDRIS DAVIES,
63, Balmoral Road, Willesden, N.W.2.

Goruchwylwyr y Gylchdaith :
Mr. JOHN RICHARDS, 10 Hillmarton Road, N.7.
Mr. S. G. JONES, 2 Kelfield Gardens, W.10.

BLAENAU FFESTINIOG A HARLECH :
Argraffwyd gan J. D. Davies a'i Gwmni, Rhedegydd

One of the last reports for City Road chapel (1936)

The ruins of City Road chapel in the late 1940s
© Wesley's Chapel

What on earth did that mean? The 1937 report made similar points about poor attendance, falling membership, and a lack of commitment.

There was surely a serious question to be asked about City Road's prospects at the end of the 1930s. The evidence suggested that the cause would not have survived another decade, such was the extent of its troubles.

The question would turn out to be irrelevant, given the events of December 1940. A night of heavy German bombing over the City of London destroyed many buildings, the Welsh Wesleyan chapel on City Road among them. A few yards away, Wesley's Chapel was saved, apparently, by a last-minute change in the direction of the wind, diverting the towering wall of flames. Bunhill Fields, the dissenters' burial ground opposite the chapel, was damaged, but it was fully restored and landscaped during the 1960s. No such restoration scheme was devised (or, it seems, requested) for City Road chapel. Its ruins were demolished after the war to make room for an office block. The little street called Oliver's Yard is still there, but there is absolutely nothing to mark the former site of City Road chapel.

Is it any wonder that this magnificent building, its short lifespan of 47 years representing an exceptional sacrifice by the London Welsh community, has been completely forgotten? There should be a memorial plaque displayed at the junction of City Road and Oliver's Yard to remind people of Eglwysbach and his vision.

City Road was not the only focus of Welsh Wesleyan activity in London. Several congregations had been worshipping in the West End, some formed as early as 1861, but it has proved rather difficult to keep track of the buildings they occupied (some for brief periods) and the long lists of circuit ministers who served.

We know that between 1871 and 1894 there was a Welsh Wesleyan chapel listed in the Post Office directories at 16 Portland Street (now called D'Arblay Street), one of the main thoroughfares running through the heart of Soho. This was the congregation which had first gathered at the YMCA in nearby Great Marlborough Street in July 1868. The 'small chapel' was on the corner of Poland Street, the name by which it was always known. In 1873, under the guidance of the Revd Lewis Jones, the officers signed a 21-year lease on the building, for an annual charge of £32. They worshipped there until the lease expired, in 1893, when they moved to the Gothic Hall,

Thomas Street. That was meant to be a temporary arrangement, but it lasted twelve years.

In 1906, the congregation secured a fourteen-year lease on Brunswick chapel, 92 Balcombe Street, Marylebone. Brunswick chapel is no longer there (it was possibly destroyed in the Second World War) and the road is now best known for one of the most notorious terrorist incidents of the 1970s: an IRA gang was caught in December 1975 after a siege at a flat in Balcombe Street, where the bombers had taken refuge.

The Brunswick congregation, under the Revd J. Wesley Felix, was still in Balcombe Street in 1921, but by 1925, under the Revd D. A. Morgan, had moved a short distance to East Street, near Baker Street. The minister's address is given as 82 East Street in the 'London Welsh Yearbook' for 1925–6. The address provides solid evidence of the link with the post-war period. East

The narrow entrance to Chiltern Street chapel (1972)
© Catrin Unwin

Street was renamed Chiltern Street in 1937, after the nearby Chiltern railway line. Tucked behind some imposing mansion blocks, this would be the home of Chiltern Street chapel – a relatively modern building, redesigned in 1947 with an adjoining flat at number 82a – until its closure in 2004. In the last years of the twentieth century, Chiltern Street was the only remaining Welsh Wesleyan chapel in London.

Was the closure inevitable? It emerged that an opportunity to give Chiltern Street a stable, long-term future had been sadly lost. In 1999, the chapel, schoolroom and flat were extensively renovated and they joined with the eight London Welsh Presbyterian Churches – formerly known as the Welsh Calvinistic Methodist Church – under the ministry of the Revd Dafydd Owen, who made his base at Chiltern Street. He explained what happened:

Attempts were made to reach Welsh students with the cooperation of the University Chaplaincy. Occasional uniting Welsh services were held which were well attended. Because the Welsh chapels in central London were faced with difficulties arising primarily from decreasing elderly membership, consideration was given to establishing an inter-denominational uniting Welsh congregation, possibly based at Chiltern Street. However, denominational loyalty and lifelong attachment to beloved chapel buildings prevailed, and an opportunity to establish an exciting new radical chapter in the story of Welsh Nonconformist witness was lost. Then, when Fred Dyer, who had given his 'life and soul' to the chapel, returned to Wales, the few remaining members were unable to carry on.

It was, therefore, a lack of members, not a lack of finances, which forced the closure of Chiltern Street, bringing to an end a long tradition of Welsh Wesleyan worship in the West End. The Revd Lord (Roger) Roberts of Llandudno, a Wesleyan minister who kindly supports all the London Welsh churches, added his perspective:

Following the destruction of the City Road chapel in 1940, most of its members worshipped at Chiltern Street. This chapel occupied the site of the old St Marylebone Workhouse. The large hall of that building became a well-used Welsh Methodist church hall. Many will remember the Wales-wide financial appeal after the war to enable 'Capel Chiltern Street' to become a most attractive and comfortable place for the Welsh-speaking Wesleyan Methodists to gather. It had seats for 150 in the hall, and three other meeting rooms. It attracted a number of Welsh people from the London area – bankers, nurses, doctors, musicians, teachers – but as the years went by, many returned to Wales, and others passed away. The once busy, if small, London Wesleyan congregation was reduced to a handful. There was a monthly evening service when members were joined by many from Holloway chapel. One minister, visiting from Wales, turned up to find the Chiltern Street chapel crowded morning and afternoon with a Chinese congregation! By paying for the hire of the chapel, which also during the week housed a special school, there were in the end few financial problems. It was the lack of members by 2004 that led to the closure and sale of the chapel. The substantial sum raised has enabled many chapels in Wales to repair and maintain their buildings – including the chapel at Eglwysbach!

The Chiltern Street complex was eventually sold to the London Centre of Self-Realization Fellowship, a group founded by the Indian yogi and guru Paramahansa Yogananda.

A smaller congregation, with an intriguing history, had been meeting in London's East End, where the Welsh Wesleyans maintained a presence for over a century, starting in the Millwall area in 1865. We have already heard how the Calvinistic Methodist congregation in Poplar became divided, driving a small faction in a Wesleyan direction, supervised by Eglwysbach himself. They worshipped in the run-down area of Duff Street, Poplar, from 1887, where they stayed for the best part of three decades, before moving much further east, to the rapidly-growing suburb of Plaistow, beyond West Ham, in 1915. There were said to be around 50 members at this time. The church, called Horeb, was in Cumberland Road, which leads today towards the A13, one of London's busiest commuter roads. This modest building was sold in 1939 to the Spiritualist Church, which still owns the site.

The search for a new home was resolved at the end of the Second World War. The Welsh Independents had started a mission branch (sponsored by King's Cross, Borough and Radnor Walk chapels) in Sibley Grove, East Ham, in 1901. It was a small iron building, with seating for fewer than 200 people, occupying a triangular piece of land at the junction of Sibley Grove and East Avenue.

The Independents had been meeting since 1899 in a house in Katherine Road, led by R. S. Williams, of the London City Mission, whose brief was to reach out to the Welsh living in the East End. A new church was formed there in 1900, and the move to Sibley Grove came the following year. This was the church led by the Revd Llewelyn Bowyer, Woolwich, for nine years from 1902. Despite the initial hopes, given the high numbers of Welsh in the area, Sibley Grove never experienced the membership surge seen elsewhere in London. In that regard, its story was very similar to that of Battersea Rise, a church which rose and fell in the first half of the twentieth century.

The Revd R. Jones Mason was inducted in 1914, staying two years, after which Sibley Grove relied on the kindness of visiting preachers, including the Revd W. E. Davies, a Baptist minister in Ilford, and the Revd Ben Davies, formerly of Pant-teg, Ystalyfera, who proved to be a true friend of Sibley Grove. The Revd J. T. Davies of Dulwich, also provided his services regularly between 1912 and 1932.

It is important to mention J. T. Davies's role as a London City missionary. The London City Mission had been formed in 1835 and it played a crucial role in the promotion of religious activity among the poor and disadvantaged

The Welsh chapel in Sibley Grove, used by Independent and Wesleyan congregations

of London. It was strictly non-denominational in outlook, with a sharp focus on improving people's understanding of the Christian message. In 1850, in response to growing demand, two missionaries were appointed to work among the Welsh in London. J. T. Davies was among the longest serving (he had been appointed in 1899) of the Welsh mission workers in London.

Sibley Grove gained significantly from their services, and there were reports of a revival in church activity in the mid-to-late 1930s, but the Second World War scattered the small congregation and the decision was made not to reopen in 1945.

This was when the building was sold to the London Welsh Methodist Circuit. There are people who remember it as a 'small church with a big heart', drawing newcomers to London throughout the late 1940s and 1950s.

Eluned Jones was one of them. She was 22 when she came to East Ham from Llangeitho in 1947 to train as a midwife. She lived in the area, and later in Essex, until the 1960s. She recalled discovering the chapel near the nurses' home in Burges Road:

> I had noticed a Wesleyan chapel in Sibley Grove, across the railway from Burges
> Road, and walked past several times during the week but there were no signs of life.
> But one Sunday evening I walked past and heard hymn singing so I went in. It was

a small, simple chapel, and a small congregation of around 20 people. A lady from the Rhondda, Lillian Jones, gave me such a warm welcome. Tom, her husband, was the organist. Their son, Cliff, was away, serving in the RAF. By 1951, Cliff and I were married.

Could there be a better example of the power of the chapel marriage bureau? Hardly. Eluned had been a few times to Falmouth Road chapel after her arrival in London, and remembered a big congregation on a Sunday night. Sibley Grove was very different:

It was a small community, but very friendly, a bit like a chapel in rural Wales. We didn't care about denominations. London was different in that sense, you went to the nearest Welsh chapel, in my experience. That was the important thing. We shared a minister with Chiltern Street. I remember Tecwyn Williams and Tecwyn Jones as pastors, and Erfyl Blainey after them in the 1960s. Mrs Blainey was headteacher of the Welsh school in London.

Even after they'd moved from London, Eluned and her family kept in touch with Sibley Grove:

Cliff conducted the choir, and we would compete against other chapels, including Leytonstone and Chiltern Street. After moving to Essex, we still made the journey by train and bus (no car at that time) and our children, Gwen and Tomos, enjoyed coming. Gwen remembers sitting with her grandfather at the organ – and his wink to signal the final hymn, his permission for her to run outside and play!

Throughout this time, the congregation rarely numbered more than 20 people. Some of the stalwarts, including Cliff's parents, retired to Wales in the early 1970s, and the effect on Sibley Grove was predictable. The site was sold, and the small chapel was demolished to make way for new housing.

The story of Sibley Grove, in many ways, perfectly encapsulates the story of the Welsh Wesleyans in London: noble ambition, notable sacrifice, non-stop struggle.

The Welsh Wesleyan Methodists have no chapel in London today, but their legacy is a valuable part of the London Welsh story. An early-morning walk along City Road, past Wesley's Chapel and the dissenting heroes of Bunhill Fields, can be a haunting, eerie experience.

The ghost of Eglwysbach is still with us.

CHAPTER 16

ANGLICAN ENCLAVES

A day spent wandering the ancient streets of the City of London is a day spent extremely well. Curiously-named alleyways and narrow lanes offer sudden glimpses of the Thames; shadowy courtyards are tucked between giant 'Walkie-Talkie' and 'Gherkin' skyscrapers; and, best of all, the dense network of City thoroughfares is gloriously studded with historic places of worship.

Many of the City's churches, designed by Sir Christopher Wren and his assistants following the Great Fire of 1666, were badly damaged during the Second World War. Of the few that escaped, the Guild Church of St Benet, Paul's Wharf, stands out as a true gem, a perfectly-preserved product of Wren's genius. This Grade I-listed building includes a fine organ, built in 1833 by J. C. Bishop, and rebuilt in the early 1970s during the tenure of the distinguished composer, Meirion Williams.

St Benet, the Metropolitan Welsh Church, has long been a prominent City presence with royal connections, occupying a site where Christians have worshipped for a thousand years. The first of several churches dedicated to St Benedict (abbreviated to St Benet) was built on the site around the year 1111, on the north bank of the Thames, located between today's Millennium Bridge and Blackfriars Bridge. Since 1556, St Benet has been the church of the College of Arms, the official heraldic authority for England, Wales and Northern Ireland.

There are strong Welsh ties to the area of Paul's Wharf, predating by several centuries the decision, in 1879, to make St Benet the headquarters of Welsh Anglicans in London. It is a wonderfully rich tradition which gives the Welsh a specific role in the story of the capital. But it is rather puzzling that those with the longest tradition of Welsh-language worship in London seem

St Benet, Paul's Wharf (Gerald Cobb, 1937)

most reluctant to advertise the fact. The Nonconformist chapels shout loudly and proudly about their origins in London, publishing books, sponsoring research, promoting their story; but the capital's Welsh Anglicans, whose origins are far older, have had relatively little to say for themselves.

St Benet and the wider community of Welsh Anglican churches in London have a great story to tell. They have made an important contribution and deserve far more credit and recognition.

If we cross Blackfriars Bridge from the south, we cannot fail to spot the spectacular dome of St Paul's Cathedral dominating the north bank. Further inspection will reveal a cluster of church spires, partially visible, in the surrounding area. One of the closest towers, built mainly in red brick, with a lead-covered steeple, is that of St Benet.

Thanks to London's planning supremos of the 1960s and 1970s, elegant St Benet now finds itself hemmed in by a traffic 'improvement' scheme of spectacular brutality. It is almost impossible to get a decent view of the church building without risking one's life in the process. It really does rank as one of the City's most ungrateful gestures to Wren and his collaborators.

Thankfully, we do have several glorious images of St Benet from a different age, a City church with room to breathe and space to occupy with dignity. The modern St Benet appears somehow to be apologising for being there.

The Revd Alfred Pryse Hawkins, who served as vicar of St Benet from 1982 until a few months before his death in 2001, produced a briefing note for the Bishop of London on the history of the church. It is an interesting document because it describes a centuries-long Welsh presence in the Paul's Wharf area, though there is little hard evidence to accompany the narrative.

His account begins by asserting that Edward I (jovially known as the 'Hammer of the Welsh') brought some of his Welsh castle-builders to London to repair the White Tower (the heart of the Tower of London) and settled them on Tower Hill nearby. By 1315, the growing numbers of Welsh were being blamed for civil disturbances, so they were moved to the area of Paul's Wharf. The theory maintains that they began to worship at St Benet.

Does this mean they worshipped in the Welsh language? There is no mention of a Welsh sermon in London until 1714 (our 1715) at St Paul's, Covent Garden, when a St David's Day service was addressed by the Revd

George Lewis. Later press reports also confirm that there were weekly Welsh-language Anglican services in the 1720s at St Dunstan-in-the-West, Fleet Street. There is no reason to think that such services were not provided elsewhere in response to demand.

As London's Welsh Nonconformist congregations grew, there were calls – at the Guild Church of St Benet – for much more stable Anglican provision in the Welsh language. 'Each request was turned down,' said Alfred Pryse Hawkins, 'because St Benet was an English parish church and it was not permissible to hold Welsh services.' The Diocese of London, it has to be said, has not always been sympathetic to the cause of Welsh-language worship.

By 1830, the Earl of Powys and some powerful Anglican friends had started a campaign to hold Welsh Prayer Book services in London. They managed to negotiate a lease on the historic church of St Etheldreda, Ely Place. Alfred Pryse Hawkins reported that 'most of the St Benet congregation moved there, leaving the rector of St Benet without a congregation'.

St Etheldreda is a very special place, the town chapel of the Bishops of Ely from about 1250 to 1570, and one of only two remaining buildings in London dating from the reign of Edward I. Its long and varied history included a period, from 1820, when it was leased to the National Society for the Education of the Poor. That venture failed, and in December 1843 it was opened for Anglican services in the Welsh language. The Welsh remained there until 1874, when the building was offered for sale, and they were outbid by the Roman Catholics, who have remained there ever since. Alfred Pryse Hawkins insisted that the Welsh were duped by a crooked solicitor (and a Roman Catholic, to boot) but the St Etheldreda website suggests that while Welsh incompetence was to blame, the Welsh were nonetheless gracious in defeat.

The Welsh Anglicans were homeless, relying on the rector of St Nicholas, Cole Abbey, for permission to hold one weekly service in Welsh, while searching for a permanent home. St Nicholas was a stone's throw from their old home, St Benet, now standing empty and almost derelict, and due for demolition. St Benet was the responsibility of the Diocese of London, which for a quarter of a century had neglected the building. The result was an initial demolition order, signed in 1854 but never acted upon, and now a second order, due to be enforced in 1876.

The interior of St Benet, Paul's Wharf
© London Metropolitan Archive

The Welsh spotted their chance and moved decisively, petitioning Queen Victoria for permission to use St Benet for worship in the Welsh language. Her Majesty's permission was granted for the church – including its pews, pulpit, altar, organ, and Communion silver – to be used 'in perpetuity' by the Welsh Anglicans, on condition that all necessary repairs and maintenance were carried out. This permission, delivered by means of an Order in Council, and bolstered by the terms of the City of London (Guild Churches) Act 1952, is still wholly valid today, much to the apparent irritation and frustration of senior figures in the Diocese of London.

The St Benet to which the Welsh returned – after an absence of 33 years – was a much poorer church. Significant sums had been received from the City authorities for the churchyard, rectory, stables, coach house, store rooms, and almshouses, which were demolished to make way for the new Queen Victoria Street, the modern route leading from Blackfriars Bridge to Mansion

House. Every penny of this money, it seems, found its way into the diocesan coffers. The newly-revived church found itself with no financial reserves, and it is to the great credit of its leaders that St Benet flourished again in the first half of the twentieth century.

One of the undoubted highlights of that flourishing period was the National Welsh Festival, a special Evensong service, based on the Welsh Book of Common Prayer, held on the Thursday before St David's Day at St Paul's Cathedral. The first was held in 1898, partly for fundraising purposes, involving some of the best Welsh preachers, and in succeeding years the cathedral was filled twice on the big day, once for the rehearsal, and then again, after tea, for the Festival Evensong. This was followed by the St David's Day concert at the Royal Albert Hall, on the Saturday evening, regularly drawing a capacity crowd of 4,500 people.

In 1947, the National Welsh Festival was held, once again, at St Paul's Cathedral, but in subsequent years, as the congregation dwindled, it moved to smaller venues such as St Martin-in-the-Fields, All Souls (Langham Place), and St Benet itself, as Alfred Pryse Hawkins explained:

In 1960, the then-incumbent of St Benet threw the Festival open to the Nonconformists, who very quickly took it over, held it in their chapels, and changed it to their usual hymn, prayer, reading format. I stopped this in 1983, and returned it to a Prayer Book Choral Evensong at St Benet. There were 80 people present at the Festival in 2000.

Order of service for the National Welsh Festival at St Paul's Cathedral (1947)

Cooperation between Welsh Anglicans and Nonconformists in London has always been patchy: so much depends on the combinations of personalities at any one period, and their relative appetites for collaboration. Alfred Pryse Hawkins, an Aberystwyth man, would have fully understood the ways of the chapel community, but it is fair to say he was not a supporter. Some of his predecessors were even less tolerant: there was (and still is, in some quarters) a view within the Anglican community that Nonconformist worship is unworthy and deficient.

The popularity of the Nonconformist chapels was seen by many Anglicans as nothing more than a prolonged emotional spasm. There was little acceptance that the wilful hostility of so many Anglican clergymen in Wales had been a prime factor in driving the masses into the arms of Howell Harris, Daniel Rowland, and their supporters. The Church of England was seen – rightly – as a very English (and, almost by definition, anti-Welsh) institution.

The biggest event of the twentieth century – in the world of the Welsh Anglicans – was the Welsh Church Act (1914) which disestablished the Church of England in Wales, creating the Church in Wales. The act was energetically promoted by Lloyd George and other Welsh patriots, but it faced ferocious opposition in parliament. It had to be bulldozed through the House of Lords by means of the Parliament Act (1911). There are still people, believe it or not, who regret its enactment, which finally took place in 1920.

The new order was broadly welcomed in Wales, but the Welsh Anglicans in London found

Canon Alfred Pryse Hawkins (1932–2001) in the garden of Dewi Sant vicarage, Paddington
© Tim Pryse-Hawkins

themselves in a less-than-ideal place. Their hybrid status caused confusion. They were often dependent on the Diocese of London, but they looked to the Church in Wales for authority in most matters. This resulted in tensions and inconsistencies.

The Revd Evan Jones, who had tended the flock at St Etheldreda, was succeeded by the Revd J. Crowle Ellis, vicar of St Benet, whose salary was paid by the Diocese of London. He was described as 'well-to-do, living in a private house in Chevening Road, Kensal Rise'. His successor, the Revd Enoch Jones ('Isylog'), also lived comfortably, 'in a large residence in Dulwich', having 'married into a great deal of money'. But his salary was paid by the Church in Wales, which treated his employment as if he were 'in the mission field'. It was all change, again, when his successor, the Revd T. J. Thomas arrived. His salary was paid by the Diocese of London, but he was housed in west London, as priest-in-charge of Eglwys Gymraeg Dewi Sant (St David's Welsh Church), Paddington Green. The Diocese of London, however, contributed nothing to the upkeep of the St David vicarage.

Enoch Jones was widely admired in the London Welsh community, and his determination to stay in London throughout the Second World War was deeply appreciated by those church members who refused or were unable to return to safety in rural Wales. Elizabeth Thomas, a lifelong member at St Benet, paid her tribute:

> Enoch was in London throughout the bombing. The Sunday after the great raid on the City in December 1940, he, the two churchwardens and my father made their way to the church. They were relieved to see it still standing in the middle of such destruction. He said a few prayers in the porch and they went home. I also remember, in the early days of the doodlebugs [German flying bombs], we were in church for the evening service and heard one coming over. My father dragged us under the gallery, Enoch was in the pulpit. After the bang he finished his sermon and the service and we went home. The London Welsh business people who stuck it out in London throughout the war – like my father, his two brothers, two sisters, my mother, her sister and my own sister (and my two brothers who were called up) – were real heroes.

Olwen Evans, Elizabeth's daughter, is a child of St Benet (she was baptised and married there) and still a loyal worshipper. She has fond memories of the past half-century:

As a small child I remember Canon Enoch Jones as the vicar. He was a bard of the Welsh Gorsedd, named 'Isylog', a very amiable man with a good sense of humour, if a little absent-minded at times! He was fortunate to be vicar when the church would be full for every Sunday service. He was succeeded by the Revd T. J. Thomas in the mid-1960s, a very kind man who cared greatly for his flock, and served as chaplain for the Putney Home for Incurables (as it was then called). After his retirement the Revd Alfred Pryse Hawkins became vicar, a most strong-willed man, who gave tireless service to St Benet, a man with a great sense of occasion and a stickler for the ritual of the church. Both Thomas and Pryse Hawkins also served as vicars of Dewi Sant, Paddington Green, and had the living of the vicarage there. Both congregations would attend each other's special services.

The long-standing pattern of shared ministry with Dewi Sant ended with Alfred Pryse Hawkins's death in 2001. There followed a period of several years during which the officers of St Benet and Dewi Sant organised their own services, but the situation created new tensions with the Diocese of London, which began to show much greater interest in the future of the congregations (and their valuable buildings).

It was clear that the arrangements lacked consistency and stability. By 2008, St Benet faced a crisis. The Bishop of London intervened in a rather dramatic way. He announced, in effect, the closure of the church, citing weak attendance, and accused the officers of failing to cooperate with the diocese on future planning. He invited the remaining worshippers to attend Dewi Sant, and signalled his desire to use St Benet for a possible 'educational project'.

This was seen by London's Welsh community as a shockingly hostile approach, made worse by the tendency of senior diocesan figures to question the validity of St Benet's status as the Metropolitan Welsh Church. The 1879 Order in Council, along with the City of London (Guild Churches) Act 1952, were made to seem painlessly disposable.

The London Welsh – most of them, let it be said, with no connection to St Benet – did not take kindly to the bishop's approach. There were strong rumours that Dr Rowan Williams, then Archbishop of Canterbury, shared those concerns. A high-profile media campaign drew attention to St Benet and its Welsh heritage. At the same time, a legal case was put together by Lloyd Lloyd, a barrister and churchwarden whose family ties to St Benet went back to the early years of the twentieth century. The result was that the diocesan plans to re-designate St Benet were dropped (but for how long, one wondered?) and a new priest-in-charge was selected by the Bishop of London.

Dr Aneirin Glyn, a young, Welsh-speaking clergyman, came from St Helen, Bishopsgate, a high-octane evangelical church in the City of London, whose conservative traditions are rather different to those of St Benet. But Aneirin and his new congregation have worked hard to reach an acceptable compromise regarding the content of services and matters of church business. His installation service in October 2011, conducted by the bishop, was attended by a big congregation, all of whom had come to wish Aneirin well, but many, it is fair to say, were also there to deliver a clear signal to the bishop that the Welsh in London valued St Benet and its traditions.

Aneirin has shared his time between the churches of St Benet and St Helen. He is, sadly, not required at Dewi Sant, which held its last service in 2009, after a long period of declining attendance. The building was leased – on a long-term basis – to a French school, which has even paid to restore the church's charming two-manual pipe organ, built by the London firm of Gray and Davison. The organ's historic value was certified by the British Institute of Organ Studies in January 2009.

Dewi Sant had started as a mission branch of St Benet, catering for a growing congregation in the western district of the capital. They first met on 26 March 1885 at the New Temperance Hall, not far from Paddington Green. Further meetings were held in a school in Marylebone, including the first public service, in May of that year, conducted by the Revd Evan Jones, vicar of St Benet. This was the start of what was called the 'West End Welsh Church Mission', which later became the first and only church specially built and consecrated for Welsh-speaking people in London.

In 1890 the members bought some land – a corner of the Paddington Green burial ground – for £5,000. The Revd J. Crowle Ellis, Penmaenmawr, appointed the first Dewi Sant chaplain in 1890 – he would move in 1897 to St Benet – played an important part in the negotiations with the Paddington Estate. The plot included a thatched property called 'Chamber's Cottage', reputed to be the oldest house in the Paddington area. They built a 'temporary iron church' – the first Welsh Anglican church to be built in the metropolis – which was dedicated on 27 July 1890 by the Archdeacon of London.

This was their home for six years, during which membership grew to 200, and attendance at Holy Communion averaged 75. It was, according to one report, the 'happy spiritual home of the London Welsh Church Community in the West'.

They were evidently in the mood to expand and secure 'a permanent and creditable church building'. They achieved their goal in 1896 by building the stone church still standing today, and converted the thatched cottage into a parsonage. The iron church structure was sold to a seamen's mission in Milford Haven.

The press reports of the fundraising launch for the new church building revealed the extent of high-level support for the enterprise. The *London Kelt* on 16 February 1895 underlined the status of the campaign, led by a well-known Welsh journalist and politician:

> *Last Thursday was held an important meeting in the drawing room of Sir John Puleston to consider the building scheme for a permanent church and vicarage. The sponsors are the Lord Bishops of Marlborough, St David's, Llandaff, St Asaph, Bangor, and Swansea. The following gentlemen are among those on the committee: Sir John T. Llewelyn, Sir John Williams, Sir John Puleston, A. J. Boscawen MP, Dr Isambard Owen, the Venerable Archdeacon of Middlesex, Canon Barker, the Revd G. Hartwell Jones, and the Rural Dean of Paddington. The chairman outlined the case and said the time had certainly come to build a permanent church. He reported that Mrs Griffith Llewellyn, Baglan Hall, Briton Ferry, had already contributed £1,000 to the fund.*

The new church was formally opened on 31 March 1897 by the Archbishop of Canterbury, Dr Frederick Temple, who had taken an interest in the project when he was Bishop of London. The building, designed by the Welsh architect Charles Evans-Vaughan – the man responsible for Falmouth Road chapel – was approached through a Gothic arch from St Mary's Terrace. It comprised a church on the first floor, with 250 seats, and a church hall with caretaker's flat on the ground floor. It was described by the Church Commissioners as a 'large late-Victorian Gothic church of yellow brick, comprising a six-bay aisled nave and two-bay chancel, with a church hall underneath'.

The parsonage, a four-bed house with a large garden, helped make

Artist's impression of the Dewi Sant
gateway (1896)
© London Metropolitan Archive

ENTRANCE GATEWAY ST DAVIDS (WELSH) CHVRCH PADDINGTON. J.P.SEDDON ARC

the Dewi Sant complex a valuable piece of real estate in a desirable part of west London. Alfred Pryse Hawkins always insisted that the entire property belonged to the trustees of St David's Church, not the diocesan authorities, whose failure to contribute anything to maintenance expenses over the years was said to prove his point. He further alleged that a clergyman working in London in the 1960s had unlawfully removed the trust and land deeds from the Dewi Sant safe, as part of an unsuccessful attempt to engineer the closure of the church. The documents, it is said, have never reappeared.

This question of the ongoing stewardship of the Dewi Sant properties – and the likely beneficiaries of any sale – has become increasingly problematic. Michael Buck, a solicitor who joined the Dewi Sant congregation in the 1960s, and became secretary of the church council, kindly provided more details:

> *The vicar, the Revd T. J. Thomas, asked me to help with various matters, including investigating the ownership of the church, as most of the records were missing. That led to an extraordinary trail, since the five Welsh-speaking churches in London were legally anomalous, a state of affairs made even more complex by the Welsh Church Act.*

The financial situation was further complicated by the existence of several trust funds, the management of which presented Mr Buck and his colleagues with a major headache:

Interior of Dewi Sant church in the 1920s

*We have striven with the Charity Commission to secure formal registration of the
Dewi Sant Memorial Trust. That is a critical stage in the process of returning to the
Church in Wales Dewi Sant's residual funds (as much as £180,000) to further
Welsh-speaking Anglican worship in Wales and beyond. In the early years from the
1890s, many people in Wales gave most generously to support and help their fellow
worshippers in London. That is the motivation for repaying past help.*

Mr Buck explained that money from the St Padarn Welsh Church Trust
and the St Rhystyd Trust Fund would be combined with the Dewi Sant
residual funds to make up the new Dewi Sant Memorial Trust. This tortuous
process has involved many hours of detailed work.

What is not in question, however, is the strong Welsh tradition of the
Dewi Sant community throughout the twentieth century. Siôn Griffiths,
whose grandfather had been treasurer of St Padarn (the Welsh church in
Holloway, north London) in the 1920s, spent eight years in Paddington
during his father's term as vicar:

*My father, Mathew Griffiths, was chaplain of Emanuel School, Wandsworth, when
he was inducted as vicar of Eglwys Dewi Sant, Paddington, in November 1955.
The church and vicarage stood in an enclave, with a spectacular, but narrow, archway
at its entrance, and anyone who entered, especially on a Sunday, was transported to*

a village in deepest Wales. The nights at that time were sufficiently quiet for me to hear the steam trains whistling their way out of Paddington station.

Siôn recalled a busy church, drawing a congregation from a wide area, throughout west London and the counties of Berkshire, Oxfordshire and Buckinghamshire:

The popular service was always Sunday evening at 6 p.m. The church was always fairly full on a normal Sunday, and packed on special occasions, such as harvest festivals. The choir consisted of young people, not top-class singers. The regular organist was Mrs Olwen Rees, who had been born and raised in London. Always a member of Dewi Sant, she knew everyone and everyone knew her! The services were in Welsh, and Sunday school was held downstairs in the hall. After the service, in the hall, supper was served. Not a meal, but rather similar to a 'funeral tea', with sandwiches and cakes, served on long trestle tables, everyone sitting down to a great social. Most of the people seemed to be involved in the dairy business, but despite the early Monday start, they would stay on Sunday nights as late as 10 or even 11 p.m.

Siôn's parents moved to Llanrhystud, on the Cardiganshire coast, in 1963, and moved later to Sandbach, Cheshire. But he insisted that their time in London had provided an exceptional experience:

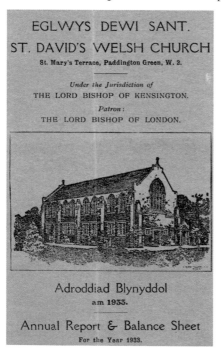

In later life, reflecting on their times in Dewi Sant, my parents came to consider this period, from 1955 to 1963, as the happiest of their lives. The unique sense of community and friendship they encountered was never ever equalled in the other places they were to live. Undoubtedly, the experience of being in exile, and in the company of their own kind, created a fellowship that was both incomparable and exceptional.

Annual report for Eglwys Dewi Sant (1933)

The London Welsh clergy in 1963, including Mathew Griffiths (fourth from left) and 'Isylog' (fourth from right)
© Siôn Griffiths

And that, in a few sentences, sums up the rewarding experience of so many Welsh people in London, in different contexts, over the centuries.

After Alfred Pryse Hawkins's death in 2001, the condition of Dewi Sant's buildings deteriorated markedly, and by 2006 it was clear that a small, elderly congregation could not cope with the work and costs involved. The handful of regular worshippers lived outside London (some a two-hour journey away) but they showed remarkable loyalty by soldiering on. It was clear, however, that they needed help. A broken-down boiler, and the need for £100,000 to be spent on 'urgent repairs to the fabric', brought matters to a head.

This was when the London Diocesan Fund stepped in, taking responsibility from 2006 for putting the building in good order and licensing the use of the premises to commercial tenants. Regular services had come to an end in 2005, but a final service was held in 2009 to mark the end of Welsh Anglican worship in the Paddington area. Eglwys Gymraeg Dewi Sant formally ceased to exist on 13 August 2013.

There was a rather poignant declaration in the booklet published to mark the half-century jubilee services at Dewi Sant in 1946:

*We will follow in the paths of those who have gone before and make their faith our
own; and when comes 1996, God will be thanked for the faith that sustained us to
keep this our inheritance intact for those who follow after.*

Keeping that inheritance intact – from this and myriad other vanished
places of worship – is still our duty today. The closure of Dewi Sant meant that
St Benet became the only remaining Anglican church in London providing
services in the Welsh language, where once there had been five.

South of the Thames, a congregation had been worshipping in
Camberwell, a sprawling working-class area lying south of the Elephant and
Castle, near the famous cricket ground at the Oval. The area had seen rapid
population growth: in 1861 there were 71,000 people living in the parish, but
by 1891 the number had grown to 235,000. There was acute overcrowding
in some areas, particularly around Camberwell Road and Camberwell New
Road, and this had driven many of the more well-to-do residents out of the
parish. This might explain the reason the Welsh Anglicans were able to secure
such an impressive home in the area.

St Mary (usually known by its Welsh name St Mair, or Santes Fair) was
initially founded as a mission in 1898. It found a home for four decades in a
large former Congregational chapel in Camberwell New Road, designed by
the architects Edward and William Habershon. The chapel – built in a rather
grand 'Gothic Revival' style – had opened in 1856. But by the early 1890s, the
congregation had dwindled, and the church building became available. This
Nonconformist place of worship – in what was described by one observer
as a 'slum area' of Camberwell – became a Welsh Anglican bastion until the
Second World War.

Alfred Pryse Hawkins maintained that the 'habit' of most of the Welsh
Anglican communities in London was to 'use Anglican churches, usually where
there was a Welsh-speaking priest willing to accommodate them', adding that
they 'never had their own appointed priest'. There has to be a question mark
over this last assertion, as the Welsh Anglican newspaper *Y Llan* frequently
provided lists of churches and their resident clergy: in November 1918, four
of the five London Welsh churches were listed with a resident priest-in-
charge. St Mair's entry was as follows:

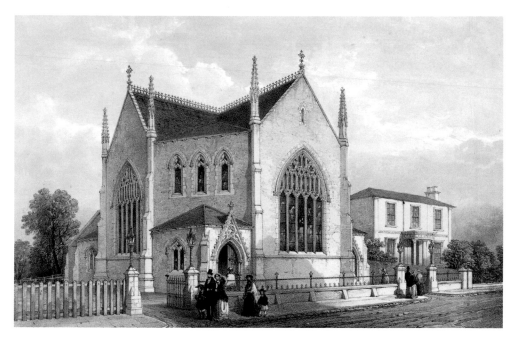

The Congregational Church, Camberwell New Road, which opened in 1856, later becoming
St Mair Welsh Church
© RIBA Library Drawings

ST. MAIR – Camberwell New Road, Camberwell, SE. Revd D. GRIFFITH,
St. Mary's Parsonage, Camberwell New Road, SE.

The vicar in question, the Revd David Griffith, was installed in 1911
and served for 22 years, the longest-serving of St Mair's clergymen, during
which time St Mair became a very active church. The *London Kelt* newspaper
(from 1899 onwards) included regular notices of special services, concerts,
eisteddfodau, lectures and meetings at the church. St Mair also held an annual
concert at the Queen's Hall, Langham Place, London's principal concert
venue for many years (the initial home of 'The Proms') with seating for
2,500 people. This surely says a good deal about the scale of the church's
ambitions.

Sadly, there is no reminder or evidence of any of that rich activity
on today's Camberwell New Road. The former site of the church is now
occupied by the Sacred Heart Roman Catholic School, tucked beside the
busy commuter railway line which leads from Camberwell to London Bridge.

The railways were part of the reason why Camberwell changed its character so dramatically in the late-nineteenth century, but the biggest change of all came in the Second World War. Camberwell, on the flight path to central London, was one of the worst-affected areas of London during the Blitz.

St Mair was one of many buildings destroyed by enemy fire in late 1940, during the ministry of the Revd D. J. Evans, so the congregation moved after the war to a church in Clapham Road, between Stockwell and Clapham High Street, and moved again, in 1948, to the Church of the Ascension, Malwood Road, Balham, where the vicar, the popular and charismatic Dr Bryn Thomas, agreed to look after the St Mair congregation as well as his own.

Bryn Thomas was a rather colourful, outspoken character who had no apparent difficulty juggling socialism, freemasonry, and his own brand of Anglo-Catholicism. He had enough spare time to conduct an affair with one of his Sunday school teachers, and soon found himself tried by a church court for 'immoral conduct' which also included allegations of sexual assault against two teenage girls. He vehemently denied the charges but was officially unfrocked by the Bishop of Southwark in 1961. It was a huge tabloid scandal at the time, and made headlines around the world.

It was sad, to say the least, that the honourable tradition of Welsh-language Anglican worship in south London came to an end in such circumstances.

North of the river, a smaller East End congregation had started worshipping in 1893 as an 'East-end Welsh Mission' in Mile End. They built a 'small iron church', dedicated to St Rhystyd, in 1914, in Whitman Road, just a short distance from the Welsh Calvinistic Methodist chapel

The vicar of St Rhystyd was president of the annual Gymanfa Ganu in 1936

The first St Padarn building, opened in 1903
© National Library of Wales

in Mile End Road. Despite its modest resources, St Rhystyd nonetheless managed to support at least five full-time priests-in-charge during the first half of the century. The church was still operating the mid-1950s, according to *Cymry Llundain Ddoe a Heddiw* (1956), holding one weekly service on Sunday evenings. The Whitman Road area was redeveloped in the 1960s as part of the Clinton Road conservation area, creating new parkland where the church of St Rhystyd once stood.

There was a much bigger congregation in north London, at St Padarn, Salterton Road, Holloway, where the vicar enjoyed more facilities, including a vicarage. The church, situated off the busy Seven Sisters Road, started as a mission venture in 1894, moving to a temporary iron church in 1903, and to a permanent building in 1912. This was a busy church, judging by many press reports of concerts, lectures and sports clubs, and it played a prominent role in London Welsh life for decades. There were at least eight full-time (and two part-time) vicars between 1897 and 1970, the longest-serving of whom was the first, the Revd William Davies, who served for eleven years from 1897. The church complex was sold in the early 1980s to the Society of St Pius X, the Catholic traditionalist movement founded by Archbishop

The St Padarn Church Committee in the 1920s

Marcel Lefebvre, and it is known today as the Church of Saints Joseph and Padarn.

It is vitally important to record the contribution of the Welsh Anglicans to the religious life of London, and of the London Welsh in particular. The earliest Welsh sermons in the capital were preached by clergymen in the city's churches, long before any Nonconformist chapels were built. It is a matter of deep regret that more detailed records of this early Welsh preaching have not been kept: they would shed much welcome light on a compelling part of our national story.

St Benet still welcomes people to its services, happily catering for those whose Welsh is not robust, and offering a warm Welsh greeting to visitors in the sublime surroundings of one of Sir Christopher Wren's original buildings.

A visit to this very special centre of worship is highly recommended.

And long may it retain its cherished status – The Metropolitan Welsh Church.

Queen Victoria would not be amused by any other outcome.

REFLECTIONS

Researching and writing *City Mission* over the past five years has been, for the most part, a heartening experience.

The pleasure has outweighed the pain, just about.

Along the way, I have enjoyed the company of some remarkable people: John Thickens, Howell Harris, 'Ginshop' Jones, Eliseus Howells, Dr Owen Thomas, Morfudd Jenkins, Elfed, Isylog, Meurig Owen, Hwfa Môn…

I am left with a powerful mix of emotions: pride in the work of the founders and pioneers; admiration for the loyalty of ministers, officers and members; and regret at the lost opportunities of the past half-century.

The Welsh have made a significant contribution to the story of London, a contribution that deserves greater recognition now that London takes pride in its status as the world's most culturally diverse capital city.

The chapels and churches are a prime element in that narrative. They have enriched the lives of many thousands of Welsh people in London, and in the process they have unquestionably enriched the cultural and religious life of Wales.

They may not be fashionable or popular features of London Welsh life today, but they still deserve our respect, approbation and gratitude for what they have achieved and contributed over the centuries.

The few that survive also deserve something else.

Our support.

There is an old proverb which asserts that a Welshman's patriotism is more evident away from home: *Gorau Cymro, Cymro oddi cartref.*

Future generations of patriotic Welsh men and women in London will not understand or forgive a failure to safeguard our religious tradition in the world's greatest city.

The time will come – sooner than we think – to decide on a single place of worship for the Welsh in London. With the right strategy and support, it could serve the capital's Welsh community for decades to come. The alternative, having no Welsh chapel or church at our disposal, would be unthinkable. No self-respecting ethnic community in London would tolerate such a grotesque failure.

It is a fact that *Cymry Llundain* – with a few exceptions – have been singularly unwilling to make bold, radical, sensible decisions about their places of worship.

That must surely change if we are to preserve our rich heritage for generations to come.

LIST OF PRINCIPAL WELSH RELIGIOUS CAUSES IN LONDON

PRESBYTERIAN CHURCH OF WALES (FORMERLY THE CALVINISTIC METHODISTS)

Jewin (*c*.1772–)

Woolwich (*c*.1790–*c*.1870)

Deptford (*c*.1799–*c*.1853)

Charing Cross Road (*c*.1831–1982)

Mile End Road (*c*.1853–1959)

Wilton Square (1853–1956)

Falmouth Road (1854–1982)

Shirland Road (1864–1988)

Holloway (1865–2004) (formed Eglwys-y-Drindod)

Islington (*c*.1869–1886)

Hammersmith (1883–1972)

Stratford (*c*.1892–1946)

Clapham Junction (1896–)

Walham Green (1897–1998)

Willesden Green (1898–1999)

Lewisham (1899–2011)

Walthamstow/Leytonstone (1903–2004) (formed Eglwys-y-Drindod)

Wood Green (1904–2004) (formed Eglwys-y-Drindod)

Ealing Green (1907–)

Sutton (1933–)

Wembley (1939–1972)

Eglwys-y-Drindod, Cockfosters (2004–)

WELSH INDEPENDENTS

Borough (*c*.1790–)

Deptford (*c*.1790–*c*.1866)

Woolwich (*c*.1790–1983)

Barrett's Grove (1846–*c*.1940)

King's Cross (1847–2006) (formed Welsh Church of Central London)

Radnor Walk (1859–2006) (formed Welsh Church of Central London)

East Ham (1899–1945)

Battersea Rise (1906–*c*.1960)

Harrow (1937–)

Luton (1938–1991)

Slough (1938–)

WELSH METHODISTS (WESLEYAN)

City Road (1812–1940)

Chiltern Street (1868–2004)

Cumberland Road (1945–*c*.1972)

WELSH BAPTISTS

Eldon Street (1817–1917)

Castle Street (1859–2006) (formed Welsh Church of Central London)

WELSH ANGLICANS

St Etheldreda (1843–1874)

St Benet (1879–)

Dewi Sant (1896–2013)

St Mair (1898–*c*.1960)

St Padarn (1894–*c*.1980)

St Rhystyd (1914–*c*.1970)

BIBLIOGRAPHY AND REFERENCES

Ackroyd, Peter. *Tudors: A History of England (Volume II)*. London: Pan, 2013.

Allen, Thomas. *The History and Antiquities of the Parish of Lambeth*. London, 1826.

Bagshaw, Samuel. *History, Gazetteer and Directory of Kent, 1847*. Sheffield: G. Ridge, 1847.

Bassett, T. M. *Bedyddwyr Cymru*. Abertawe: Tŷ Ilston, 1977.

Beken, P. & Jones, S. *Dragon in Exile*. London: Springwood Books, 1985.

Brechin, Derek. *Georgian London (Discovering London 6)*. London: Macdonald, 1969.

Carr, G. 'Bwrlwm bywyd y Cymry yn Llundain yn y ddeunawfed ganrif', in *Cof Cenedl XI*. Llandysul: Gomer, 1996.

Census of Great Britain, 1851: Religious Worship in England and Wales. London: Routledge, 1854.

Clwyd, Hafina. *Buwch ar y lein: detholiad o ddyddiaduron Llundain 1957–1964*. Cardiff: Honno, 1987.

Crosland, T. W. H. *Taffy was a Welshman*. London, 1912.

Daniels, Peter. *In Search of Welshness: Recollections and Reflections*. Talybont: Y Lolfa, 2011.

David, T. 'The rise and fall of the London Welsh', *Planet* (1991).

Davies, Ben (Gol.) *Llawlyfr Cyfarfodydd Llundain*. Llandysul: Undeb yr Annibynwyr Cymraeg, 1937.

Davies, E. T. *Religion and Society in the Nineteenth Century*. Llandybïe: Christopher Davies, 1981.

Davies, Ieuan. *Trwy Lygaid Tymblwr – A Gweinidog!* Abertawe: Ieuan Davies, 2007.

Davies, John. *Hanes Cymru*. Caerdydd: Gwasg Prifysgol Cymru, 1993.

Davies, John E. ('Rhuddwawr') *Canmlwyddiant Cymanfa'r Pasc: Methodistiaid Calfinaidd Llundain*. Dinbych, 1912.

Davies, William. *Canmlwyddiant Cymdeithas Genhadol Llundain 1895*. Llundain: Cymdeithas Genhadol Llundain, 1895.

Dews, Nathan. *History of Deptford*. London: Simpkin Marshall, 1884.

Edwards, E. 'The Welsh School in London', *Transactions of the Honourable Society of Cymmrodorion*, New Series 1, 2000.

Edwards, Hugh. *Y Deugain Mlynedd Hyn: sef Adgofion mewn cysylltiad a Methodistiaeth Llundain*. Aberystwyth, 1894.

Edwards, Huw T. *Tros y Tresi*. Dinbych: Gwasg Gee, 1956.

Elias, T. *Y Porthmyn Cymreig*. Llanrwst: Gwasg Carreg Gwalch, 1987.

Ellis, T. I. *Cofiant Thomas Edward Ellis (Cyfrol 1)*. Liverpool: Hugh Evans a'i Feibion, 1944.

Ellis, T. I. *Cofiant Thomas Edward Ellis (Cyfrol 2)*. Liverpool: Hugh Evans a'i Feibion, 1948.

Ellis T. I. *Ym Mer fy Esgyrn*. Lerpwl: Gwasg y Brython, 1955.

Ellis, T. I. *Dilyn Llwybrau*. Llandybïe: Christopher Davies, 1967.

Ellis, T. I. *Crwydro Llundain*. Llandybïe: Christopher Davies, 1971.

Evans, Beriah Gwynfe. *Diwygwyr Cymru*. Caernarfon: Beriah Gwynfe Evans, 1900.

Evans, Caradoc. *Nothing to Pay*. London: Faber & Faber, 1930.

Evans, E. Gwyn. *Y Ganrif Gyntaf (1849–1949)*. Llundain: Eglwys Charing Cross Road, 1951.

Evans, E. Keri. *Cofiant Dr Joseph Parry*. Cardiff: The Educational Publishing Company, 1921.

Evans, M. 'Cow-keeper in Cockney London', *East London Family Historical Society* (1980).

Evans, W. G. 'Equal opportunities for girls and women in Victorian Wales: the contribution of the London-Welsh', *Transactions of the Honourable Society of Cymmrodorion*, New Series 2, 1996.

Evans, William. *Cofiant y Parchg William Evans, Tonyrefail*. Newport, 1892.

Francis, J. O. 'London-Welsh Papers', *The Welsh Outlook*, VII (1920).

Francis-Jones, Gwyneth. *Cows, Cardis and Cockneys*. Talybont: Y Lolfa, 1984.

George, M. Dorothy. *London Life in the Eighteenth Century*. London: Peregrine Books, 1966.

Godwin, George. *London Shadows*. London: Routledge, 1854.

Griffiths, Peter Hughes. *Llais o Lundain: Ysgrifau Myfyrdod*. Lerpwl: Hugh Evans a'i Feibion, 1912.

Hanes ac Egwyddorion Annibynwyr Cymru. Abertawe: Undeb yr Annibynwyr Cymraeg, 1939.

Hanes Clapham Junction, Llundain 1896–1996. Llundain: Eglwys Clapham Junction, 1996.

Hanes, Cyfansoddiad, Rheolau Disgybliaethol, ynghyd a Chyffes Ffydd y Corff o Fethodistiaid Calfinaidd yng Nghymru. Salford: John Roberts (dros Y Gymanfa Gyffredinol), 1876.

Hill, Douglas. *Regency London (Discovering London 7)*. London: Macdonald, 1969.

Hughes, D. R. 'Hanes achosion crefyddol Cymreig Llundain', *Y Ddolen*, (1) 4 (1926).

Hughes, D. R. *Yma ac Acw*. Dinbych: Gwasg Gee, 1944.

Hughes, Huw Price. 'John Wesley', *Nineteenth Century: a monthly review*. 29:169 (March 1891).

Hughes, John. *Methodistiaeth Cymru Cyf. I, II, III*. Wrexham: Hughes a'i Fab, 1851–6.

Hughes, T. & Roberts, J. P. *Cofiant y Parch. John Evans, Eglwysbach (yn cynnwys ei 'adgofion')*. Bangor: Llyfrfa Wesleyaidd, 1903.

Huws, Ifor O. (Gol.) *Hanes Eglwys Radnor Walk, Llundain (1859–1959)*. Llandysul: Gwasg Gomer, 1959.

Jenkins, Geraint H. *The Foundations of Modern Wales 1642–1780*. Oxford: Clarendon Press, 1987.

Jenkins, Geraint H. (Gol.) *Iaith Carreg Fy Aelwyd (Iaith a Chymuned yn y Bedwaredd Ganrif ar Bymtheg)*. Caerdydd: Gwasg Prifysgol Cymru, 1998.

Jenkins, Geraint H. *A Concise History of Wales*. Cambridge: Cambridge University Press, 2007.

Jenkins, Morfudd. *Hanes Eglwys Gymraeg Harrow 1937–1987*. Llundain: Eglwys Gymraeg Harrow, 1987.

Jenkins, Nigel. *Gwalia in Khasia*. Llandysul: Gomer, 1996.

Jenkins, R. T. *Hanes Cymru yn y Ddeunawfed Ganrif.* Caerdydd: Gwasg Prifysgol Cymru, 1928.

Jenkins, R. T. *Yr Apêl at Hanes.* Wrexham: Hughes a'i Fab, 1931.

Jenkins, R. T. *Hanes Cymru yn y Bedwaredd Ganrif ar Bymtheg.* Caerdydd: Gwasg Prifysgol Cymru, 1933.

Jenkins, R. T. & Ramage, Helen M. *A History of the Honourable Society of Cymmrodorion and of the Gwyneddigion and Cymreigyddion Societies (1751–1951).* London: The Honourable Society of Cymmrodorion, 1951.

John, Walter P. & Hughes, Gwilym T. *Hanes Castle Street a'r Bedyddwyr Cymraeg yn Llundain.* Llandysul: Gwasg Gomer, 1959.

Jones, D. G. *Cofiant y Parchedig Edward Matthews o Eweni.* Denbigh, 1893.

Jones, D. G. & Judges, A. V. 'London's population in the late seventeenth century', *Economic History Review,* VI (1935), pp. 45–63.

Jones, Emrys. 'The Welsh in London in the seventeenth and eighteenth centuries', *Welsh History Review,* (10) 4 (1981), pp. 461–79.

Jones, Emrys. 'The Welsh in London in the nineteenth century', *Cambria,* (12) 1 (1985), pp. 149–69.

Jones, Emrys. 'The Welsh language in England, *c.*1800–1914', in G. H. Jenkins (Ed.), *Language and Community in the Nineteenth Century,* (Cardiff, 1998), pp. 231–60.

Jones, Emrys (Ed.) *The Welsh in London 1500–2000.* Cardiff: University of Wales Press, 2001.

Jones, H. M. 'Cofnodion Cymreigyddion Llundain', *Y Llenor* (1938).

Jones, Hugh. *Hanes Wesleyaeth Gymreig.* Bangor: Llyfrfa Wesleyaidd, 1911–13.

Jones, Huw Llewelyn (Gol.) *Camre Canrif Holloway, Llundain 1865–1965.* Caernarfon: Llyfrfa'r Cyfundeb, 1965.

Jones, John Gwynfor. *Her y Ffydd: Ddoe, Heddiw ac Yfory (Hanes Henaduriaeth Dwyrain Morgannwg 1876–2005).* Caerdydd: Henaduriaeth Dwyrain Morgannwg, 2006.

Jones, John Gwynfor (Gol.) *Y Twf a'r Cadarnhau (c.1814–1914) Hanes Methodistiaeth Galfinaidd Cymru, Cyfrol III.* Caernarfon: Gwasg Pantycelyn, 2011.

Jones, M. H. *Crynodeb o Hanes Eglwys y Methodistiaid Calfinaidd yn Jerusalem, Ton Pentre.* Ystrad, 1920.

Jones, R. Lewis. *Cerdded y Lein*. Dinbych: Gwasg Tŷ ar y Graig, 1970.

Jones, R. M. & Rees, D. B. *The Liverpool Welsh and their Religion*. Liverpool, 1984.

Jones, R. Tudur. *Hanes Annibynwyr Cymru*. Abertawe: Gwasg John Penri, 1966.

Jones, R. Tudur. *Ffydd ac Argyfwng Cenedl (Cyfrol 1)*. Abertawe: Tŷ John Penri, 1981.

Jones, R. Tudur. *Ffydd ac Argyfwng Cenedl (Cyfrol 2)*. Abertawe: Tŷ John Penri, 1982.

Jones, R. W. *Y Ddwy Ganrif Hyn: Trem ar Hanes y Methodistiaid Calfinaidd o 1735 hyd 1935*. Caernarfon: Llyfrfa'r Cyfundeb, 1935.

Jones, Thomas. *Welsh Broth*. London, 1950.

Jones, T. *Leeks and Daffodils*. Newtown, 1942.

Jones, T. Emlyn. *London-Welsh Memories*. Merthyr Tydfil: Merthyr Express, 1943.

Kingsford, C. L. *John Stow's Survey of London, reprinted from the 1603 edition*. London: Centre for Metropolitan History, 1908.

Kirby, R. S. *Wonderful Museum: Or, Magazine of Remarkable Characters (Volume 1)*. London: T. Keating, 1803.

Knowles, Anne Kelly. *Calvinists Incorporated: Welsh Immigrants on Ohio's Frontier*. Chicago: University of Chicago Press, 1997.

Leathart, William Davies. *The Origin And Progress Of The Gwyneddigion Society Of London*. London: Hugh Pierce Hughes, 1831.

Lewis, George. *Pregeth a bregethwyd ar y dydd cyntaf o fis Mawrth yn y Flwyddyn 1714, Yr hwn oedd Ddydd Gwyl St. Dafydd. Gan George Lewis, M.A. Caplan i'r gwir Barchedig Arglwydd Ioan Escob Bangor. Argraphedig yn Llundain gan Edm. Powel, Ac ar werth gan Charles King yn Westminster Hall, achan Edm: Powel yn Blach-fryres yn Llundain 1715*. London, 1715.

Lewis, W. *Pwlpud Methodistaidd Dwyrain Morgannwg, 1893*. Manchester: J. Roberts and Sons, 1893.

Linnard, William. 'Merched y gerddi yn Llundain ac yng Nghymru', *Ceredigion* (9) 3 (1982).

Llawlyfr Rheolau Eglwys Methodistiaid Calfinaidd Cymru neu Eglwys Bresbyteraidd Cymru. Caernarfon: Llyfrfa'r Methodistiaid Calfinaidd, 1958.

Lloyd, Dewi F. (Gol.) *Cymry Llundain Ddoe a Heddiw*. Llundain: Undeb Cymdeithasau Diwylliannol Cymraeg Llundain, 1956.

Lloyd, J. E. & Jenkins, R. T. *The Dictionary of Welsh Biography down to 1940*. London: Blackwell for the Honourable Society of Cymmrodorion, 1959.

Lockie, John. *Lockie's Topography of London*. London, 1810.

Manning, O. & Bray, W. *History and Antiquities of the County of Surrey*. London, 1814.

Millward, E. G. (Gol.) *Cerddi Jac Glan-y-gors*. Y Bala: Cyhoeddiadau Barddas, 2003.

Morgan, J. J. *Cofiant Edward Matthews, Ewenni*. Mold, 1922.

Morgan, Kenneth O. *Rebirth of a Nation: Wales, 1880–1980*. Oxford: OUP, 1981.

Morgan, Prys. *The Eighteenth Century Renaissance*. Llandybïe: Christopher Davies (Publishers), 1981.

Morgan, Prys (Ed.) *The Tempus History of Wales*. Stroud: Tempus Publishing, 2001.

Morris, John Hughes. *Hanes Methodistiaeth Liverpool*. Liverpool: Hugh Evans a'i Feibion, 1932.

Morris, William (Gol.) *Deg o Enwogion (Ail Gyfres)*. Caernarfon: Llyfrfa'r Cyfundeb, 1965.

Morris, William (Gol.) *Ysgolion A Cholegau Y Methodistiaid Calfinaidd*. Caernarfon: Llyfrfa'r MC, 1973.

Mudie-Smith, Richard (Ed.) *The Religious Life of London*. London: Hodder and Stoughton, 1904.

Norton, Graham. *Victorian London (Discovering London 8)*. London: Macdonald, 1969.

Owen, Meurig. 'Llyfr bedyddiadau Eglwys Wilderness Row a Jewin Crescent, Llundain, 1799–1875', *Cylchgrawn Cymdeithas Hanes y Methodistiaid Calfinaidd,* 23 (1999).

Owen, Meurig. 'The Welsh Church in Deptford 1800–66', *Lewisham Local History Society Transactions*. London, 1979.

Owen, Meurig. *Tros y Bont*. Dinbych: Gwasg Gee, 1989.

Owen, Meurig. *Ymofyn am yr Hen Lwybrau*. Dinbych: Gwasg Gee, 2001.

Owen, Meurig (Gol.) *Yr Achos yn Lewisham, Llundain 1899–1999*. Dinbych: Gwasg Gee, 1999.

Owen, Oswald Rees. *Moreia, Walthamstow (Hanes yr Achos 1903–1953)*. Llundain: Eglwys Bresbyteraidd Cymru, 1953.

Owen, Robert. 'Ymfudiadau o Gymru i Lundain a hanes y bywyd Cymreig yn Llundain hyd at 1815' (Eisteddfod Genedlaethol Bae Colwyn, 1947), Bangor MSS 7343/4.

Owen, W. T. (Gol.) *Capel Elfed (Hanes Eglwys y Tabernacl, King's Cross)*. Abertawe: Gwasg John Penri, 1989.

Parry, David Hughes. *O Bentref Llanelhaearn i Ddinas Llundain*. Caernarfon: Llyfrfa'r Methodistiaid Calfinaidd, 1972.

Parry, E. Wynne (Gol.) *Cofiant a phregethau y diweddar Barch. David Charles Davies*. Wrexham: Hughes a'i Fab, 1896.

Pearse, Malpas. *Stuart London (Discovering London 5)*. London: Macdonald, 1969.

Phillips, Geraint. *Dyn heb ei gyffelyb yn y byd: Owain Myfyr a'i gysylltiadau llenyddol*. Cardiff: University of Wales Press, 2010.

Powell, D. W. 'History of the Cymmrodorion', *Transactions of the Honourable Society of Cymmrodorion*, New Series 1, 2000.

Prichard, Caradog. *Un Nos Ola Leuad*. Dinbych: Gwasg Gee, 1961.

Pritchard, W. *Cofiant a Phregethau y Parch. Richard Owen, y 'Diwygiwr'*. Amlwch, 1889.

Rees, Thomas. *Hanes Ymneilltuaeth yng Nghymru*. Port Talbot: Cynghrair Eglwysi Rhydd ac Efengylaidd Cymru, 1912.

Rees, Thomas & Thomas, John. *Hanes Eglwysi Annibynnol Cymru (Cyfrolau I–IV)*. Lerpwl: Hughes a'i Fab, 1871– .

Rhys, John. *Celtic Britain*. London: SPCK, 1884.

Rhys, Robert. *James Hughes, 'Iago Trichrug'*. Caernarfon: Gwasg Pantycelyn, 2007.

Roberts, Gomer M. *Y Ddinas Gadarn (Hanes Eglwys Jewin, Llundain)*. Llundain: Pwyllgor Dathlu Daucanmlwyddiant Eglwys Jewin, Llundain, 1974.

Roberts, J. Herbert. *Hanner Can Mlwyddiant yr Achos yn Ealing Green 1907–1957*. Llundain: Eglwys Bresbyteraidd Cymru, 1957.

Roberts, John. *Methodistiaeth Galfinaidd Cymru, Ymgais at Athroniaeth ei Hanes (Darlith Davies 1930)*. Llundain: Gwasg Gymraeg Foyle, 1931.

Smith, David. *Wales! Wales?* London: Allen & Unwin, 1984.

Smith, David. *Wales: A Question for History*. Bridgend: Seren Books, 1999.

Smith, David. *In the Frame: Memory in Society Wales 1910–2010*. Swansea: Parthian Books, 2010.

Stanford, Edward. *Library Map of London and its Suburbs*. London: Edward Stanford, 1862.

The Works of the Rev. John Wesley (Volume III). London: John Mason, 1829.

Thomas, M. Wynn. *In the Shadow of the Pulpit*. Cardiff: University of Wales Press, 2010.

Thickens, John (Gol.) *'Hanes ac Atgof', Jiwbili Eglwys Jewin*. Llundain: Henaduriaeth Llundain, 1929.

Thickens, John. *Howel Harris yn Llundain (Y Gyfrol Gyntaf 1739–1740) Darlith Davies 1934*. Caernarfon: Argraffdy'r Methodistiaid Calfinaidd, 1938.

Thomas, Thomas. *Hynodion Hen Bregethwyr Cymru Gydag Hanesion Difyrus Am Danynt*. Wrexham: Hughes and Son, 1872.

Timpson, Thomas. *Church History of Kent From The Earliest Period To The Year 1858*. London: Ward, 1859.

Vincent, W. T. *The Records of the Woolwich District*. London: Jackson and Virtue, 1890.

Williams, G. A. *The Welsh in their History*. Croom Helm, 1982.

Williams, G. J. 'Bywyd Cymry Llundain yng nghyfnod Owain Myfyr', *Y Llenor* (1939).

Williams, Glanmor. *Wales and the Reformation*. Cardiff: University of Wales Press, 1997.

Williams, Gwyn A. *When Was Wales?* London: Penguin Books, 1985.

Williams, John ('Cenadwr Cymreig'). *Cymry Llundain*. Caernarfon: John Davies, *c.*1867.

Williams, John ('JW'). *Hynt Gwerinwr*. Lerpwl: Hugh Evans a'i Feibion, 1943.

Williams, John ('JW' London). *The Story of a Country Man (translated from the Welsh by E. Pennant Jones)*. Hailsham: E. Pennant Jones, 1997.

Williams, Llywelyn (Gol.) *Hanes Eglwys y Tabernacl, King's Cross 1847–1947*. Llundain: W. Griffiths a'i Frodyr, 1947.

Williams, R. Bramwell. *Hanes Capel-y-Lôn, Slough (1938–1998)*. Abertawe: Gwasg John Penri, 1998.

Williams-Davies, John. 'Merched y Gerddi', *Ceredigion* (8) 3 (1978).

INDEX

AN ASTERISK FOLLOWING A PAGE NUMBER
INDICATES AN ILLUSTRATION OR PHOTOGRAPH